THE CHESAPEAKE
REGION

The Chesapeake Region

FODOR'S TRAVEL PUBLICATIONS, INC.
New York & London

Copyright © 1990 by Fodor's Travel Publications, Inc.

Fodor's is a trademark of Fodor's Travel Publications, Inc.

All rights reserved under International and Pan-American Copyright Conventions.
Published in the United States by Fodor's Travel Publications, Inc., a subsidiary of
Random House, Inc., New York, and simultaneously in Canada by Random House of
Canada Limited, Toronto. Distributed by Random House, Inc., New York.

*No maps, illustrations, or other portions of this book may be reproduced in any form without
written permission from the publisher.*

ISBN 0–679–01756–9

Parts of this guide appear in *Fodor's Virginia 1990.*

Fodor's The Chesapeake Region

Editor: Vernon Nahrgang
Area Editor: Francis X. Rocca
Editorial Contributors: Edgar and Patricia Cheatham, James Day, Steve
  Doherty, Eleanor and James Louttit, Eric Smith, Rodney N. Smith
Maps: Burmar Technical Corp.
Drawings: Amy Harold
Cover Photograph: Patrick Eden/Stock Photos

Cover Design: Vignelli Associates

Special Sales

Fodor's Travel Publications are available at special discounts for bulk purchases
(100 copies or more) for sales promotions or premiums. Special editions,
including personalized covers, excerpts of existing guides, and corporate
imprints, can be created in large quantities for special needs. For more
information, write to Special Marketing, Fodor's Travel Publications, 201 East
50th Street, New York, NY 10022. Inquiries from the United Kingdom should
be sent to Fodor's Travel Publications, 30–32 Bedford Square, London WC1B
3SG.

MANUFACTURED IN THE UNITED STATES OF AMERICA
10 9 8 7 6 5 4 3 2 1

CONTENTS

PLANNING YOUR TRIP

When to Go, 11; How to Get There, 11; Tourist Information, 13; Tips for British Visitors, 14; Hints for Motorists, 14; Boats and Boating, 15; Information for Disabled Travelers, 16; Time Zone and Area Codes, 16; Additional Reading, 16; Senior-Citizen Discounts, 17; Places to Stay, 17; Places to Eat, 19; Tipping, 20; Seasonal Events, 21; Swimming, 25; Ferry Rides and Cruises, 26; Parks and Forests, 28; Canoeing, 28; Fishing, 28; Hunting, 29; Crabbing, 29; Yacht Chartering, 29; Colonial Sites, 31

THE CHESAPEAKE REGION

FOREWORD

Captain John Smith was delighted by the natural wonders of the Chesapeake when he toured the Bay in 1608. Smith, in time, committed his impressions to print—and thereby became the first Chesapeake travel writer. History and progress have added many "wonders" since Smith sailed these waters: Baltimore's rejuvenated Inner Harbor, picturesque Annapolis, two mighty Bay bridges, historic St. Mary's City, Colonial Williamsburg—the list could go on and on.

While every care has been taken to assure the accuracy of the information in this guide, the passage of time will always bring change, and consequently the publisher cannot accept responsibility for errors that may occur.

All prices and opening times quoted here are based on information available to us at press time. Hours and admission fees may change, however, and the prudent traveler will avoid inconvenience by calling ahead.

Fodor's wants to hear about your travel experiences, both pleasant and unpleasant. When a hotel or restaurant fails to live up to its billing, let us know and we will investigate the complaint and revise our entries where the facts warrant it.

Send your letters to the editors of Fodor's Travel Publications, 201 E. 50th Street, New York, NY 10022.

MAP OF
THE CHESAPEAKE
REGION

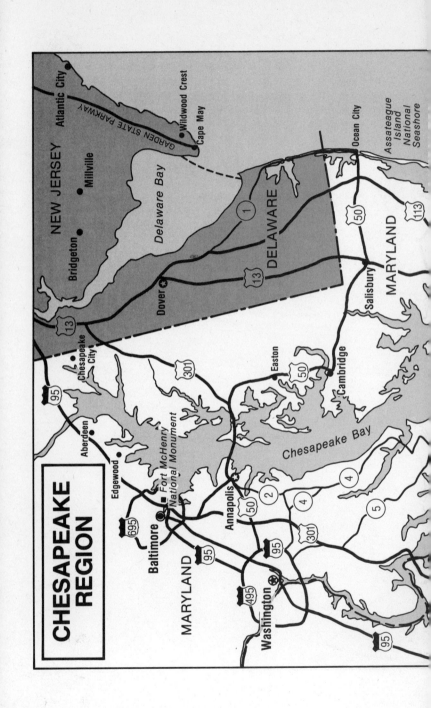

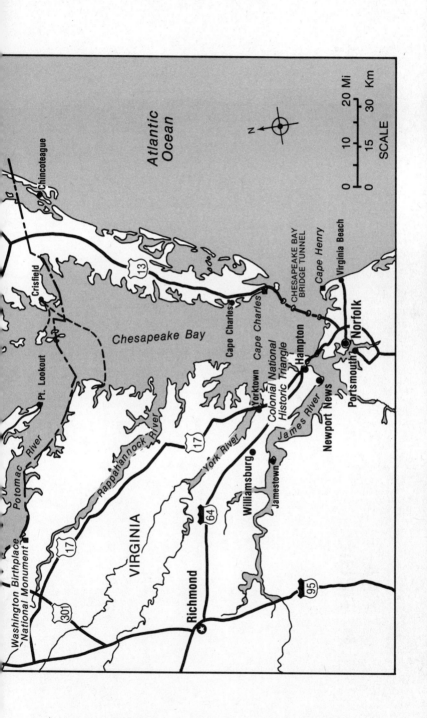

INTRODUCTION

by
JAMES LOUTTIT

It all started when the Atlantic drowned the Susquehanna.

Ten thousand years ago, give or take a few centuries, there was no Bay. Starting somewhere in the mountains to the north, there was only the river, flowing cold and gently south to the sea. Melting glaciers changed all that. Slowly, inexorably, rising ocean tidal waters drowned the lower reaches of the river and formed what is today the major inlet on the Eastern Seaboard—a great shallow filigree of a bay that is almost 200 miles long but seldom more than 20 miles wide. The Susquehanna now flows *into* the Bay, as do some 45 other rivers and streams. These include (to name but a few) Virginia's Rappahannock, York, and James in the south, Maryland's Patuxent, Choptank, Chester, and Sassafras in the north, and the mighty Potomac in between. Combined, they and their lesser sisters join the Atlantic to form America's largest estuary—a gentle blending of fresh river and salty sea that spreads over 3,277 square miles, has an average depth of 21 feet, and embraces a tidal shoreline of almost 6,000 miles.

The Chesapeake Vacationland begins at the water's edge, and all that is most important to the Bay is but a few short miles from its shores. Visitors have recognized this happy fact since this great bay was formed some ten thousand years ago.

About 8000 B.C. or So

The first tourists to the Chesapeake were probably Midwesterners—nomadic Indian deer hunters who drifted in when the Susquehanna was still giving ground to the Bay. This may have been as early as 8,000 B.C.; they were certainly there four thousand years later. Not too surprising, they liked what they saw—and they stayed. These Stone Age travelers, with their straight black hair, dark eyes, and red-brown skin, were the descendants of earlier prehistoric wanderers who had migrated eastward across the Bering Strait "bridge" more than 20 thousand years before, spreading slowly to the south and then eastward across the Great Plains. Their descendants, in turn, later became the Powhatan Confederacy, a scattered group of some 30 Eastern Woodlands tribes whose loose "family" tie was the Algonquian language. (Other than the common thread of language, there is little evidence that they liked each other very much—and there is *no* evidence they wanted anything to do with those English-speaking strangers who would someday move into the Bay.)

The Powhatan, in time, were comfortably ensconced in some 200 palisaded villages along coastal Virginia and around the shores of Chesapeake Bay. Now out of the Stone Age, they still hunted rabbits and deer in the woodlands, but now they also raised corn and enjoyed the bountiful fruits of their bay-front homes—the fish, crabs, and oysters that would someday make the Chesapeake famous. This was the Good Life: a mild climate, plenty to eat, and only an occasional tribal squabble to keep the juices flowing. But like all things, good or bad, it was bound to change; somewhere beyond the eastern horizon a new breed of adventurer was beginning to eye the Powhatan's watery paradise.

1492 and All That

Columbus, we know, sailed westward from Spain in 1492 and discovered America. Then, for the next few centuries, Spanish soldiers, priests, and adventurers busied themselves in South and Central America (and even in Florida, Texas, New Mexico, and California), converting the natives, looking for gold, and reintroducing the horse to the place the horse had started but was now totally extinct. Spain's influence in the New World was enormous, but her adventurers sometimes neglected or ignored some of the better touring places—the Chesapeake, for example. It took a ragtag crew of Englishmen to capitalize on this oversight.

The British Are Coming

Spaniards visited the Chesapeake in the early 1500s, and Giovanni de Verrazano, sailing for France, probably sailed into the bay in 1524 on his way north to New York Harbor, but the bay remained relatively peaceful through most of that century. Although English seadogs Drake, Gilbert, and Raleigh were harassing Spanish shipping in the Americas, the British Crown gave little serious thought to New World colonization until her captains had smashed the Spanish Armada in 1588. Two feeble attempts had been made a few years before, but each had been a failure.

The first attempt by Englishmen to settle in the New World was made in 1585, when Sir Walter dispatched a small band of settlers westward across the Atlantic. Those first English colonists landed on Roanoke Island between North Carolina's Albermarle and Pamlico Sounds. They sailed home to England in 1586. A second group tried again in the same place the following year, but they had disappeared without a trace when the busy folks back home finally got around to sending them supplies in 1591. That second desperate little band has gone down in history as a sad footnote: The Lost Colony of Roanoke.

True to character, the British tried again, this time landing further north at Jamestown (Virginia), near the entrance to the great Bay. It was anything but roses, but this third colony survived. Established May 14, 1607, by the London Company, this first *permanent* English settlement on a peninsula (now an island) in the James River fought disease, starvation, and hostile Indians until supplies and more settlers finally arrived. Seven months after the original 105 settlers landed, only 32 were still alive. Baron Thomas West De la Warr (note *that* name) arrived in 1610 and persuaded Jamestown's surviving colonists to hang on. It's hard to imagine exactly what De la Warr said to convince them that things could possibly be worse back in England, but the good baron prevailed—the colonists stayed and the colony did indeed survive. One of America's first states (the *first* of the original 13 colonies to ratify the Constitution) now bears De la Warr's name.

If it was Baron De la Warr who finally persuaded those early colonists to remain, it was tough-minded Captain John Smith who kept them going during the "starveing tyme" between 1607 and 1609. And, believe it or not, that celebrated story of Smith's capture by Chief Powhatan (Wahunsonacock) and his rescue by the chief's daughter, Pocahontas, is probably true. John Rolfe, who began cultivating tobacco in Virginia in 1612, helped ensure the struggling colony's survival when he married Pocahontas in 1614 and took his Indian bride back to England two years later. The Smith–Pocahontas–Rolfe triangle is yet another intriguing fragment of early American history, and one can't help but wonder if an Indian princess, not Martha Washington, wasn't truly America's *first* First Lady?

Captain Smith was a busy fellow during those early years of the Virginia Colony—cajoling his dispirited fellow colonists not to lose hope and prodding them when they did, but also finding time to explore the great Bay to the north in 1608. Smith charted the Bay and wrote colorful descriptions of what he saw, but it was another strong-willed Englishman, William Claiborne, who became the first European to settle in present-day Maryland. Claiborne, also of Virginia, established a fur-trading post on Kent Island in the Upper Bay in 1631. (The Chesapeake Bay Bridge, US 50, today crosses over Kent Island, linking Maryland's Western and Eastern Shores.)

In 1632, King Charles I of England gave the whole region to George Calvert, the first Lord Baltimore, but George died before the king signed the charter. It was then chartered to George's son, Cecil, the second Lord Baltimore. These chartered lands were named "Maryland" in honor of Queen Henrietta Maria, wife of King Charles.

The first Maryland colonists arrived two years later (1634) aboard two small ships, *Ark* and *Dove.* They landed on St. Clements Island in the Potomac on the western shore, not far down the Bay from Claiborne's Kent Island trading post. The new colonists established St. Maries Citty (St. Mary's City in St. Mary's County). Although Claiborne's settlement was now part of the colony, the doughty trader refused to accept Lord Baltimore's authority. In 1654, five years after the colony passed a religious toleration act, Claiborne seized control. He held onto the colony for four years, but the crown prevailed and Claiborne returned Maryland to Lord Baltimore in 1658. A Protestant group led by John Coode took over in 1689, demanding that England take control of the government, which it did in 1691.

What those original Algonquin inhabitants thought of all this isn't hard to imagine. Most soon decided the old neighborhood wasn't what it used to be, packed up, and moved out, leaving little behind but some of their tribal names—Patuxent, Choptank, Portobago, Wicomico, and others.

Three "Home" Wars

The American Revolution, the War of 1812, and the Civil War all touched the Chesapeake—sometimes lightly, often with hammer blows. A great natural bay, with its rivers and harbors, it is a magnet for the peaceful—and for the aggressive. The same attributes that attracted its first settlers, Indian or European, made the Chesapeake a natural target in times of war.

Neither state has a monopoly on historic sites from America's first three "home" wars. If the last decisive battle of the Revolution was fought at Yorktown, Virginia in 1781, one of the first cargoes of British tea was burned with the British ship *Peggy Stewart* in Annapolis harbor in 1774.

The British returned to the Chesapeake in 1814, during the War of 1812, winning early victories against England's former colonies. British troops eventually burned the young nation's Capitol and White House in Washington, but they later suffered a major defeat at Fort McHenry near Baltimore. Neither side had much heart for the war after that.

Although both Virginia and Maryland were slave states, the two found themselves on opposite sides during the Civil War, 1861–1865. After Virginia joined the Confederacy, the fate of Washington, D.C., depended on whether Maryland remained in the Union. It finally did, although many Marylanders fought for the Confederacy. Many of the biggest and the bloodiest battles of the war took place in Virginia, but several major campaigns were fought in Maryland. The first duel between two ironclads, the *Monitor* and the *Merrimac,* was fought to a draw in Chesapeake Bay off Newport News, Virginia. Battle sites, museums, and historic monuments from each of these three wars are discussed in greater detail in later chapters.

The Chesapeake Today

Change is inevitable, and there have been changes, but much of the Bay and its surrounding tidal lands remain as they were three or four hundred years ago.

Thousands of miles of natural woodland still fringe the Bay, forests and scrub pines spreading outwards from the low-lying shores. Great reaches of Chesapeake Bay are much the same as Captain Smith saw it in 1608, disturbed only by an occasional reminder that this *is* the 20th century and change *is* inevitable.

In the Upper Bay, Baltimore rises proudly above its rejuvenated Inner Harbor, a happy reminder of the way things were and what they can be; while in the south, near the wide mouth of the great Bay, Norfolk strives to blend in harmony our past, our present, and our future.

Two great bridges now span the Bay, engineering marvels that would have sent Captain Smith reeling. In the north, near Annapolis, the twin graceful arches of the William Preston Lane, Jr. Memorial Bridge link Maryland's Eastern and Western shores; while in the south, near the ocean entrance to the Bay, the Chesapeake Bay Bridge and Tunnel complex ties Norfolk's Cape Henry with Delmarva's Cape Charles.

Along the middle reaches of the Chesapeake, where Maryland's Calvert Cliffs Nuclear Plant is a modern symbol of the Atomic Age, dozens of quiet hamlets and small backwater ports still look much as they did centuries ago. The past and the present are usually at peace with each other in the Chesapeake—and this, as much as anything, bodes well for our future and the future of the Bay.

Chesapeake Weather

Few things are perfect; few *places* are perfect. So, face it—
Chesapeake weather is good, but it's not perfect.

That inveterate traveler, Captain John Smith, described it this
way:

"The sommer is hot as in Spaine. The winter colde as in France
or England. The heat of sommer is in June, July, and August, but
commonly the coole breeses assuage the vehemencie of the heat."

In other words, translating from Smith's Olde English: Neither
a tiger, nor a pussycat.

Smith was right; "the heat of sommer" is indeed in June, July,
and August. The Chesapeake has a long summer season, at least
a month longer on either end than neighboring areas to the north.
The "normal" temperature in Baltimore, in the Upper Bay, ranges
from 54.2 (degrees Fahrenheit) in April, to an average high of 76.8
in July, and back to 57 in October. Norfolk, at the lower end of
the Bay, has "normal" averages of 58 in April, 78.8 in July, and
62 in October.

Smith was also right about those "coole breeses." The breezes
are generally southerly (that is, they head south) during a Chesapeake summer. Calms are frequent, especially at night and in the
morning. In early summer, and again in the fall, winds usually
blow up or down the Bay. Rainfall is relatively light during those
early and late-season months. It is heaviest in June, July, and August, when occasional violent thunderstorms shatter the midsum-
mer calms.

Captain Smith described a brief but blustery early-summer Chesapeake thundersquall as "an extreme gust of wind, raine, thunder
and lightning (and) with great danger we escaped the unmerciful
raging of that ocean-like water."

"Wind, raine, thunder and lightning"—guaranteed to earn your
respect, and useful for cooling things off. The good captain knew
what he was talking about. Chesapeake Bay thundersqualls are leg-
endary, but they seldom last long, and they do "assuage the vehemencie of the heat."

There is very little fog during a Chesapeake summer, but those
long clear hot spells encourage a variety of unpleasant critters—
especially sea nettles (poisonous jellyfish) and mosquitoes. Nettles
can be a real nuisance in warm, quiet waters, while mosquitoes are
likely to be found (actually, *they* find *you*) where the land is marshy
and when the weather is damp. Mosquitoes are likely to be thickest
in early summer, especially in the marshlands below the Choptank
on Maryland's Eastern Shore.

On the other side of the coin, the Chesapeake's unique blending
of fresh and salt water, and its temperate location between the
colder north and the hotter south, make the Bay a near-perfect
breeding or nesting home for a wide variety of fish and fowl—and

a mecca for anglers and hunters. Half a million geese invade the fields and wet lands of the Eastern Shore during the peak of the Canadian migration. And last but not least of the Chesapeake's native—and famous—inhabitants are its shellfish. If the Oyster is King of the Chesapeake, the Crab is its Prime Minister. They need the Bay's perfectly proportioned waters, and the Bay needs them; neither would be the same without the other.

Perhaps it's not perfect, but the waters and surrounding tidelands of Chesapeake Bay are a unique tourist magnet. Easily reached and easily explored, the Chesapeake Vacationland has something for everyone—major cities and tiny villages, ocean beaches and quiet backwaters, "theme" parks and historic sites, and an abundance of wonderful food, from Maryland crab to Virginia ham.

PLANNING
YOUR
TRIP

PLANNING YOUR TRIP

WHEN TO GO. The Chesapeake lies in the mid-Atlantic region, definitely offering a "Southern" climate during the summer months, with appreciable humidity, yet having a rather mild spring and fall. "A good time to visit" spans nine to ten months of the year. Water has a strongly moderating influence on temperature; it's often warmer inland, but it's more humid near the water. A spring or fall vacation has its advantages if you don't mind slipping into a sweater or windbreaker when it becomes cool in the late afternoon—there is a welcome decrease in the size of crowds at most attractions and historical sites during the off-season months. Also, there are often price decreases during the "off" season.

The other side of the weather coin is that you *will,* as noted, encounter sticky heat during the summer. Washington, near the Chesapeake, and Baltimore on the Bay are famous—or infamous—for their humidity, and that condition applies to the whole Chesapeake area. The saving grace, at least some of the time, is that when you're on or near the water a cooling breeze often takes some of the sting out of the heat.

As for Places to See and Things to Do, there's a jam-packed Calendar of Events in both states from one end of the year to the other. A visitor won't find winter an inappropriate time for a Chesapeake vacation.

Weather in the Bay area is relatively mild throughout the year. Winters average 45°F; summers are in the 80°F range, but the humidity often makes it feel much warmer.

HOW TO GET THERE. If you're coming from the Northeast or from Southern states, and have the time to skirt the entire Bay on your vacation, the logical starting points are Havre de Grace or Baltimore in the north, and Norfolk in the south. If you're driving and choose one of these, a complete circuit of the Bay will land you at your starting point for the trip home. From the northwest (Pennsylvania) or west (West Virginia), the logical starting points are Baltimore or Washington, D.C. If available vacation time makes a circuit of the Bay too ambitious, you can tour *half* the Bay area, say the upper half for northern visitors and the lower half for Southerners, thus saving driving time that can be used visiting sites. But keep in mind that the *two* Bay crossings are almost 150 miles apart (the Bay bridge at Annapolis and the Bridge-Tunnel at Norfolk), so if you drive very far north from Norfolk, or south from Baltimore or Annapolis, you will have a fairly long haul by road before you reach the next crossing. On the Bay's Western Shore, the Potomac River is the dividing line between the two states, and it's so broad at its mouth that there are no bridges until you've driven 45 miles upriver.

Don't count on a "shorefront" drive where you will always have the Bay in sight. There are only a few places where this is possible. The best way to see the Bay by car is to visit the waterfront towns that attract you and stop at or near them for lodgings and meals.

As for accessibility, the Bay area is well served from all directions by Interstate highways and excellent U.S. and state roads: from the north, by I-81, I-83, and state roads; from the northeast, the same two interstates and I-95; from the west, I-64, I-70, and US 50 are the best choices, and from the south, the lower end of I-95 is the natural route. It skirts the Bay's Western Shore from top to bottom, while US 13 and 50 bisect the Eastern Shore, north to south (and vice versa, of course).

Northern visitors who approach the Eastern Shore of the Bay (after crossing the Delaware Memorial Bridge from New Jersey into Maryland), follow US 301 to reach US 50, which curves down the Delmarva Peninsula, inland but parallel to the Bay as far as Salisbury, Maryland, where it meets US 13. US 13 soon dips south into Virginia for an easy drive to the Bay Bridge and Tunnel, which crosses the mouth of the Chesapeake to Norfolk.

New Jersey motorists may find it interesting, even quicker, to take the toll ferry from Cape May to Cape Henlopen, DE, rather than crossing the Delaware further north at the Memorial Bridge. And from the South, those bound for the Bay's Eastern Shore can choose any highway leading to Norfolk; especially Rtes. 17, 13, and 58. Rtes. 17 and 13 cross at Norfolk, with Rte. 17 tending northwest up Virginia's North Neck until it meets US 301 near Port Royal.

By Bus. There are four major cities on or near the Bay where one might logically start a tour: Baltimore, Washington, Annapolis, and Norfolk. But it must be said that after you have arrived at one of these cities, by Greyhound or Trailways, any real appreciation of the Bay's attractions pretty much requires a car. The sole exception might be a split-week spent in Baltimore and Annapolis, arriving in one, and a few days later taking a bus to finish the week in the other.

By Train. Reliable and frequent Amtrak service is available to the cities listed above (except Annapolis), but the visitor still faces the same problem mentioned above: reaching the Bay's waterfront restaurants, colonial sites, and historic landmarks demands a car.

By Air. The best arrival points, those served by most major airlines, are the Baltimore-Washington International Airport, lying midway between those two cities, National Airport in Washington, and Norfolk. The obvious choice for foreign visitors arriving on an international flight is Baltimore-Washington International. From there it would be convenient to include a few days in the nation's capital before beginning a Chesapeake Bay tour at Baltimore's restored Inner Harbor, with its shops, ships, and seafood, or a bit further south at historic Annapolis.

TOURIST INFORMATION. For additional information to plan your Chesapeake trip, the following addresses will be helpful. They are listed with Maryland first, by Western Shore counties that face the Bay, then Eastern Shore; after that, the useful Virginia addresses. NOTE: When writing for tourist information about the Virginia section of the Delmarva Peninsula, specify that you're interested in *Virginia's* Eastern Shore.

Maryland

Western Shore. *Baltimore City*—Baltimore Office of Promotion & Tourism, 34 Market Pl., Suite 310, Baltimore, MD 21201; (301) 752–8632 or 837–INFO (24-hr. information). *Harford County*—Office of Economic Development, 29 W. Courtland St., Bel Air, MD 21014; (301) 838–6000. *Baltimore County*—Chamber of Commerce, 100 W. Pennsylvania Ave., Towson, MD 21204; (301) 825–6200. *Annapolis & Anne Arundel County*—Annapolis Tourism Office, 160 Duke of Gloucester St., Annapolis 21401; (301) 263–7940. Anne Arundel County Office of Economic Development, Arundel Center, 44 Calvert St., Annapolis 21401; (301) 280–1122. Tri-County Council for Southern Maryland, Box 1634, Charlotte Hall, MD 20622; (301) 884–2144.

Eastern Shore (MD). *Cecil County*—Office of Planning, County Office Bldg., Rm. 300, Elkton, MD 21921; (301) 398–0200, Ext. 144. *Kent, Queen Anne's & Talbot Counties*—Tourism Council of the Upper Chesapeake, 208 N. Commerce St., Centreville, MD 21617; (301) 758–2300. *Dorchester County*—Dorchester County Tourism, Box 307, Cambridge, MD 21613; (301) 228–3234. *Wicomico County*—Convention & Visitor's Bureau, Civic Center, Glen Ave. Ext., Salisbury, MD 21801; (301) 548–4914. *Somerset County*—Tourism Commission, Box 243, Princess Anne, MD 21853; (301) 651–2968.

Ocean City. Ocean City Visitors and Convention Bureau, 4001 Coastal Hwy., Ocean City, MD 21842; (301) 289–8181.

Virginia

Virginia's comprehensive tourism program offers nearly 600 pamphlets to visitors on all areas and activities of the state. Many fascinating Colonial, Revolutionary War, and Civil War sites lie in Virginia and a fair number of these are close to the Bay. Here are some useful addresses for information on your Virginia trip: Virginia Travel Council, Box 15067, Richmond, VA 23227; (804) 266–0444, or Virginia Div. of Tourism, 202 N. Ninth St., Suite 500, Richmond, VA 23219; (804) 786–4484.

When writing or calling for assistance, be sure to describe your primary interests, so either states' tourism offices can send you the most approriate material.

TIPS FOR BRITISH VISITORS. Passports. You will need a valid 10-year passport (cost £15). You will not need a visa if you are staying for less than 90 days, have a return ticket, and are flying with a participating airline. There are some exceptions to this, so check with your travel agent or with the *United States Embassy,* Visa and Immigration Department, 5 Upper Grosvenor St., London W1A 2JB (tel. 01–499 3443).

Vaccinations. No vaccinations are required for entry into the U.S.

Customs. If you are 21 or over, you can take into the U.S.: 200 cigarettes or 50 cigars or 3 lbs. of tobacco (combination of proportionate parts permitted); and 1 U.S. quart of alcohol. In addition, every visitor, including minors, is allowed duty-free gifts to a value of $100. No alcohol or cigarettes may be included in this gift exemption, but up to 100 cigars may be. Be careful not to take in meat or meat products, seeds, plants, fruits, etc. Avoid narcotics like the plague. Returning to the U.K., you may bring home: (1) 200 cigarettes or 100 cigarillos or 50 cigars or 250 grams of tobacco; (2) two liters of table wine and, in addition, (a) one liter of alcohol over 22% by volume (most spirits), (b) two liters of alcohol under 22% by volume (fortified or sparkling wine), or (c) two more liters of table wine; (3) 50 grams of perfume and ¼ liter of toilet water; and (4) other goods up to a value of £32.

Insurance. We heartily recommend that you insure yourself to cover health and motoring mishaps, with *Europ Assistance,* 252 High St., Croydon CRO 1NF (tel. 01–680 1234). Their excellent service is all the more valuable when you consider the possible costs of health care in the U.S. It is also wise to insure yourself against trip cancellation and loss of luggage.

Air Fares. We suggest you explore the current scene for budget flight possibilities—APEX and other fares offer considerable saving over the full price. Quite frankly, only business travelers who don't have to watch the price of their tickets fly full price these days—and find themselves sitting right beside APEX passengers! At press time (mid-1989), APEX roundtrip fares to Baltimore from London cost from £353, to Richmond from £479, and to Norfolk from £517. Also check the small ads in daily and Sunday newspapers for last-minute discount fares.

Electricity. 100 volts. You should take along an adapter, since American razor and hair-dryer sockets require flat two-prong plugs.

HINTS FOR MOTORISTS. Both Maryland and Virginia, of course, have the 55 mph speed limit (except where posted 65 mph on some rural Interstate highways). Maryland has a reputation for being tough on speeders: a word to the wise should be sufficient! Remember, you're on vacation, out to have fun, see interesting sights, and *relax*. There's no need for a heavy foot on the gas pedal.

Highway Information Centers

On the Road in Maryland. Once you have arrived in Maryland, there are four highway information centers available to make your trip a success: 1. On I-95, near Laurel (up north), in the Rest Area at Mile Marker 37, serving southbound and northbound traffic; it's open Memorial Day to Labor Day, 8:30–6:30, but is closed Thanksgiving, Christmas, New Year's Day, and Easter. 2. On I-95 in Cecil County, in the Rest Area at Mile Marker 29, serving traffic headed both ways; open weekdays 9–5; weekends and holidays 8–4; closed same holidays as above. 3. State House Visitors' Center, in Maryland State House, State Circle, Annapolis; open daily 9–5; closed same holidays as above. 4. US 13 Information Center, located on Route 13 (Eastern Shore), 2 mi. north of the Virginia state line on the Delmarva Peninsula.

On the Road in Virginia. There are 10 locations in Virginia where the motorist can get help in planning a Chesapeake tour, and where the wide selection of brochures mentioned above are available. They are located as follows: *Northern Region*—On I-81 in Clear Brook, and on I-66 in Manassas; *Northeastern Region*—on I-95 in Fredericksburg; *Tidewater Region*—On US 13 in New Church (Delmarva); *South-Central Region*—On I-95 in Skippers, and on I-85 in Bracey; *Southwest Region*—On I-81 in Bristol, and on I-77 in Lambsburg; *Western Region*—On I-64 in Covington. In general terms, this means there is a Welcome Center on every interstate highway just inside the Virginia state line.

BOATS AND BOATING. When considering the Chesapeake, visitors should put boats and boating at (or near) the top of their list of attractions and things to do. To the recreational sailor, the Bay is a cruising ground par excellence with its hundreds of sheltered anchorages tucked in behind all those points of land—quiet places to relax at the end of the cruising day. To the boat *lover,* the Bay is dotted with hundreds of boatbuilders, charter boat operators, fishing boat rental stations, yacht brokers, new-boat dealers, yacht clubs, commercial vessels, and boatyards where a visitor can browse just for the pleasure of looking at boats. Boats of all kinds, for many purposes, is what the Bay and its people are all about. Yet boats are only part of the Chesapeake picture. To the lover of good food, especially regional seafood specialties and time-proven Colonial dishes, the Chesapeake is dotted along both shores with charming rural inns, urban restaurants, and waterfront "eateries" that offer gourmet seafood dishes made from the day's catches in the Bay—fish, crab, clams, and oysters.

Boat- and water-lovers intent on absorbing the Bay's nautical ambiance but also interested in the hallowed sites of great events in history, need only journey inland a few miles from the water to discover much of America's past. When Captain John Smith explored the Bay from Jamestown in 1608 he was so delighted by what he found—protected coves, abundant seafood, tree-covered islands, and gentle woods and fields—that he named one of the islands after himself. (It lies between Smith Point, VA, and Crisfield, MD, and visitors can reach it by ferry.) Allowing for some changes over nearly four centuries, today's visitor will find Chesapeake Bay no less entrancing.

INFORMATION FOR DISABLED TRAVELERS. Both Maryland and Virginia, which play host to hordes of visitors every year, have made significant strides in adapting their attractions to the needs of the disabled. The Maryland Travel Guide (Office of Tourism Development, 217 E. Redwood St., Baltimore, MD 21202; (301) 333–6611), for instance, lists for the handicapped the facilities that have been incorporated into public and private attractions. These include such conveniences as barrier-free access, ramps, handrails, reserved parking spaces, and accessible phones, elevators, bathrooms, drinking fountains, assembly areas, and turnstiles. Naturally all these are not offered at *every* site, but the program continues along with the awareness of its importance, especially in new construction.

In Virginia, special efforts have been made to accommodate the disabled visitor. The many state attractions that have been made accessible include air shows, national battlefields, vineyards, state and national parks, churches, plantations, botanical gardens, Indian reservations, wildlife refuges, museums, zoological parks, theaters, boat cruises, and seashore areas. A helpful brochure for planning a trip is "Tips For The Disabled Traveler," available from: Div. of Tourism, 202 N. Ninth St., Suite 500, Richmond, VA 23219; (804) 786–2051.

TIME ZONE AND AREA CODES. Both states are in the eastern standard time zone, and go on and off daylight saving time in April and October. Maryland has only one telephone area code (301) for the entire state, but Virginia has two, (703) in the western and northern part, and (804) in the south and along the Eastern Shore, i.e., the Chesapeake area.

ADDITIONAL READING. For those who like to do a little "homework" before a trip, here are a few useful books:

Maryland. *Maryland: A Bicentennial History,* by Carl Bode, published by W. W. Norton, New York, 1978.

Maryland Folklore and Folklife, by George C. Carey, published by Cornell Maritime Press, 1970.

Portrait of a Free State, by Donald M. Dozen, published by Cornell Maritime Press, 1976.

For a fictionalized but fine rendering of the Bay's special flavor, don't forget James Michener's best-seller, *Chesapeake.*

And for lovers of crab, *The Official Crab Eater's Guide,* by Whitey Schmidt, Marian Hartnett Press, Alexandria, VA, 1985.

Virginia. *Virginia, A Guide to the Old Dominion,* by Hans Hannau, Oxford Univ. Press, New York, 1940.

Virginia, by Hans Hannau, Doubleday, Garden City, NY, 1966.

Virginia Beautiful, by Wallace Nutting, EPM Publications, McLean, VA, 1974.

The Bay. *Bay Country,* by Tom Horton, published by Ticknor & Fields, 1988.

Beautiful Swimmers: Watermen, Crabs, and the Chesapeake Bay, by William W. Warner, published by Atlantic Monthly Press, 1975 (Penguin paperback).

Chesapeake Bay Magazine, available at local newsstands, offers interesting articles on all aspects of Bay life. The magazine also lists restaurants and current events and provides a sweeping survey of everything the Bay area has to offer.

SENIOR-CITIZEN DISCOUNTS. Senior citizens may in some cases receive special discounts on lodgings. The Days Inn chain offers various discounts to those 55 and older. Holiday Inns extend a discount to members of the American Association of Retired Persons or its subsidiary, the National Retired Teachers Association; write the AARP or the NRTA at 3200 E. Carson St., Lakewood, CA 90712. The amounts and availability of discounts change, so it's wise to check in advance with these organizations or with the hotel or motel chain. The National Council of Senior Citizens, 925 15th St., N.W., Washington, D.C. 20005, is always working to develop low-cost travel opportunities for it members.

PLACES TO STAY. Accommodations around the Chesapeake vary widely and wildly in price. In major cities and popular tourist centers such as Baltimore, Williamsburg, Annapolis, and Norfolk, you can expect hotel and motel rooms to compare closely with simmilar city accommodations in the rest of the mid-Atlantic region. The same holds true for fashionable or long-established inns. This rule-of-thumb applies on both sides of the Bay. In less-densely populated areas (where taxes and real estate values are lower), also on both sides of the Bay near quiet ports and smaller towns, you'll often find lower nightly rates. (See below for a general scale of rates.) Although there are bargains to be found, and occasional rip-offs, you generally get pretty much what you pay for. This is especially true in major touring areas, where there are large selections of accommodations in each price range.

The key to selecting the *right* place for you to stay is "balance"—that is, balancing your needs, desires, and preferences against your ability or willingness to pay. If you insist on a central location, be prepared to pay extra for the convenience. On the other hand, if location is not important to you, you'll probably enjoy substantial savings.

If you prefer full-service accommodations (restaurants, lounges, room service), again be prepared to pay extra. Here, you should be aware that most hotels and motels are near or adjacent to restaurants.

If an accommodation's ambiance and amenities are important to you, recognize in advance that you'll pay for those, too. But if "a view of the garden" and extra-large and fluffy bath towels rank low on your list of priorities, your travel dollars will almost certainly stretch a bit farther. Whatever your preference, reserve your accommodations well in advance, especially during peak seasons. Weighing what you want against what you'll pay is good travel insurance against future disappointment.

In the Practical Information sections you will find fairly comprehensive selections of Places to Stay. These selections are arranged by price category under separate general location headings around the Chesapeake. Each of the listings has one or more of the following general price designations: *Deluxe,* $100 or more; *Expensive,* $75–$100; *Moderate,* $45–$75; and *Inexpensive,* under $45. This *very general* pricing structure is based on double occupancy for one night; it applies except where noted.

Most major hotels and motels accept major credit cards; others may accept a few or none at all. Many of our listings include those cards that are acceptable at a particular hotel, motel, or chain. These are indicated by the following abbreviations at the end of each selection: AE, American Express; CB, Carte Blanche; DC, Diners Club; MC, MasterCard; and V, Visa.

A few additional words of caution are appropriate here:

• Our selection of listings, while fairly comprehensive, is not complete; new facilities are added each year, while others go out of business or change their names. If you discover an exceptional place that we've overlooked, we would be delighted to hear about it. By the same token, if you disagree with any of our selections, we would appreciate hearing that, too. Our aim throughout is to give you the widest possible choice of locations, facilities, services, and prices—but we are realistic enough to know that it's impossible to please every traveler every time; the best we can do is try.

• Our pricing structure—*Inexpensive* through *Deluxe*—is a general one. Rates may change seasonally or at the discretion of management, and a facility listed in one price category may slip into another while we're on press or before you read or use this guide. Even service may slip, or improve, sometimes in less than a year.

• Although our four general price ranges are based on current lodging trends, plus our years of personal experience, each of us differs as to what we need, what we will pay, and whether we truly believe that where we sleep and change our clothes is really all *that* important. Only you can make those decisions. We can, as we have done, provide broad guidelines, recognizing that a moderate price to one traveler may seem wildly extravagant to another or "a real bargain" to yet a third.

• Each of our hotel-motel-campground listings includes addresses and telephone numbers (often toll-free 800 numbers). Because these numbers are possibly the most valuable part of the total listing, we recommend you make use of them by calling for more details than our abbreviated descriptions can provide. Above all call well in advance to make a firm reservation. The time and money spent before your trip can save you hours—even days—of aggravation later. In fact, it just might *make* your trip!

PLACES TO EAT. The Chesapeake area is highly regarded for its regional seafood specialties in both Maryland and Virginia. Crabs caught in the Bay are justly famous (in the form of crab cakes, especially) and it's said around the Bay that any Chesapeake chef worthy of the name knows at least 20 ways to prepare crab. The upper end of the Bay, Maryland's part, is famous for its oysters—although sad to relate the supply may be thinning dangerously—and these are enjoyed on the half shell, in stews, fried and—mixed with spices and baked—as appetizers. Both ends of the Bay are renowned for fish dishes—broiled or fried—and this includes black drum, channel bass, flounder, bluefish, weakfish, plus a whole range of others that come from the ocean.

Down in Virginia waters, you'll enjoy almost the same menus as you'll find further north, with minor variations from one place to another. Besides seafood, Virginia is also famous for its ham, especially the smoked Smithfield variety, which has a reputation more than two centuries old. (Of course, Southern Maryland is justifiably proud of *its* local ham.) Many surviving dishes from Colonial cooks are still served. Don't be afraid to try them; you'll probably be delighted. *Crab Norfolk,* seasoned with salt, red and black pepper, and vinegar, then baked *en casserole,* is a favorite at the lower end of the Bay. At Smithfield, where those wonderful hams come from, they claim the flavor comes from allowing the hogs to roam free in the fields until autumn, when they are let into the peanut fields to fatten. It's the peanuts and the special curing method that give them their distinctive flavor. Virginia is also renowned for spoonbread, fried chicken, and beef from Black Angus cattle.

Over on the Bay's Eastern Shore, in both states, you'll find the menus leaning strongly toward seafood. Delmarva natives are incredulous at anyone who doesn't love fish, oysters, and crab. In this area there's also a regional dish called *White Potato Pie.* It's

made with potatoes and tomatoes, skillfully blended with milk,
butter, eggs, sugar, lemon, cinnamon, and nutmeg. Try it; it's a
delight.

For those not excited by seafood, be assured that restaurant
menus will always include plenty of entrees that you might find
anywhere else in the country. The waitress or waiter may look at
you strangely, but the cook will do his best.

Immediately following Places to Stay in the Practical Information sections, you will find a selection of Places to Eat. We don't
claim that our selections are all-inclusive; instead, we have attempted to provide a broad and well-rounded selection of "safe"
places to eat—a varied selection that hopefully will satisfy every
taste and pocketbook.

Our restaurant listings, although abbreviated, include addresses
and telephone numbers, as well as the following general price designations: *Deluxe,* over $30; *Expensive,* $20–$30; *Moderate,* $10–
$20; and *Inexpensive,* under $10. Most of the selections also include
one or more credit-card designations—AE (American Express),
CB (Carte Blanche), DC (Diners Club), MC (MasterCard), or V
(Visa). But be aware that all establishments reserve the right to
change their minds, and a credit card that was acceptable when
we compiled our lists may not be acceptable later. When in doubt,
ask when you reserve a table or before you sit down to dine.

Restaurants around Chesapeake Bay are in business primarily
to serve the touring public, and there is neither joy nor profit in
turning away potential customers. Yet, as anywhere else, this is
occasionally necessary, much to the regret of the restaurant's staff
and the chagrin of the disappointed customer. Rejection, if it
amounts to that, may result from two sources: lack of a reservation
or improper attire. Some restaurants accept credit cards, others do
not; some restaurants insist on advance bookings, while others
won't accept them; and some restaurants are fussy about their customers' dress, while others couldn't care less. Wherever possible,
we have tried to give you the guidance you need, but keep in mind
that rules sometimes change, and a phone call in advance is a wise
move.

TIPPING. Whom to tip, how much, and when, are some of the
more confusing aspects of travel. There are no written laws or
hard-and-fast rules to govern the practice—merely custom and our
own inclination. Unlike much of Europe, where a service charge
is added automatically to most restaurant (and some hotel) bills,
few restaurants in the United States have adopted this practice. In
the rare instance where one has, that fact should be noted on the
menu and again on your final bill. When in doubt, *ask;* you may
add to the tip, but you are not expected to pay double. Fifteen percent of your total food and beverage bill (excluding any tax) is still
universally acceptable throughout the United States, and this, of

course, includes the Bay area. In general, tip as you would at home. Since the virtual disappearance of the half-dollar coin, a dollar bill per suitcase is appropriate for bellhops, or for the doorman who makes an extra effort to hail and help you into a cab. However, if there is a long line of waiting cabs, 50 cents is sufficient for the simple task of helping you into a taxi. For a local cab ride, 15 to 20 percent of the fare is a reasonably generous tip, and it may even earn you a smile. Many establishments add a fixed room-service charge, usually 10 to 15 percent. It is not out of line to add a bit extra, especially for prompt and courteous service. And finally, there are those unsung and often neglected heroines (and an occasional hero)—the housekeepers and chambermaids who make up your bed, collect your trash, and straighten your room. A tip for a special service performed on request is not inappropriate, and if your stay was especially pleasant, leaving a modest monetary gift when you check out is a nice way to show your appreciation.

SEASONAL EVENTS. The number of things to see and do all around the edge of the Chesapeake, in both Maryland and Virginia, for all 12 months of the year, is simply staggering. The following selection is a *summary* only of a year's events, and we have only included those that have been conducted for several years running. Each state publishes its own official *Calendar of Events* complete with dates and details. To get the most up-to-date information, contact: **Maryland**—Office of Tourism Development, 217 E. Redwood St. Baltimore, MD 21202; (301) 333–6611. **Virginia**—Virginia Div. of Tourism, 202 N. Ninth St., Suite 500, Richmond, VA 23219; (804) 786–4484.

January. As might be expected, Maryland's January events are principally indoors, such as an antiques show at Annapolis, a Lee-Jackson Confederate Memorial Service in Baltimore, and the Nautical and Wildlife Festival Art Show in Ocean City. The Chesapeake Bay Boat Show, the Mid-Atlantic's largest and oldest boating exposition, is held in Baltimore. In Virginia, most January events by coincidence are inland, away from the Bay. Newport News and Hampton Roads have their Wildlife & Waterfowl Festival, and the Antiques Forum is held in Williamsburg.

February. Maryland opens the month with the Anne Arundel County Agricultural Week in Annapolis (exhibits, demonstrations, products) held at the Annapolis Mall, while Baltimore has the annual ACC Craft Fair (Baltimore Convention Center) and Salisbury holds a Mardi Gras late in the month. In Virginia, Alexandria, Williamsburg, Mount Vernon, and Washington's birthplace celebrate the first president's birthday with banquets and balls, tours, demonstrations, and parades. Mid to late February. The big Mid-Atlantic Sport & Boat Show is held in Virginia Beach this month.

March. Baltimore celebrates St. Patrick's Day and Maryland Day this month, while St. Mary's has its own Maryland Days (2, not 1) later. In Virginia, not to be outdone, Norfolk holds its own St. Patrick's Day Celebration, now an annual affair.

April. This month, spring comes to most of the Chesapeake, and that's evident by the swing to outdoor activities. Easter, horticulture, and the joy of spring are the themes for celebrations in cities and hamlets around the Bay. These range from a spring arts and crafts show, a vacation and recreation expo, and an Arbor Day tree-planting celebration at Ocean City to a daffodil show in Edgewater's London Town Publik House & Gardens, a flower fair in Cambridge, fish and fowl day in Snow Hill, and Salisbury's spring festival, a block party on Riverwalk. Farther south in Virginia, Jamestown opens its summer-long celebration of the first English colony in America, featuring the *Godspeed,* a reproduction of one of the three sailing vessels that made the 1607 voyage to these shores. Norfolk holds an Annual Children's Easter Festival (one of Norfolk's Festevents), and at Chincoteague, over on the Delmarva Peninsula, there's a Decoy Carver Festival, at which local carvers competed for top honors. Norfolk fills April's third weekend with its highly regarded International Azalea Festival, saluting NATO member nations.

May. Maryland listed 105 events in May last year and Virginia 51, so it's clear when spring has arrived on the Chesapeake. Virginia opens the month with the Annual Seafood Festival in Chincoteague, while Jamestown celebrates "Settlement Day" on with crafts, games, music, and military drills at the Jamestown Festival Park (fee). At Norfolk, the Ghent Arts Festival, held on Mother's Day weekend, features painting, sculpture, tapestries, leather goods, and photography at an outdoor location. Chincoteague *starts* the town's summer programs (running into early Sept.) at the Memorial Wildlife Refuge with nature walks, movies, lectures, and family activities. In Maryland, the May festivities often start with Baltimore's Flower Mart, a rite of spring dating back to 1911, offering visitors plants, flowers, arts, crafts, food, and entertainment at Mt. Vernon Place. Over in Ocean City (Delmarva), the Sweet Adelines Competition & Show fills a weekend with barbershop quartets and choruses. Baltimore holds its May Day celebration, a traditional folk event with a Maypole dance, at the Cloisters Children's Museum and there is a weekend Spring Festival at Havre de Grace's Steppingstone Museum, offering a horse and carriage show, exhibits of rural tools and crafts of the 1880–1920 period, and entertainment. Baltimore holds its Antiques Show at the city's Museum of Art, while in Annapolis, late in the month, the U.S. Naval Academy's 6-day Commissioning Week includes parades, athletic events, and a performance of jet-fighter acrobatics by the Blue Angels, all leading up to the graduation of the Academy's midshipmen. Also in May there is the annual Running of the Preakness Stakes (the middle event of thoroughbred racing's Triple Crown) at Pimlico Race Course. In the latter half of May, Baltimore holds a Bach Festival and Annapolis has its Roses & May Flowers Day.

June. This is another big month in Maryland and Virginia. Virginia starts with Harborfest at Norfolk, featuring tall ships, sailboat races, entertainment, children's activities, and seafood specialties. Portsmouth, Norfolk's neighbor across the harbor, holds its Annual Seawall Art Festival. About a week later, Colonial Beach (up the Potomac from the Bay) has its Annual Potomac River Festival. Virginia Beach stages its Boardwalk Art Show in June, featuring the works of artists and artisans along eight blocks of waterfront. In Maryland, Baltimore begins a summer-long series of ethnic festivals called Showcase of Nations (through Sept.), stages its Dundalk Outdoor Art Show, and celebrates Confederate Memorial Day. At Hooper's Island (Eastern Shore), Fishing Tournament is sponsored by the fire department. Then Cambridge, also on the Eastern Shore, has its Strawberry Festival. At the lower end of Maryland's part of Delmarva, Pocomoke City has a Cypress Festival. Bay crabs reign supreme in June when the St. Mary's County Crab Festival is held at Paw Paw Hollow Land in Leonardtown, with arts and crafts and entertainment.

July. On or around July 4, both states stage celebrations of Independence Day at so many locations you probably couldn't miss one wherever you are. Virtually all include parades, fireworks, contests, children's activities, and patriotic music. In Wachapreague, VA, they load the first two weeks with their Annual Art Show and Annual Eastern Shore Marlin Club Tournament. Nearby, in Chincoteague, the famous ponies of Assateague Island are herded (by local firemen) on their swim across the channel to the mainland, where an auction is held for all visitors who want to buy a pony. In Maryland, July's variety of attractions continues with a Canal Day Festival at the far northern end of the Bay in Chesapeake City, and at Baltimore with the Chesapeake Turtle Derby (10 classes racing for prizes and the crowning of a Grand Champ). Crisfield—on the Bay—holds its Chamber of Commerce Fishing Tournament, offering thousands in prize money for the best catches in three categories: trout, flounder, and croaker. In St. Mary's City (Western Shore, near the Potomac), the final two weeks of the month are given over to the Bay County Camp of the Theater Arts, and across the Bay, Easton holds the Talbot County Fair. A late July Eastern Shore special attraction in Cambridge is the Sail Regatta, followed by a Power Boat Regatta (races and a boat show).

August. At the lower end of the Bay, Norfolk stages its annual Town Point Jazz Festival and Virginia Beach hosts a two-day East Coast surfing championship and a folk arts festival. Portsmouth lays out its tempting all-you-can-eat Annual Seafood Outing. Across the Bay on the Eastern Shore, Wachapreague has an Annual Fish Fry. Cambridge also has a Seafood "Feast-i-val," and the Dorchester (county) Fest on the Choptank River, an antique show with arts and crafts, Nanticoke Indians, bike races, tours, and water activities, is held at the Long Wharf and Armory. At Annapolis, there is the Kennel Club Dog Show & Obedience Trial and the Governor's Cup Yacht Race, Annapolis to St. Mary's, the largest yacht race on the Bay. Boats are for fishing in Ocean City, which has Small Boat Fishing Tournaments on weekends and hosts the $45,000 White Marlin Open and the annual White Marlin Open (August into September). Baltimore's Little Italy has its St. Gabriel's Festival this month, while North Beach has Bayfest, where Chesapeake Bay crabs are sometimes raced but mostly steamed and eaten. Crisfield's National Hard Crab Derby is held at the end of August or the beginning of September.

September. In Maryland, Cambridge opens with its Weekend Tennis Classic and Salt Water Festival, both annuals, Annapolis has a Seafood Festival, and Baltimore holds its city fair and Defenders' Day Celebration (the anniversary of the Battle of Baltimore—War of 1812). Closing out the month, Havre de Grace has its Fall Harvest Festival, while Ocean City celebrates its yearly Sunfest and then an annual Beachcomber Funrun. County fairs are held in St. Mary's (Leonardtown) and Anne Arundel (Crownsville) during the month. In Virginia, Cape Charles (Delmarva) holds Cape Charles Day (parades, marathon, and local arts and crafts, a flea market, and the "finest clam fritters around"), while Virginia Beach stages its Annual Neptune Festival (sand castle contests, parades, and entertainment). Norfolk stages its Elizabeth River Blues Festival, Poquoson has a Seafood Festival, and Hampton celebrates Hampton Bay Days on the waterfront.

October. This month hardly feels like autumn in the Bay area, so it's no surprise that Virginia is still active with outdoor events through the month. Inland, off the Bay, it is fall foliage time, with harvest festivals (for apples, molasses, and tobacco), but in Chincoteague on the Eastern Shore, the big repeat event is an Oyster Festival ("oysters cooked every way"). During October, Yorktown celebrates Yorktown Days, Newport News stages a Fall Festival, and Norfolk presents its Annual Halloween Celebration at Festevents, an adult costume ball with music, dancing, and food. In Maryland, Annapolis is the magnet for small-boat sailors as the Sailboat and Powerboat Shows take over the town for four days each at the City Dock. At St. Michael's (Eastern Shore, below the Bay bridge), the Mid-Atlantic Small Craft Festival, where boats are judged and raced, offers diversions for the kids and food for all. At St. Mary's City (back on the Western Shore), there is the Old State House Quilt Show, held at the Reconstructed State House of 1676. Baltimore calls its autumn event Festival-On-The-Hill (in the city's premier Victorian neighborhood, Bolton Hill), and Solomons, a popular Bay port, stages its Patuxent River Appreciation Days (nautical exhibits, boat rides, parade, and local foods). At Edgewater, the Needlework Show features a competition of outstanding needlework from the area, while down in St. Mary's City the two-day Grand Militia Muster reenacts 17th-century battles, drills, and parades. Baltimore's Halloween Parade closes out the month, but Ghost Walks, Halloween Parties and Happenings, and Halloween Festivals are held on both shores of the Bay late in the month.

November. In Maryland, Easton (just inland from St. Michaels on the Bay) holds a three-day Waterfowl Festival (featuring decoys and waterfowl art, guns, and a goose-calling contest), so you know that the millions of migratory birds that visit the Chesapeake each fall are expected soon. In Cambridge there is an Antique Show & Sale at the American Legion Post, and Baltimore holds its Mayor's Thanksgiving Celebration. In Virginia, Urbanna (up the Rappahannock from the Bay), holds an Oyster Festival with a parade, a 10K race, arts & crafts, and "special foods." Over on the Eastern Shore again, Chincoteague celebrates Waterfowl Week (right up to Dec. 1), at which nature trails at the Wildlife Refuge are open "as Canada and Snow Geese migrate south."

December. This is the month of Christmas, and both states load their calendars with Yuletide celebrations. Christmas festivities vary from carol and choral singing, tree lightings, candlelight tours, hot cider, and wassail cups to madrigal singers, courtly dancing, and recreated 18th-century customs. Norfolk also holds its Annual Waterfront New Year's Eve Festival (music, dancing, and fireworks) at Festevents. And in Maryland, St. Mary's Christmas Madrigal Evenings, Christmas in Annapolis, and Ocean City's annual Christmas Parade are especially noteworthy. Baltimore closes out the year's events with a New Year's Eve Extravaganza, with dozens of celebrations throughout the city, culminating in a fireworks display at the Inner Harbor.

It may be a cliché, but it's nevertheless true that the Chesapeake has something of interest or entertainment going on for every visitor all year long. And remember, the listings above are only a *sampling* of what the two new calendars will include. This, then, would be a good time to write for *next year's* official calendars of events. For **Maryland,** write to Office of Tourism Development, 217 E. Redwood St., Baltimore, MD 21202. The **Virginia** calendar may be obtained from The Virginia Division of Tourism, 202 North Ninth St., Suite 500, Richmond, VA 23219.

SWIMMING. The impulse to go swimming in the Chesapeake, with the water beckoning at every turn, is practically irresistible. **A Warning:** During hot summer months, the Bay is often plagued with jellyfish and nettles, whose sting is more painful than a bee's and fairly long-lasting. To some it can be dangerous. So, swim with caution; not all Bay areas are equally infested. For some visitors, the motel pool may be the better choice. The alternative, for those who enjoy surf swimming, are the ocean beaches on the Delmarva Peninsula in both states and the Atlantic shore at Virginia Beach.

FERRY RIDES AND CRUISES. Of the Chesapeake port towns that offer boat rides, the principal ones are those large enough to attract tourists in numbers or those with historical sites that are reachable only by water. In Maryland, you can find cruises from an hour to a day to a full week aboard a cruise ship. Some of the most popular are half a day long, with lunch or dinner aboard. They offer anything from a tour of harbor sights (Baltimore and Annapolis), a trip to an offshore historical site (Fort McHenry in Baltimore harbor), a sightseeing jaunt along the waterfront and backwaters (Annapolis), a trip to an offshore island (St. Clement or Smith I.), or a live-aboard, week-long cruise that takes in a vast portion of the Bay (Baltimore to Colonial Williamsburg and return). Such cruises have schedules running from just the summer months, or from April through Oct., or all year long. Many have guides who present a narrative description of the sights as you cruise. Here's a rundown of boat trips offered in Maryland waters:

Chesapeake Bay. Seven-day cruises on Chesapeake Bay, with stops at Bay ports. Weekly from Inner Harbor, Constellation Dock, Pier 1 at Pratt St., American Cruise Lines. Phone (800) 556–7450.

Baltimore. Six cruises from 20 min. to a full day to the 1-week trip mentioned above. *Clipper City,* excursions aboard a topsail schooner, 575–7930; Harbor Charter offers hour and a half Inner Harbor cruises, 962–1171; *Lady Baltimore* and *Bay Lady,* day cruises to Annapolis and luncheon and dinner cruises, Harbor Cruises Ltd., 727–3113 or 347–3552; *Baltimore Defender* and *Baltimore Patriot,* Inner Harbor and Ft. McHenry cruises, Maryland Tours, Inc., 685–4288; and Schooner *Nighthawk,* 3-hour cruises aboard a two-masted schooner, 327–SAIL. Cruises are also available through Harbor Cruises Ltd., 301 Light St., Inner Harbor, Baltimore, MD 21202, (301) 727–3113.)

Annapolis. A variety of cruises, long and short. For sailing schedules, contact: Chesapeake Marine Tours, 268–7600; The *Lady Baltimore,* 727–3113.

Southern Maryland (Lower Western Shore). Three cruises: 1 hr. 40 min. from Pt. Lookout State Park to Smith I. (Somers Cove Marina, Crisfield, MD 21817, (301) 425–2771.) Tour boat for groups for cruises from Colton Pt. to St. Clements I. (Potomac River Museum, Colton Pt., MD 20626, (301) 769–2222.) One-hour excursions aboard a Chesapeake Bay (sailing) bugeye, with guide describing the 1814 Battle of Leonard's Creek against the British. Calvert Marine Museum, Solomons, MD 20688, (301) 326–2042.

Eastern Shore. 35 min. cruise across Tangier Sound to Smith I. (Capt. Jason, Box 642, Tylerton, MD 21866, (301) 425–2351.) 1-hr. 15-min. cruise to Smith I. with lunch & bus tour of Ewell, the "capital" of the island. (Somers Cove Marina, address as above.) 1-hr. cruise to Smith I. (Island Belle II, Box 67, Ewell, MD 21824, (301) 425–4271.) Narrated 1½-hr. cruise on Miles R., from

Chesapeake Bay Maritime Museum at St. Michaels. (Patriot Cruises, Box 1206, St. Michael's, MD 21663, (301) 745–3100.) 1½-hr. cruises across Tangier Sd. to Tangier I. with box lunches available. (Steven Thomas, Crisfield, MD 21817, (301) 968–2338.) 1½-hr. cruise to Smith I. with dining at an island restaurant. (Harborside Restaurant, Ewell, MD 21824, (301) 425–2201.)

Ocean City Area (Listed by boat and type of cruise). *Angler,* summer months, evening cruises of Ocean City waters; (301) 289–7424. *Capt. Bunting,* summer months, cruises of Ocean City waters from the Atlantic, (301) 289–6720. *Mariner,* June–Labor Day, cruises on the Atlantic, (301) 289–9125. *Miss Ocean City,* summer months, cruises on the Atlantic, (301) 289–8234. *Starfish,* mid-July to Labor Day, evening scenic cruises on Ocean City waters, (301) 289–8547. Also, Bay and Atlantic cruises through: Talbot Street Pier, Inc., 289–9125, and Bahia Marina, 289–7438 *(Tortuga).*

Here are cruises in the Virginia part of the Bay:

Norfolk & Portsmouth: Boat tours (May thru Oct.) of the harbor, including the U.S. Navy Base at Norfolk and its array of warships. *Chesapeake City:* Boat tours to Lake Drummond in the Great Dismal Swamp National Wildlife Refuge. *Jamestown:* Ferry to Smith's Fort Plantation (historic site). *Smith Point:* Passenger ferries to Smith I. and Crisfield, MD. *Reedville:* Ferry to Tangier I. and on to Crisfield, MD. For information on cruise routes and schedules, write or call: Virginia Div. of Tourism, 202 N. Ninth St., Suite 500, Richmond, VA 23219, (804) 786–4484.

Small Boat Rentals. Some waterfront motels have outboard-powered skiff or daysailers (open sailboats) available for rental to their guests. Otherwise, dozens of waterfront locations all around the Bay have fishing stations that rent boats by the day or half-day. Even if you're not an angler, if you've handled an outboard boat before, a half-day rental is a fine way to get a waterside view of a place that interests you. If you have kids along, don't expect the outboard motors provided to be powerful enough to tow a waterskier. The fishing station operators usually limit rentals to 15-horsepower motors to prevent seagoing "cowboys" from damaging the boats.

Boat-Launching Ramps. For visitors intent on spending a good deal of time on the bay, for fishing or exploring, and who bring along their own boat and motor on a trailer there are literally hundreds of public launching ramps around the Bay.

Charter Fishing Boats. For those attracted by ocean fishing, over on the Delmarva Peninsula facing the Atlantic, there are "head" boats (up to 30 fishermen) and "charter" boats (up to 6) operating out of the major coastal towns. The cost ranges from about $15 (half day) to $25 (full day) for the head boats, and the most popular places are: *Maryland*—Chesapeake Beach, Ridge, and Ocean City. *Virginia*—Chincoteague, Wachapreague, Sanford, Quinby, and Cape Charles on the Delmarva Peninsula, and Little Creek, Lynnhaven, and Rudee Inlet on the Norfolk side of the Bay.

PARKS AND FORESTS. Both states are heavily dotted with state parks, forests, and both public and private campgrounds. If you are planning a family vacation with a trailer, camper, or RV, you will find dozens of camping sites on or near the Bay. For detailed information about parks and campsites, write or call as follows: *Maryland*—Office of Tourism Development, 217 E. Redwood St., Baltimore, MD 21202; (301) 333–6611. *Virginia*—Div. of Parks & Recreation, 203 Governor St., Richmond, VA 23219; (804) 786–2134 (reservation information) or 786–1712 (general information). NOTE: *Early* reservations are *essential.*

In all, Virginia has 23 recreational and 6 historical state parks, and 6 natural areas, plus 32 private campgrounds in the Tidewater and Eastern Shore area. Maryland lists 18 state parks and 27 private campgrounds in the Annapolis, Southern, Eastern Shore and Ocean City areas.

CANOEING. Both states, with all their rivers flowing into the Chesapeake, offer a full range of challenge to the canoeist—novice, intermediate, and expert. The Western Shore offers the most opportunities, especially on Virginia rivers—the Potomac, Rappahannock, York, and James. The visitor can choose a river and a time of year to match his skills with the degree of challenge he wants to confront. Rivers are highest and swiftest in the early spring during the winter runoff. Both states offer detailed information, including sources of canoe rental, as follows: "Virginia—A Great Place to Canoe" (pamphlet) from Div. of Tourism, Bell Tower on Capitol Sq., 101 N. Ninth St., Richmond, VA 23219, (804) 786–4484. In Maryland, the principal canoeing rivers are the Choptank and Marshyhope Rivers, and Tuckahoe Creek.

FISHING. As of Jan. 1, 1985, a license was required to fish in the Maryland waters of the Chesapeake. A license may be purchased for $5 from: Dept. of Natural Resources, Box 1869, Annapolis, MD 21404; (301) 974–3211. Or, you may get your license at a sporting goods store when you reach the Bay. A typical cost is $7 for a 1-week tourist license.

No license is required for fishing in Virginia waters of the Bay, but one is mandatory for fishing freshwater streams and rivers.

In Maryland waters, these are the principal catches: black drum (Tangier Sd., mid-May to mid-June, and off Tilghman I., mid-June to late Aug.); red drum or channel bass (Tangier Sd., same season as above); flounder (Tangier Sd., entire summer); bluefish (entire Bay, Apr. through Dec.); also, white perch, weakfish, croaker, and trout; largemouth bass (1–3 lbs., in the Eastern Shore's tidewater rivers—Choptank, Nanticoke, Pocomoke, and Wicomico).

Virginia lists 32 species to lure the angler—18 in the Bay and 15 in the ocean. The Bay varieties include: black drum, channel bass, cobia, tarpon, striped bass, speckled trout, croaker, spot, weakfish, flounder, spadefish, and porgy; and in the Atlantic, sheepshead, tautog, sea bass, bluefish, sailfish, blue and white marlin, tuna, wahoo, king mackerel, dolphin, false albacore, amberjack, and swordfish.

In addition to its wide variety of fish, Virginia has a special enticement for visiting anglers. Each year the state conducts a Salt Water Fishing Tournament, which runs from May 1 through Nov. 30 (no charge), which awards 3,500 Citation wall plaques for catches meeting minimum tournament standards. Details for qualification are available at all harbors.

HUNTING. Maryland's Eastern Shore is the finest duck and goose hunting region on the Atlantic Flyway. Each year, more than half a million Canada and snow geese, ducks, and other species of migratory game birds winter on the fields and marshes along Chesapeake Bay. For detailed information on hunting and licenses, contact: Dept. of Natural Resources, Licensing and Consumer Services, Box 1869, Annapolis 21404. Hunting licenses are also available through sporting goods stores. For a guide to Public Hunting Areas, regulations, seasons, and bag limits, contact: Dept. of Natural Resources, Maryland Forest, Park, and Wildlife Service, Tawes State Office Building, Annapolis 21401, (301) 974–3195.

CRABBING. There are few things more enduring and endearing than the feisty Chesapeake Bay blue crab. Served in restaurants, they're a mouth-watering delight, but when *you* catch them they are truly superb. The crabbing season lasts from Apr. 1 through Dec. 31. Non-commercial crabbers may take up to a bushel, but no more than two bushels per boat (with two or more occupants). It is legal to use five collapsible traps per person without a license. For details, write to Dept. of Natural Resources, Tidewater Admin., 69 Prince George St., Annapolis, MD 21401 for *The Happy Crabber* and *Maryland Blue Crab Fact Sheet,* both free.

YACHT CHARTERING. If you're bound for the Chesapeake with a principal aim of chartering a sail or power yacht, perhaps for your entire vacation, but have never done so before, here is some useful information: 1) There are several ways to charter (rent) a yacht: "bareboat" (just you and your crew aboard); with captain; or, with captain *and* crew. Naturally, with captain and crew, there must be berths for all, which suggests a fairly large boat and higher charter fee. Consider the extra cost as you make your plans. 2) You must be an experienced sailor to take out a yacht—power or sail— and charterers will check you out thoroughly before they give you a yacht. Some charter operations also offer sailing lessons, so if you have *some* experience, you may be able to take lessons for a few days until you qualify to take out the yacht alone. Or you may sail with a captain for a few days, until he feels you are qualified, then put him ashore and continue the cruise alone. 3) Make sure the yacht is covered by an insurance policy providing thorough coverage for the responsibility you are assuming. Remember, if you damage or sink the boat, you're responsible; an insurance policy is your only protection. 4) The yacht will be "fully" equipped when you depart on a bareboat charter—from sailing rig and deck equipment to the last teaspoon in the galley—and you will have to sign for this inventory. Make sure you *see* every item on the list with someone from the operation *before* you sign for all of it. The list will be checked again on your return and you'll be responsible for any missing items. 5) In addition to the yacht's charter fee, you'll have to pay a "security deposit" (cash, certified check, or in some cases a credit card). These deposits vary in amount, depending on the size of yacht and amount of charter fee, but a boat of 30–35 feet can cost $600 or more. Naturally, this is all returnable if there is no damage or loss. 6) Sizes of yachts available: There's no way to pin this down exactly, as different outfits use boats made by different builders. But a good range is 25 to 45 feet, suitable for 2 to 6 persons. 7) Cost: Weekly charter fees, for the boat (regardless of how many will be aboard) range between $600 and $1,800, depending on size of boat. The fee for a 30-ft. sailboat (bareboat) is about $600. A captain aboard a boat will add about $150 a day. 8) *Make your arrangements well in advance* to insure getting the boat you want and out of the starting port you have chosen. The prime chartering period is mid-May through Oct. (See the list below for representative charter operations.) 9) Lay out a "rough" itinerary of Chesapeake ports you'd like to visit *before you go,* and do this with charts purchased at home from your local U.S. Government chart outlet; charts *are* available in the Bay area, of course, but sometimes summer demand causes marinas to run out of the one you need and you'll waste time chasing around to find it. 10) For a complete guide to charter operations in the Chesapeake, write to: Chesapeake Bay Yacht Charter Assn., Box 4022, Annapolis, MD 21403, and request their brochure listing member companies. 11) To get a sweeping sense of all you can see and do while sailing, you may want to purchase "Guide to Cruising Chesapeake Bay," available for $22.95 plus $3 postage from: Chesapeake Bay Magazine, 1819 Bay Ridge Ave., Suite 200, Annapolis, MD 21403. You can order by phone, too, (301) 263–2662, charging the guide to your VISA or MasterCard.

Most of the yacht charter operations listed below will send detailed information on boats available, accommodations, charter rates, deposits, insurance, experience requirements, and sailing lessons if offered. Charter companies come and go; if you don't find one operating at your destination, companies elsewhere on the Bay can advise you. All firms listed below offer sailboats exclusively, unless otherwise indicated:

The Sailing Emporium, Green Lane, Rock Hall, MD 21661, (301) 778–1342; *Gratitude Boat Charters,* Lawton Ave., Rock Hall,

MD 21661 (301) 639-7111; *Pelorus Yacht Sales,* Rte. 1, Bayside
Ave., Rock Hall, MD 21661, (301) 639-2151; *La Vida Yacht Charters,* Rte. 2, Box 759E, Chestertown, MD 21620, (301) 778-6330;
North East-Wind Yacht Charter, 326 First St., Annapolis, MD
21403, (301) 267-6333 or (800) 638-5139; *Nauticat Motorsailers,*
222 Severn Ave., Annapolis, MD 21403, (301) 268-7700; *Chesapeake Yacht Charters,* 1700 Bowleys Quarters Rd., Baltimore, MD
21220, (301) 335-6677; *Tradewind Charters, Inc.,* 2 E. Fayette St.,
Baltimore, MD 21202, (301) 467-7788; *White Rock Yachting Center,* 1402 Colony Rd., Pasadena, MD 21122, (301) 261-1167; *Lippencott Sailing Yachts,* Rte. 1, Box 545, Grasonville, MD 21638,
(301) 827-9300; *Commonwealth Yachts,* Box 1070, Gloucester Pt.,
VA 23062, (804) 642-2150; *Huntly Yacht Charters* (power & sail),
R.D. 1, Box 301, Wernersville, PA 19565, (215) 678-2628 or (800)
322-9224; *Baileywick,* Box 710, Solomon's, MD 20688, (301) 326-
3115.

COLONIAL SITES. For the visitor to the Chesapeake who is
also fascinated by the Colonial era in the American story, the Bay
offers dozens of opportunities to see history first hand. Wander just
a few miles inland from the Bay or its tributaries and you step into
the center of Colonial and Revolutionary War history.

If we consider the Bay area as divided—by nature and state
boundaries—into four sections, the Eastern and Western Shores
of both Virginia and Maryland, the Western Shore of Virginia offers the maximum convenient opportunity to visit a range of colonial sites while focussing primarily on the Bay. What follows is a
generous sampling of such sites just off the Bay, but it should be
emphasized that there are historic buildings, homes, inns, military
headquarters, and battlegrounds all around the rim of the Bay,
though in smaller concentrations than on Virginia's Western
Shore. The explanation is simple: It is here, between Norfolk and
the Potomac River where the first permanent English colony was
established, that many of the area's most famous plantations were
begun, and that the climactic final battle of the American Revolution was fought. (It is worth noting that you have only to range
a little further inland to reach the part of Virginia where dozens
of Civil War battles were fought. In fact, 60 percent of *all* the battles in that war were fought on Virginia soil.)

So we begin with Virginia's Tidewater region, that stretch of
shore between Norfolk and the Potomac, and pick up the start of
a historic site tour:

In Norfolk itself, there's the *Hermitage Foundation Museum* (a
splendid collection of Oriental objects, and a picnic ground); then
the *Adam Thoroughgood House* (built in 1636, the oldest standing
brick house in America); next, the *Willoughby-Baylor House* (built
1794); and finally, the *House of Moses Myers,* one of America's first
millionaires and the first Jewish resident of Norfolk.

Going north across Norfolk harbor to Hampton, you'll find the 63-acre expanse of *Fort Monroe,* a hexagonal bastion surrounded by a moat; here, over a 150-year span, distinguished prisoners such as Indian chief Black Hawk and Confederate President Jefferson Davis were incarcerated.

A bit to the northwest, in Newport News, the *Mariner's Museum* is—while not Colonial—a must-see stop for maritime/nautical buffs. The museum has the outstanding Crabtree Collection of Miniature Ships, other models, marine paintings, figureheads, and nautical memorabilia.

Driving west for 23 miles on I-64 brings you to the Colonial Parkway and the state Information Centers at Jamestown, Colonial Williamsburg, and Yorktown. In Jamestown, there's a walking tour that includes the settlement's original church tower and the foundations of many of the earliest buildings. A mile away is Jamestown Settlement, formerly known as Jamestown Festival Park (built by the state in 1957), where the visitor can go aboard reproductions of the *Susan Constant, Godspeed,* and *Discovery,* the three tiny ships that carried the first settlers here.

In Williamsburg, 60 years of painstaking restoration (with Rockefeller family funds) has returned Virginia's second capital to a startlingly accurate reproduction of life in Colonial days; especially popular with visitors are the bakery, the print shop, the blacksmith's forge, and the wig-maker's shop. And it's fascinating to walk along the broad main thoroughfare from the magnificent capitol building at one end to the College of William and Mary at the other (America's second-oldest, founded in 1693), passing as you stroll guides, soldiers, and shopkeepers, all garbed in authentic Colonial dress.

Not far from Williamsburg—only a few minutes' drive—is *Yorktown,* where combined American and French forces, commanded by General George Washington, defeated British General Lord Cornwallis on Oct. 19, 1781, and brought a successful end to the American Revolution. At the Yorktown Information Center, you can trace the steps in this final climactic battle against the British redoubt, and see tents used by Washington's troops and a diorama of the battle.

Depending on how far inland you want to drive on State Rte. 5 toward Richmond, as it winds roughly along the James River (the total distance is 51 mi.), you can see the greatest concentration of great houses and plantations anywhere in the U.S. Six miles east of Williamsburg (on Rte. 60) is *Carter's Grove,* a 1750 mansion built by wealthy Robert "King" Carter, whose home is considered one of the most beautiful in America. At Jamestown, you can take a ferry across the James to *Smith's Fort Plantation,* and see the foundations of the breastworks built in 1609 by Capt. John Smith. On these grounds is the *Rolfe-Warren House,* a brick structure built in 1652.

Moving west from Williamsburg, you encounter a procession of famous Colonial homes. First is *Sherwood Forest,* built by President John Tyler, who fancied himself a "political Robin Hood." Then comes *Bel Air,* built in 1670, one of the oldest frame dwellings in the country. Following that is *Evelynton,* a brick mansion built on land that once belonged to the Byrds of Virginia. (You may visit Bel Air by appointment only; Evelynton is open daily.) The great William Byrd II himself—diarist, member of the Colonial governor's council, explorer, and founder of Richmond—once owned 179,000 acres of Virginia land and lived nearby in *Westover.*

Next in the sequence is *Berkeley,* the home of Benjamin Harrison, V, a signer of the Declaration of Independence, and his son, President William Henry Harrison. Last in the series along Rte. 5 is *Shirley Plantation,* a home that has been in the Hill-Carter family for nine generations, since 1723. This was the home of Robert E. Lee's mother, Anne Hill Carter, and it still contains many of the original furnishings.

The section of Virginia lying between the Rappahannock and Potomac Rivers is renowned for producing U.S. presidents and statesmen. In this area, King George County gave us President James Madison, and Westmoreland County was the birthplace of George Washington, James Monroe, and Robert E. Lee. The Lee house, *Stratford Hall,* was started in 1725 by Thomas Lee. All told, this home produced 12 members of the Virginia House of Burgesses, four governors, the Revolution's Light Horse Harry Lee (Washington's cavalry commander), and the Confederacy's Robert E. Lee. Stratford Hall was built of brick shipped from England, in the shape of a capital H. It measures 60 by 90 feet. Its 1,500 acres are still worked as they were in Colonial times. The house overlooks the Potomac, only 8 miles from Wakefield, the birthplace of George Washington.

Wakefield is an approximation of Washington's home (the original burned down on Christmas Day, 1779), and was rebuilt by the National Park Service. Many of the original furnishings were saved and may be seen at Wakefield.

For those willing to wander further, or for those approaching from the west, Virginia has *many* more fascinating colonial sites. South of Appomattox (west of Petersburg on US 460) lies *Red Hill Shrine,* the home of the great patriot Patrick Henry. *Staunton* (I-65, NW of Richmond) is the family home of President Woodrow Wilson, and near Leesburg (NW of Washington, D.C., on Rte. 7) is *Oatlands Plantation,* a classical revival mansion built in 1800 by George Carter, the great-grandson of "King" Carter, whose mansion is near Williamsburg. The bricks and lumber for this great home were produced on this 3,400-acre plantation, and the terraced formal gardens are among the finest examples of early Virginia landscape design. Also near Leesburg is *Morven Park,* with a mile-long tree-lined drive leading to the house, the former home of Gov. Westmoreland Davis, with its Greek revival portico, a Jacobean dining room, a French drawing room and a library. The house is furnished with intricately carved furniture, oriental rugs, 16th-century tapestries, and rare porcelain, china, and silverware.

As you circle the Bay, visiting the places that attract you the most, dozens of signs, historical markers on highways, and Maryland and Virginia highway information centers will lie along your wandering route. Each will help guide you to historical sites that span over 350 years of America's past. You won't be bored around Chesapeake Bay, but you may have a problem finding enough time to see all the sights and do all the things that are waiting there for you.

Excellent touring maps may be obtained from visitor centers in the two states, both on the road or in major cities; or from Maryland and Virginia tourism offices (see Touring Information, above). The various state touring maps are uniformly informative, and, best of all, they're free!

THE CHESAPEAKE
REGION

TOURING THE CHESAPEAKE BAY AREA

by
STEVE DOHERTY

Ask any 100 visitors to the Chesapeake Bay why they are there
and you'll probably get 100 different answers. Every traveler has
favorite things to see and do and just about every one of those
things can be found in and around "the Bay." For sports enthusi-
asts, there's swimming, boating, fishing, hunting, horse racing, and
horseback riding. Hobbyists can find arts, antiques, flowers, sand
castles, dog shows, and—would you belive?—duck decoy carving
contests!

Interested in history? There's the Jamestown-Williamsburg-
Yorktown "Historic Triangle," George Washington's birthplace,
Annapolis, Fort McHenry, museums, plantations, and old seaport
towns. If you enjoy the city life, Baltimore is at the north end and
Norfolk at the south.

The scenery includes farmlands in Delmarva, tiny hidden fishing
villages in secluded coves, wild ponies on barren sandy banks, and
white sails on blue water. Your experiences in the Chesapeake Bay
area might include watching smart young midshipmen on parade

at the U.S. Naval Academy in Annapolis, a ride over and under the Bay where the Chesapeake joins the Atlantic, or a sumptuous feast of very-recently-caught seafood or long-and-lovingly-cured Virginia ham. Read on, and you'll find *your* reason to visit the Chesapeake.

Geography

Chesapeake Bay is a unique topographical feature of the U.S. East Coast. Two hundred miles long from north to south, it is the largest inland body of water on the Atlantic Coast. (Small-boat sailors will note that Long Island Sound, while impressive as a body of protected water, is only 150 miles long.) The Chesapeake runs north and south, roughly parallel to the Atlantic. It is actually an estuary flowing into the ocean and, by penetrating deep into the land interior, has had a vital role in the development of this mid-Atlantic region. Visualize how long it would have taken to develop the vast land area touching the Chesapeake if there had been no Bay and only rutted, muddy wagon roads for transportation.

It's hard to exaggerate the importance of the Bay as a Colonial "water highway" for freight, farm produce, mail, and passengers. The early American cities were East Coast ports, with easy access to the Atlantic. Among these were Charleston, South Carolina; Norfolk, Virginia; Baltimore, Maryland; New York City; and Boston, Massachusetts. Even Philadelphia, so pivotal in America's early history, was easily reached by any ship that proceeded up Delaware Bay until it became a river.

Norfolk, just inside the mouth of the Bay, was an obvious site for a city, and Baltimore has been a major seaport since Colonial days, simply because the Chesapeake was navigable for 150 miles north of the ocean. But the Chesapeake's importance goes beyond that. Even locally it shaped the way this part of the nation developed.

At the lower (Virginia) end of this great bay, when that state was still an English colony in the early 1600s, its first settlement was at Jamestown, which was also the capital. Virginia's second capital was Williamsburg. Both were on the banks of the James River, within easy reach of the Bay. Even after the capital was moved to Richmond more than a century later, that city was still reachable via the James.

Further north, in Maryland, it's the same story. The Maryland colony was founded in 1634, 27 years after Jamestown. Its capital was later established at Annapolis, facing east on the Chesapeake. Not only were Norfolk, Williamsburg, Richmond, Annapolis, and Baltimore within easy sailing distance of each other and of all the small waterfront towns that lay between, but perhaps more important, each could easily reach the national capital at Washington, D.C. by proceeding up the Potomac River from the Bay. During the Civil War Abraham Lincoln sometimes used the Bay as a quick route to the front lines so he could have face-to-face conferences with his commanders. Once he departed the White House surreptitiously (so as not to alarm the capital's populace where Confederate forces were less than 100 miles away), proceeded down the Potomac to the Bay in a fast steamboat, ran south to the James River, and then up that river to General U. S. Grant's headquarters outside Richmond. Within 24 hours he was back in the Oval Office, with no one in Washington aware he had been away.

The rivers that flow into the Chesapeake are an important part the Bay's transportation network. And there are a lot of them! Starting in the extreme north, the Susquehanna flows from Pennsylvania into the narrow upper end. Down the Bay's Western Shore, eight rivers empty into its waters from Maryland: Gunpowder, Back, Patapsco, Magothy, Severn, South, West, and Patuxent. Then there is the broad Potomac, which is the state line between Maryland and Virginia. In Virginia, four more rivers flow into the Bay: Rappahannock, Piankatank, York, and James. (The two most southerly rivers, first discovered by the early settlers, were named after English royalty, while the two further north were named later for local Indian tribes.)

On the Bay's Eastern Shore, eight more rivers feed the Bay. All are in Maryland. They are Bohemia, Sassafras, Chester, Eastern, Tred Avon, Choptank, Nanticoke, and Wicomico.

A visitor may be surprised to learn that Maryland has more than 3,100 miles of shoreline, but only 31 miles of it faces the Atlantic. This startling fact is explained by the many sounds and caves that form the Bay's jagged shoreline. There are literally hundreds of places on the Eastern Shore where two neighbors, facing each other's houses across a short expanse of water, can visit each other in minutes by boat, while the trip *around* the inlet could take an hour or more by car. (In Colonial times, that same journey would have taken a day or more by wagon.)

It will *not* surprise the visitor to the Chesapeake, therefore, to learn that in this topography where hundreds of fingers of water poke into the land from all directions, the *boat* still ranks high on the scale of must "things" to own, and a dock often exceeds a garage in importance. For the visitor, the boat is the "transport of delight" that will open up the wonders and pleasures of the Chesapeake.

As an inlet of the ocean, the Bay pulses with the ebb and flow of the ocean's tides, although the Atlantic, with such a mighty basin to fill and empty twice each day, achieves a tidal range of only 2 to 3 feet from high to low. For large ships, smaller commercial vessels operating between local ports, the "watermen" who earn their living on Bay waters, and for small-boat recreational sailors, this small tidal range is a blessing. While sailors to the north and south of the Chesapeake—from Maine to Georgia—contend with tides that rise and fall 6 to 8 feet, and must have floating docks to accommodate the change, Chesapeake sailors simply moore their boats with a careful arrangement of docking lines.

The Chesapeake is more than a boon to water transportation. Being *salt* water—because of the ebb and flow of the tide—the Bay is home to a marvelous variety of seafood—the fish, clams, crabs, and oysters that have been taken out of the Bay for centuries. At the time of the earliest settlements, the water was so pure and the Bay so full of seafood that had reproduced for centuries undisturbed (with the exception of small amounts consumed by local Indians) that boatloads of seafood were the "miracle" that helped Jamestown survive until its first crops were harvested. The Bay has continued to provide such delicacies right up to the present, although warnings are beginning to appear.

Some years ago, when the internal combustion engine was developed and the sailboats of the Bay were first converted to power, it became evident that Chesapeake oysters, which were being shipped in ice all over the country, would not last long if powerboats were allowed to dredge them off the bottom. So a law was passed that oysters could only be dredged by boats under *sail power alone.* And so it remains today, to the delight of visitors, who occasionally see them working offshore or watch them returning to their home ports at night.

Industrial pollution is another threat to Bay waters, but it is gratifying to report that surrounding states and the federal government are making a concerted and costly effort to curtail contamination. Unless they succeed, one of the Chesapeake's greatest gifts, its seafood, will be lost to the Bay's residents and to millions of others along the Eastern Seaboard.

Geographically, the Chesapeake ebbs and flows through two states, the upper 60 percent of it in Maryland, the lower 40 percent in Virginia. The dividing line lies—like the border between North and South Korea—on the 38th Parallel of Latitude. On the Western Shore, the state line follows the Potomac River. Let's look at the land around the Chesapeake. Later chapters will follow this clockwise exploration of the Bay.

Maryland was founded as a English colony in 1634 by Cecil Calvert, the second Lord Baltimore. It was named for Queen Henrietta Maria. Calvert was a Roman Catholic who believed in religious freedom, and the new colony was open to all faiths. The settlements were ruled by succeeding Lords Baltimore through the Colonial period. During the American Revolution, the Second Continental Congress met briefly in Baltimore. The new federal government sat for a time in Annapolis, until the state gave land for the District of Columbia.

During the War of 1812, while watching ships of the Royal Navy shell Fort McHenry in Baltimore Harbor, Francis Scott Key wrote the words to the "Star Spangled Banner," and the song became our national anthem. By that time, Maryland was already known as the "Old Line State," a nickname given it when George Washington praised the heroic "troops of the line" for their fighting prowess during the Revolution. Half a century later, during America's Civil War, 60 percent of the battles were fought in Virginia, but several major engagements took place in Maryland, including one of the bloodiest: Antietam.

Maryland has a population of 4.3 million, with nearly 9 out of 10 citizens living in rural areas. The state has its highest point at Backbone Mt. (3,360 ft.), and its lowest, sea level, on its Atlantic shore. Maryland's motto is *Fatti Machii Parole Femine* ("Manly deeds, womanly words"), and the state song is "Maryland, My Maryland" (to the melody of the German "O, Tannenbaum"). Maryland's state bird, not surprisingly, is the Baltimore Oriole, its flower is the Black-Eyed Susan, and its tree is the White Oak.

On its farms, Maryland grows corn, soybeans, and tobacco, and produces milk, broilers, and beef cattle. In its factories, the output is electric and electronic equipment, machinery, chemicals, transportation equipment, printed materials, paper products, and clothing; and from its mines, clay, stone, coal, sand, and gravel.

Virginia, at the southern end of the Chesapeake, has nearly four times the land area of Maryland (40,817 to 10,577 square miles), with a high point in its western mountains at Mt. Rogers (5,729 ft.), and a low point, like Maryland, on the Atlantic Shore. The population of the "Old Dominion" is 5.6 million. Virginia was named for Elizabeth I, the "Virgin Queen" of England. As noted above, Jamestown (1607), on the James River, was the first permanent English settlement in America. When Virginia entered the Union on June 25, 1788, it covered an enormous land area that extended all the way to the Mississippi River. This area was eventually carved up into eight of our present states.

Small details of interest are: state flower—American dogwood; state bird—Cardinal; state dog—Foxhound; state motto—*Sic Semper Tyrannis* ("Thus always to tyrants"); and state song—"Carry Me Back to Old Virginia."

The Lure of the Chesapeake

When you arrive at the Bay, you'll find that the focus, carried over from the area's earliest days, is on *water,* all the things you can do in, on, and around the water. And that means boats. Not *only* boats, of course, because a great many attractions are *at* the water's edge—fishing piers, waterfront restaurants, port facilities, fishing stations, art galleries, craft fairs, and theaters. But if you want to enjoy the Chesapeake to the fullest, make sure you include boats in your plans.

In many Chesapeake port towns, a boat ride is simply the *best* way to get from here to there or to see the sights, perhaps the only way to get the full picture. Many towns and cities—Baltimore and Annapolis come to mind—recognize this and their harbor boat tours are among their most popular offerings. Most boat rides run an hour or less, but you *can* find longer boat tours. Some boat rides will take you out on the Bay for a whole day (with lunch or dinner aboard), and you can even cruise for a week, living aboard as you would on a mini ocean liner.

For visitors who arrive already in love with boats—perhaps owning one back home—the problem is not where to find them, but how to keep boating activities within your available time.

Let's say you've taken in Baltimore—done the Inner Harbor tour; gone aboard the U.S. Navy's first ship, the U.S.S. *Constellation;* toured the fabulous new Aquarium; explored the shops; and sampled the restaurant fare—and now you are ready to move on. Head south!

About 50 miles south on Rte. 2 lies Annapolis, the state capital, site of many historic buildings, home of the U.S. Naval Academy, and headquarters of more "boating activity" than you can wave an oar at. Here, in the summer season, you may see a sailing regatta, take a harbor ride, rent a boat for fishing, charter a sailboat for a day or a week of sailing on your own, check out dozens of yacht brokers (for a used boat) or boat dealers (for a new one), or thump hulls the way car buffs love to kick tires at auto shows. If you're a boat person, wander from showroom to boatyard and back to showroom to see which one of them is offering your next "dreamboat." If you're already a boat-owner, the next step in your cruising life is a custom-built boat and you can easily spend an entire Chesapeake vacation discussing your requirements (and the cost) with boatbuilders in and around the Annapolis area. They're tucked into every nook and cranny around the Severn and South Rivers, which flow into the Bay on either side of town.

In spite of this small port-town's Colonial heritage, it's no exaggeration to say that Annapolis is the most boat- and boating-oriented town on the U.S. East Coast. (Although Newport, Rhode Island, might take exception.) If you're there in mid-October, when *two* four-day boat shows are held (Sail, then Power), back to back, you'll understand why Chesapeake Bay sailors are called "serious boating people." Wherever there isn't a boat dealer or charter operation or boatyard, you'll find a sail loft or a ship's chandlery offering all sorts of salty and sophisticated yacht gear. If you are planning to attend the Annapolis boat shows, make sure you make your lodging reservation *not less than six months in advance;* Annapolis is awash with yachting types during the middle two weekends in October!

Across the Bay (via the bridge), two real boating towns recommend themselves to the boat-lover. Set in the more placid country of the Eastern Shore and home ports to many beautifully maintained wood boats of classical vintage, these towns are Cambridge and Oxford, both dating back to Colonial days, as their English names suggest. After crossing the Bay Bridge, drive south on US

50. Oxford is west of US 50, on Rte. 333. Cambridge is farther south on US 50, across the Choptank River. Both towns are renowned for gracious inns offering comfortable "Old World" accommodations and menus filled with Chesapeake gourmet delicacies.

The remainder of the Eastern Shore, down through the rest of Maryland and Virginia to Cape Charles and the Bay Bridge and Tunnel complex, is a quiet agricultural region, with many small farms, some large estates, and few towns of any real size. The shoreline through here is cut by rivers that flow through marshland to the Bay. Each peninsula formed by two rivers is as jagged as an octopus—miles and miles of twisting shoreline, creating dozens of small bays and sounds. It's a watery playground made in heaven for the small-boat sailor, the professional "waterman" who makes his living from the Bay's offerings, and for the amateur who cruises for pleasure or fishes for sport. Dozens of country roads end at the water's edge, where you may find a small boatyard, a town dock, a public launching ramp, a small boat club—or just a few boats tied up to stakes, waiting there until their owners are free to go fishing or sailing again. In almost every town, however small, you'll find some type of "eatery," from a simple lunch stand on the water's edge to a pleasant Bay-front restaurant. Count on it—each will be serving fresh-caught seafood from the Bay.

If you cross the Delmarva Peninsula toward the ocean (from Cambridge, take US 50 to Salisbury and stay on it till you reach the ocean), you can visit Ocean City, Maryland's only seaside resort. Ocean City is for swimming in ocean surf (10 miles of beach) or strolling along the Boardwalk. Then, turning south again toward Cape Charles, you can stop at Chincoteague, Virginia, to savor Tom's Cove oysters, touted by the natives as "the best in the world." And here at Chincoteague, in the fall of the year, you may be on hand when the wild ponies that live on Assateague Island are herded for a swim to the mainland, where they are auctioned off to the highest bidders. You can go ocean fishing here on a "head boat" (up to 30 people) or a "charter boat" (up to 6), and you can do the same further down the coast in Wachapreague, as you head for the Bay Bridge-Tunnel.

For those who like a taste of small-town flavor, pause a while at Oyster (pronounced "Orster" locally)—perhaps for lunch—to take in the daily routine of folks who face the ocean with their backs to the Bay, and make a living from both. In Oyster you'll find piles of oyster shells that are higher than your head down by the waterfront, evidence from decades of making a living from the town's namesake. And here there's a wonderful seafood festival every year in the autumn.

After that, your next jump south will take you over *and* under the Bay on the toll bridge-tunnel into Norfolk. There, in the harbor you can take a boat trip and see the U.S. Navy's mothballed fleet and vessels of every description crisscrossing the Bay and harbor. In nearby Virginia Beach, Hampton, and Newport News, you'll find a wide range of cultural activities, historic sites, and, yes, more seafood restaurants. As you cross another (toll) bridge-tunnel to Hampton and drive northward, you should be aware that just a few miles inland to the west, Virginia offers a great concentration of famous historical sites (more on these below).

If you turn northward on US 17, veering eastward back toward the Bay, and across the Piankatank River, you'll arrive in Deltaville, a town widely known as the capital of wooden boatbuilding on Virginia's Western Shore. For those who like to study local types and see steel and wood boats under construction, more than half a dozen boatyards are turning out yachts and the boats that local watermen use for their work on the Bay. There's more of the same if you follow the Rappahannock River upstream to Urbanna, but if you don't want to wander too far inland, you can cross the Piankatank on the Rte. 3 bridge into Lancaster and Northumberland counties. This region, like that south of it, is tobacco country, and here you will find Reedville and Smith Point, where you can catch ferries bound across the Bay with stops at islands in mid-Bay. Interstate 64, north out of Norfolk, will take you to that historic trio—Jamestown, Williamsburg, and Yorktown.

Further north in Virginia's Northern Neck, the next river crossing is over the wide Potomac, where there are no bridges until you reach US 301. For those who wish to take in some American history, a "detour" up Virginia Rte. 202 will bring you close to Stratford Hall, the birthplace of Robert E. Lee. (See more later on historic sites.) Either way, when you reach US 301, you can turn north again, cross the Potomac (toll bridge), and reenter Maryland. At this point you'll be about 50 miles south of Annapolis, the end of this imaginary circuit of the Bay. If you use this plan and arrive back at Annapolis with time left to spend, you can easily fill the remaining days taking in bypassed events and attractions in Maryland's capital.

MARYLAND'S WESTERN SHORE

Three Southern Counties—Calvert, Charles, and St. Marys

by
JAMES LOUTTIT

Maryland was born on these gentle shores.

The date was March 25, 1634; the place St. Clement's Island in the Potomac, just off Colton Point.

The Indians were there first, but their lease was running out. John Smith inspected the property in 1608, but the captain had a lot of things on his mind and didn't stay very long. William Claiborne of Virginia had staked a claim to a nice piece of bay-front property on Kent Island in 1631. He was still there when the first Maryland colonists landed from *Ark* and *Dove* three years later. Claiborne fixed the newcomers with a jaundiced eye, not sure that he didn't prefer the Powhatans to his new neighbors from England. Trader Claiborne stuck around long enough to become a royal pain in the breeches to his king and to Lord Baltimore, but that's another story.

The new arrivals were also in Maryland to stay. Devout Catholics, they first erected a cross on St. Clement's Island, then built a small fort—a "pallizado of one hundred and twentie yards square"—when they moved to the mainland a little while later. Within a short time settlers had scattered over several miles of the peninsula between the Chesapeake and the Potomac, and had founded St. Maries Citty, which would be Maryland's Colonial capital for 60 years. Historic St. Marys City today features an interpretive museum and visitor center, a reconstruction of Maryland's first state house, archaeological digs, and living-history exhibits.

Tucked away between bay and river, Maryland's most historic region is all-too-often its forgotten shore, but Southern Marylanders are proud of their roots and they are changing that; there are more touring attractions in the area each year. Especially noteworthy is *Maryland Dove,* a replica of Lord Baltimore's square-rigged *Dove,* which is docked on St. Mary's River, St. Marys City.

Maryland's three Southern Counties, are a quiet, sparsely populated land of tobacco fields, 18th-century towns, and stately tidewater plantations. The region is also a gastronomical delight, for this is also the natural home of the oyster and crab and Southern Maryland stuffed ham. Southern Maryland celebrates its tobacco crop—the early cavaliers' "green gold"—each spring, March till May, when the warehouses in Upper Marlboro, Hughesville, and Waldorf are crowded with buyers, sellers, and tourists and ring with the singsong chant of tobacco auctioneers. Additional celebrations of Maryland's history are the Patuxent River Appreciation Days (October), the St. Marys County Oyster Festival (also October), the "No Foolin" Antiques Show in March, and the crab year-round.

Southern Maryland—on the Bay's Western Shore—should be enjoyed at your leisure, but be prepared to let your belt out at least one notch, two for a longer stay.

Unless you have a yacht and plenty of time, the best way to see the Southern Counties is by car. Turn onto side roads as often as you like to sample the leisurely pleasures of tree-lined lanes, country hamlets, and unexpected waterscapes.

Each season has its own beauty to offer, although the long, moderate Tidewater springs and falls are most suited for auto travel. Try to include a stopover at the growing recreation center of Solomons by the mouth of the Patuxent River, where the seafood restaurants are outnumbered only by the sailboats.

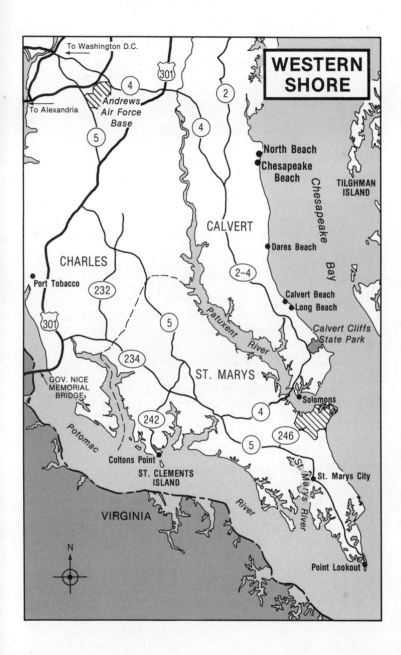

To Washington D.C.

US 301

4

2

To Alexandria

Andrews Air Force Base

5

4

● **North Beach**
● **Chesapeake Beach**

TILGHMAN ISLAND

CALVERT

Chesapeake Bay

● Dares Beach

CHARLES

2-4

● Port Tobacco

232

● Calvert Beach
● Long Beach

US 301

5

Patuxent River

Calvert Cliffs State Park

234

ST. MARYS

GOV. NICE MEMORIAL BRIDGE

242

4

● Solomons

Potomac

5

246

Coltons Point ●

ST. CLEMENTS ISLAND

St. Marys River

● St. Marys City

VIRGINIA

River

N

● Point Lookout

WESTERN SHORE

PRACTICAL INFORMATION FOR
MARYLAND'S WESTERN SHORE

Note: The area code for all Maryland is 301.

PLACES TO STAY

MOTELS AND INNS. Maryland's three southern counties—Calvert, Charless, and St. Mary's—are a rural area of the Western Shore, with numerous small towns and hamlets but no major urban centers. Although there are many small motels throughout the region, there are few major motel complexes complete with full-line restaurants. The following is a selection only of those that are available.

Calvert County

Holiday Inn Conference Center & Marina. *Moderate to Expensive.* VA Rtes. 2–4, Solomons; 326–6311; 170 rooms. A full-line hotel with pool and conference facilities and boat rentals at nearby marina. AE, DC, MC, V.

Comfort Inn. *Moderate.* Lore Rd., Solomons; 326–6303 or (800) 228–5150. 60 rooms, with pool and restaurant. AE, DC, MC, V.

Bowen's Inn. *Inexpensive to Moderate.* Main St., Solomons, 326–2214. Nine hotel units, with marina and restaurant nearby. MC, V.

Charles County

Holiday Inn of Waldorf. *Moderate.* US 301 and St. Patrick's Dr., 20601; 645–8200 or (800) HOLIDAY. 193 units in a three-story motel. Pool, restaurant, and bar. AE, DC, MC, V.

Days Inn Hotel. *Moderate.* US 301N, Waldorf; 932–9200 or (800) 325–2525. 100 rooms, with meeting facilities. Restaurant adjacent. AE, DC, MC, V.

EconoLodge. *Inexpensive.* US 301 at Acton Lane, Waldorf; 645–0022 or (800) 446–6900. 92 rooms, with a restaurant nearby. AE, DC, MC, V.

Martha Washington Motel. *Inexpensive.* US 301, Waldorf; 645–1200. 50 rooms. Outdoor pool. Restaurant nearby. AE, CB, DC, MC, V.

Lafayette Motel. *Inexpensive.* US 301, Bel Alton, 934–8233. 38 motel units, with a restaurant nearby. AE, MC, V.

La Plata Motel. *Inexpensive.* US 301, La Plata; 934–8121 or 934–8122. 40 motel units, restaurant nearby. AE, MC, V.

St. Marys County

Patuxent Inn. *Moderate.* VA 235, near Patuxent Naval Air Test Center, Lexington Park, 20653; 862–4100. 120 hotel rooms, with outdoor pool, restaurant, jogging track, two tennis courts. Tennis and golf packages. AE, CB, DC, MC, V.

Belvedere Motor Inn. *Inexpensive to Moderate.* 60 Main St., Lexington Park; 863–6666. 166 units, including efficiencies. Outdoor pool, restaurant, with tennis nearby. AE, CB, DC, MC, V.

A & E Motel. *Inexpensive.* 412 Great Falls Rd., Lexington Park; 863–7411. 35 rooms. Restaurant nearby. AE, MC, V.

Lord Calvert Motel. *Inexpensive.* Rte. 235, Lexington Park, 863–8131. 29 motel units, with outdoor pool. Restaurant nearby. MC, V.

Lexington Park Super 8 Motel. *Inexpensive.* 290 Three Notch Rd., California (VA 235); 862–9822 or (800) 843–1991. 62 rooms, with meeting facilities. No major credit cards.

PLACES TO EAT

RESTAURANTS. The emphasis as a general rule is on good food, not decor, in Calvert, Charles, and St. Marys Counties. And, still as a general rule, that good food will be fresh from the Bay or nearby farms. This is the Land of the Oyster and Crab, and few will complain about that. The following is of course a selection only of the numerous seafood and general restaurants that dot the area, especially near the Bay.

Calvert County

Old Field Inn. *Expensive.* 485 Main St., Prince Frederick; 535–1054. Local seafood, American and Continental cuisine in comfortable Victorian house. Reservations recommended. Dinner only Sat., brunch and dinner Sun. AE, MC, V.

Crabhouse. *Moderate.* Rtes. 2 and 4, Solomons; 326–2800. Open year round, seven days a week, dinner only Mon.–Thurs., and lunch and dinner Fri.–Sun. Spicy Maryland steamed crabs and every other way. The Crabhouse is an old firehouse with a nice harbor view. No credit cards.

St. Marys County

Evan's Crab House. *Moderate.* St. George's Island; 994–2299. Hard shell crab and soft shell crab sandwiches. Open all year, closed Mondays, 4 P.M. to 11 P.M. weekdays, from noon till 11 P.M. weekends. Dockage available on St. George's Creek. No credit cards.

Farthing's Ordinary. *Moderate to Expensive.* A reconstructed 17th-century inn, with outbuildings, open for dining (see Historic

St. Marys City in "Things to See and Do," below); 862–0990. MC,
V.

THINGS TO SEE AND DO

TOURING INFORMATION. General. *Charles County* Public
Information Officer, Box B, La Plata, MD 20646 (645–0580); *Cal-
vert County* Tourism, 175 Main St., Prince Frederick, MD 20678
(535–1600); *St. Marys* County Chamber of Commerce, Rte. 5, Box
41–A, Mechanicsville, MD 20659 (884–5555). **Fishing.** *Calvert
County* Dept. of Economic Development, 175 Main St., Prince
Frederick, MD 20678 (535–1600, Ext. 211); *Charles* and *St. Marys*
Counties, same as above.

Calvert County

Battle Creek Cypress Swamp Sanctuary. One of the northern-
most stands of bald cypress in America, the swamp is located on
Grays Rd., off Rte. 506. Self-guided elevated tours. Open 10 A.M.
to 5 P.M. Tuesday through Saturday, 1 P.M. to 5 P.M. Sunday. Visitors
center (535–5327).
  Bayside Beaches. Two excellent Calvert County beaches are:
Chesapeake Beach, opposite the intersection of Rtes. 260 and 261.
Picnic tables. Fee. *North Beach,* between 3rd and 7th Sts. on Rte.
261. Free.
  Bugeye Cruise. Hour-long excursions aboard an 1899 Chesa-
peake Bay bugeye. May–Oct., Wed.–Sun., 2 P.M. Adults $3.50, chil-
dren $2.50. Contact the *Wm. B. Tennison,* Calvert Marine Muse-
um, Solomons. Phone 326–2042 for details.
  Calvert Cliffs State Park. Rtes. 2 and 4, south of Lusby. Thirty
miles of the Chesapeake's western shore, first described by Captain
Smith. Famous for its Miocene fossils, 15 to 30 million years old.
Scavenging permitted but no digging allowed on cliffs. Open
March through October, sunrise to sunset. 326–6578.
  Calvert Cliffs Nuclear Power Plant Museum. Rtes. 2 and 4,
Lusby. Dioramas and exhibits in a converted tobacco barn. Open
9 A.M. to 5 P.M., closed Christmas. 586–2200. Free.
  Calvert Marine Museum. Rte. 2, Solomons. Local maritime his-
tory and fossils from Calvert Cliffs Drum Point Lighthouse and
cruises on a converted 1899 bugeye, *Wm. B. Tennison.* Open daily,
326–2042. Donations accepted. During the fall and winter, September through March, visitors can see working oyster boats at
Broomes Island, Chesapeake Beach, and Solomons Island.
  Chesapeake Beach Railway Museum. Rte. 261, Chesapeake
Beach. Housed in old railway station; exhibits depict a turn-of-the-
century resort. Open daily 1 P.M. to 4 P.M. 257–3892. Free.
  Cove Point Light Station. Cove Point Rd., Rte. 497, off Rtes.
2 and 4, Cove Point. Oldest lighthouse on the Bay, with a great
view of the Chesapeake and Calvert Cliffs. 326–3254. Free.

Jefferson Patterson Park and Museum. Nearly 70 archaeological sites on 2½ miles of Patuxent River shoreline. Located on Mackall Rd. (Rte. 265), Port Republic. Location of Battle of St. Leonard's Creek, largest naval engagement in Maryland waters during War of 1812. Museum and visitors center. Open Apr. 15–Oct. 15, Wednesday through Sunday, 10–5. For information, call 586–0050.

Charles County

Cedarville State Forest. South of Cedarville, off MD 301, this natural forest area offers camping sites, freshwater fishing, hiking, and nature trails. Phone 888–1622 for details.

Dr. Mudd's House. Back a fair piece from the water, but an interesting side trip, Dr. Samuel A. Mudd's restored farm home is on Rte. 232, Bryantown. Dr. Mudd's descendants will show you where the unlucky doctor set John Wilkes Booth's broken leg after the actor had shot President Lincoln. Open weekends, 12–4, April till late November. 645–2870 or 934–8464. Adults $3, children 75¢.

1819 Charles County Courthouse. A reconstructed Federal courthouse in Port Tobacco, with tobacco and archaeological exhibits. Closed January and February. 934–4313. Admission.

Historic Port Tobacco. Rtes. 6 and 427, several miles west of US 301, Port Tobacco is the site of the first permanent English settlement in Charles County. Historic Federal-style courthouse (Chapel Point Rd.) and museum, 10 till 4, Wednesday through Saturday, and at noon Sunday, June through August; Saturday and Sunday only April–May, September–December. Closed January–March. 934–4313. Admission.

Popes Creek. Once the gathering place for local Indians, who sat on the north bank of the Potomac and ate shellfish and crabs, this tiny community is now a gathering place for locals and tourists, who sit on the north bank of the Potomac and eat shellfish and crabs. The riverfront site of several seafood houses and restaurants, Popes Creek is located 3 miles south of Faulkner on US 301.

Tobacco Auctions. Upper Marlboro, Waldorf, and Hughesville, mid-March through the first week in May. Open Monday through Thursday, 9 A.M. until the last leaf's sold. 782–4594. Free.

Smallwood's Retreat. This restored Colonial tidewater plantation is located in Smallwood State Park, Rison, quite a way up the Potomac from the Bay. Outbuildings illustrate 18th-century plantation life. House open weekends. 743–7613. Free.

St. Marys County

Cecil's Mill. This three-story mill and country store in Great Mills, off Rte. 5, houses a crafts shop, where some 90 artisans demonstrate and sell local arts and handicrafts. Open Friday to Sunday, 10–5, mid-March till November. Closed Thanksgiving. 994–1510 or 994–1770.

Chancellor's Point Natural History Area. St. Marys City. Sixty-six acres of woodland, marsh, beach, and bluff on St. Mary's River. Open daily except Christmas, sunrise to sunset.

Godiah Spray Tobacco Plantation. St. Marys City. This is a working reconstruction of a 17th-century tobacco farm. Living history presentations during the summer. The plantation is part of Historic St. Marys City (see below). 862–0990 or 862–0960. Admission.

Historic St. Marys City. An outdoor history museum on 800 acres on the site of Maryland's first settlement and first capital. The museum's visitors center is housed in a complex of restored farm houses (862–0990) and includes information, a gift shop, and exhibits. Other Historic St. Marys City features are State House of 1676, *Maryland Dove,* Godiah Spray Tobacco Plantation, Chancellor's Point Natural History Center, Old Trinity Church, built in the early 1800s with bricks salvaged from the original State House of 1676, and Farthing's Ordinary Inn. This focal point of early Maryland history is open weekends, 10–5, mid-March to May and September to November; daily, 10–5, June to September. 862–0990. Adults $4, senior citizens $2, children $1.50.

Old Jail Museum. Dating back to 1858, the Old Jail in Leonardtown now houses the headquarters, museum, and library of St. Marys Historical Society. Open Tuesday–Saturday, 10–4. Closed Christmas week. Phone 475–2467. Free.

Point Lookout State Park and Fort Lincoln. Civil War exhibits at the visitors center (Rte. 5) and the Point Lookout Confederate Cemetery, where prisoners were interred. The earthen fort was built by Confederate POWs. Open daily except Thanksgiving and Christmas week. 872–5688. Free.

St. Clement's Island. Off Colton Point, Rte. 242. A 40-foot cross—not the original!—marks the spot the first settlers landed from *Ark* and *Dove* in 1634. Boat tours available at St. Clement's Island-Potomac Museum, Friday–Sunday, 12–4, June–September. The museum on Bay View Road, Colton Point, has exhibits spanning 12,000 years. Open weekdays, 9–4, weekends, 12–4; closed Monday and Tuesday in winter. 769–2222.

St. Mary's River State Park. North of MD 5 on Rte. 471, the park offers boating, freshwater fishing, hunting, and hiking. Call 872–5688 for information.

Smith Island Cruise. One hour and 40 minute cruises from Point Lookout State Park, see above, to Smith Island and return. Memorial Day–Labor Day, daily, 10:30 A.M.–4 P.M. Phone 425–2771 for details.

Sotterley on the Patuxent. A lovely Georgian mansion and plantation (1717) off Rte. 245 near Hollywood. English country gardens. Open June through September, 11 A.M. to 5 P.M., and by appointment in spring and fall. 373–2280. Adults $4, senior citizens $3, children $1.50.

ANNAPOLIS

by
ELEANOR LOUTTIT

The Indians were there first, of course. But only occasionally. There was a nice little river and some creeks, tidal beaches for shell-gathering to make wampum, oyster beds everywhere, and a half-day's canoe trip across the Bay to visit the folks. There were so many places like it along the edge of that 200-mile bay, east side and west side, that it wasn't even bothersome when a group of white families moved in and settled on the land between the nice little rivers. After all, there had been other white settlers in patches around the Bay for at least a man's lifetime. The Indians simply moved off.

They had no realization, or much concern, that the whole area had been given to Cecil Calvert, second Baron of Baltimore. The lovely forests, beaches, and fields around the river had been given the name of Calvert's wife, Anne Arundel's County.

First settled by Puritans and called Providence, this harbor-side village prospered and grew, spreading south of the Severn River. In 20 years it became an important cargo landing place called Anne Arundel Town or Arundelton. Twenty-five years later the town became an official entry port of the colony of Maryland, and in 1695 when it became the capital of the Maryland Colony, its name

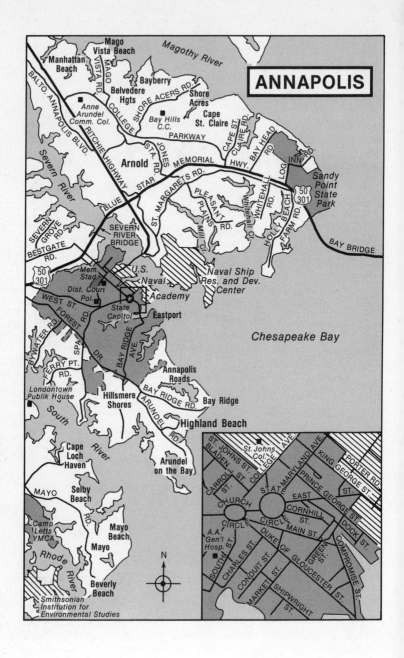

was changed to Annapolis, City of Anne, daughter of William and Mary, Princess of England who later would be Queen Anne. In 1708 the town on the Severn was named a city by charter. It quickly grew into an important center for commerce and society in the colony. Maryland's first newspaper was published in Annapolis in 1727.

The Maryland State House was built in 1772 and it was there that the young Congress of the United States met from November 1783 to August 1784. George Washington resigned as Commander-in-Chief of the Continental Army in the State House in December 1783, and in early 1784 Congress there signed the Treaty of Paris that ended the Revolutionary War.

Annapolis was familiar with the great and the near-great by the time Congress moved out. It settled back complacently to commerce and building and hardly turned a hair when, in 1845, the United States Naval Academy was founded on the Severn to "create a select group of gentlemen and scholar officers." After all, St. John's College had already been there 150 years. The first Superintendent of the then "Naval School on the Severn" was Franklin Buchanan. In a short time, a four-year curriculum with summer training cruises was initiated. The Civil War split the Academy in microcosm as it split the country. Classmates separated to face each another at another time and place as enemies. The Academy's buildings, from which the cadets had moved to Newport, Rhode Island, became hospitals for the battlefields of Virginia. Otherwise Annapolis was little disturbed by the Civil War.

With the emergence of Baltimore as the principal port of the Chesapeake, Annapolis settled into being an agricultural center and a seafood harvesting market. It is still the capital of the State of Maryland, using the oldest state house in the nation as the meeting place for its legislature. Annapolis' chief raison d'etre is the Academy, but its growing importance as a tourist-attracting hub keeps this city of 32,000 energetic.

EXPLORING ANNAPOLIS

Annapolis is primarily a walking town but to get there almost requires a car. The Washington-Baltimore International Airport is the closest commercial airport but Washington National Airport is not much farther away. Municipal parking is provided at various locations but on-street parking is very strictly limited to two hours. There is a shuttle bus service between the Navy/Marine Stadium parking lot and downtown.

The town is sprinkled with historical buildings: residential, commercial, and governmental. Many are privately owned and unavailable for viewing. All the dozen or so that can be visited were built in the mid-1700s and have seen some restoration. The **Maryland State House** is particularly proud of its historical significance both as the first peacetime capitol building of the United States and as the oldest capitol building in continuous legislative use. Within a half-dozen blocks of the State House are the exquisitely restored **Paca House** and **Gardens, Brice House, Chase-Lloyd House,** and **Hammond-Harwood House.** Five historic hostelries in the city have been restored for use as taverns and inns. These cluster around Church Circle and State Circle in the center of the town. These charming country-inns-in-town range in size from the four guest rooms, restaurant, and tavern of the **Reynolds Tavern** to the 51 guest rooms, meeting rooms, and banquet room of the **Governor Calvert House.** Also on State Circle is the old **Treasury,** the oldest legislative building in use in Maryland.

A short walk from State Circle along North Street will bring the visitor to the south corner of **St. John's College** with its lovely campus bounded by St. John's Street, College Avenue, College Creek, and King George Street. The latter, if taken in the opposite direction (i.e., south) leads at its other end to the visitors' gate of the **United States Naval Academy.** The campus is impressive but serene. It is hard, however, to resist a thrill at the sight of all those arrow-straight young leaders-to-be in their neat uniforms. Between Gate 3 of the Academy and State Circle is Maryland Avenue, three blocks of shops, galleries, and antique dealers housed in buildings barely changed from the turn of the century.

The maybe not as historical but very much enjoyable area of Annapolis is centered around **City Dock.** Here the **Market Space** is surrounded by hotels, restaurants, shops, and boats, boats, boats. Charter boats, tour boats, fishing boats, working boats, and playing boats. Ferries, dinghys, yachts, canoes, power launches, and, as this writer found delightedly one early morning, even a 52-foot schooner moored beside the balcony of a second floor room in the Hilton Inn above City Dock.

PRACTICAL INFORMATION FOR ANNAPOLIS

Note: The area code for all Maryland is 301.

TOURING INFORMATION. For the latest touring information, including the current Calendar of Annual Events, contact: Tourism Council of Annapolis and Anne Arundel County, 6 Dock St., Annapolis 21401; 268–TOUR. There is also a Visitor Information Center at City Dock.

PLACES TO STAY

HOTELS, MOTELS, AND INNS. Annapolis is small and rooms are sometimes scarce, especially during the summer season, when the Boat Show is in town, or when the Naval Academy is graduating a new class. Book early and hope for the best, but don't be surprised if your motel is a very long hike from the water.

Governor Calvert House. *Deluxe.* 58 State Circle, 263–2461. A Historic Inn of Annapolis. 51 rooms, some restored Victorian. Restaurant nearby. Underground parking. AE, CB, DC, MC, V.

Robert Johnson House. *Deluxe.* 23 State Circle, 263–2641. 30 rooms in a four-story hotel. Rates less off-season. Continental breakfasts. AE, CB, DC, MC, V.

Hilton Inn. *Expensive to Deluxe.* On the harbor, with boats, boats, and boats below your window and the Academy only a stone's throw away. 80 Compromise, at St. Mary's St., 268–7555 or (800) 445–8667. 135 rooms in an attractive, efficient inn. Waterfront bar and penthouse restaurant. AE, DC, MC, V.

Maryland Inn. *Expensive to Deluxe.* 16 Church Circle, at Main, 263–2641. Built in the late 1700s and restored in 1953, this charming red-brick, three-story inn has 44 rooms. Bar and Treaty of Paris restaurant. AE, CB, DC, MC, V.

Radisson Annapolis. *Expensive to Deluxe.* 126 West St.; 263–7777. 217 rooms. No pool and not on the water, but this newest and largest hotel in the city is only two blocks from the downtown historic district. Rooms and striking cherrywood lobby have Victorian flair; also meeting rooms, banquet facility, and three ballrooms. Restaurant and bar on premises. 34 rooms on 2-floor Plaza Club level. Concierge and private lounge. AE, DC, MC, V.

Ramada Inn. *Expensive to Deluxe.* 173 Jennifer Rd., 21401; 266–3131 (3 miles west on Rte. 50 at Crownsville exit); 197 rooms. Full convention center, elegant restaurant and lounge, indoor pool. AE, DC, MC, V.

Holiday Inn. *Expensive.* Out of the harbor area, but convenient; near US 50 and 301; 210 Holiday Ct., Rtes. 301 and 450, 21401; 224–3150. A full-line, attractive motel, with 218 rooms. Bar. AE, DC, MC, V.

Gibson's Lodgings. *Moderate to Expensive.* 110 and 114 Prince George St., 268–5555. An interesting 14-room inn, with off-street parking and restaurant nearby. Breakfast. AE, MC, V.

Howard Johnson. *Moderate to Expensive.* 170 Revell Hwy., 757–1600. 100-unit motel, with a restaurant and pool. AE, DC, MC, V.

Academy Motel. *Moderate.* 200 Revell Hwy., 757–2222. 40 rooms, with restaurant nearby. AE, CB, DC, MC, V.

Annapolis Terrace Hotel. *Moderate.* 71 Revell Hwy., 757–3030. 51 units, with outdoor pool. AE, CB, DC, MC, V.

EconoLodge. *Moderate.* 591 Revell Hwy. (US 50 and 301), 974–4440 or (800) 446–6900. 74 rooms. AE, MC, V.

Thr-Rift Inn. *Moderate.* 2542 Riva Rd., 224–2800 or (800) 636–5179. 150 rooms, three miles west on US 50. Restaurant nearby. AE, CB, DC, MC, V.

PLACES TO EAT

RESTAURANTS. Annapolis has no shortage of excellent restaurants. Not too surprising, Bay fish and crab are featured fare, but if seafood isn't your thing, there's something for every taste. The following is a list of selected restaurants; there isn't space to list them all. We've given special mention to a few that the editors feel are especially noteworthy, either for the food, the view, or the decor; you're certain to find some favorites of your own.

San Remo. *Deluxe.* 186 Main St.; 263–0949. Northern Italian cuisine in quiet, elegant surroundings. Reservations required. Open daily, lunch and dinner. Dinner only Sat. AE, MC, V.

Chart House. *Expensive.* 300 2nd St. (across harbor in Eastport); 269–6992. Part of the chain, but the chain's formula is good—good food in generous portions on the water, with boats in their slips and a harbor view just beyond your table. Chart House restaurants feature a comfortable lounge, where you can sip your pre-dinner cocktail while waiting for your table in the restaurant's sprawling, busy dining room. Seafood, of course. Reservations not a must, but a good idea. Dinner only, except Sun. brunch and dinner. Major credit cards.

Harbour House. *Moderate to Expensive.* 87 Prince George St., just off City Dock; 268–0771. Open from shortly before noon until almost midnight. Harbor House is in a building designed to look like an old dock warehouse. Fish, and on-site baking. Outdoor dining, May–Oct. AE, MC, V.

Hilton Inn (Penthouse Restaurant). *Moderate to Expensive.* Hilton Inn, on the harbor, above the City Dock, 268–7555. Although not noted for its menu, the Hilton's top-floor restaurant offers one of the most spectacular harbor views in town. Maryland crab featured, but the menu is fairly international. AE, CB, DC, MC, V.

Lester's. *Moderate to Expensive.* 173 Jennifer Rd., Ramada Inn; 266–3131. Varied menu, with bar and wine list. Children's menu. Sunday brunch. Seafood the specialty, with excellent Maryland crab cakes. AE, CB, DC, MC, V.

Middleton's Tavern. *Moderate to Expensive.* 2 Market Pl., overlooking the harbor; 263–3323. Stuffed sole and black bean soup, with a salad bar. Open till 1 A.M., with a bar that's open till 2. Outdoor dining at a restored 1750 building. AE, MC, V.

Treaty of Paris Restaurant. *Moderate to Expensive.* Maryland Inn, Main St. and Church Circle; 263–2641. Breakfast, lunch, and dinner, with a continental menu. Reservations a must. Restaurant and King of France Tavern worthy of note. Outdoor dining in season. AE, CB, DC, MC, V.

McGarvey's Saloon & Oyster Bar. *Moderate.* 8 Market Space, across from City Dock; 263–5700. The kind of casual, cheerful place where you see businessmen rubbing elbows with boaters just in from a day's cruise. Serves dynamite hamburgers and the best eggs Benedict in town. Open daily, lunch and dinner. AE, MC, V.

Rustic Inn. *Moderate.* 1803 West St.; 263–2626. A pleasantly varied menu, from Bay seafood to beef and veal. Bar. Closed Thanksgiving, Christmas Eve, Christmas Day. Two floors, with cabaret upstairs. AE, MC, V.

Slightly Out of Town

Carrol's Creek Cafe. *Expensive.* 410 Severn Ave., across the bridge in Eastport; 263–8102. Fresh Bay seafood, some Cajun style. Bar. Outdoor dining in season. On the water. Lunch, dinner, and Sun. brunch. AE, MC, V.

Chesapeake Inn. *Moderate to Expensive.* Two miles west of the Bay Bridge on US 50 and 301, 321 Revell Hwy., 757–1717. A Chesapeake standby, Busch's Chesapeake Inn features on-site baking and crab imperial. Bar. Open from 11 till 11, later on Saturday. Rustic, nautical decor. AE, CB, DC, MC, V.

Fred's. *Moderate to Expensive.* 2348 Solomons Island Rd., at Parole, 224–2386. Italian-American, from veal parmigiana to crab cakes in a Victorian setting. Closed Thanksgiving, Christmas. AE, CB, DC, MC, V.

Hemingway's. *Moderate to Expensive.* (See Eastern Shore) Hemingway's bayfront restaurant and crab house is on Pier One Road near the eastern end of the Bay Bridge, Stevensville. Outdoor dining with a super view of the Bay. Soft shell crab—of course! 643–2722. AE, DC, MC, V.

Whitehall Inn. *Moderate.* Seven miles east of town on US 50 and 301, a mile and a half west of the Bay Bridge; Revell Hwy.; 757–3737. 11 till 10, Sunday at noon. Flounder and crab, plus chicken, in an attractive rustic decor. Open daily, lunch and dinner. AE, DC, MC, V.

Damon's. *Inexpensive to Moderate.* Rte. 2, 3 mi. north of US 50/301 at Old Jones Station Road; 647–4300. "Damon's is The Place for Ribs," specializing in barbecued baby-back ribs but also serving chicken and steak. Closed major holidays. AE, MC, V.

THINGS TO SEE AND DO

THE HARBOR. It all starts at the harbor, and the harbor is why it's all there. Annapolis is a nautical town, loaded to the gunnels with docks, marinas, seafood restaurants, yacht chandleries, and the U.S. Naval Academy. Home port or a mecca for Bay sailors,

Annapolis is also a major stopover haven for yachtsmen cruising north or south along the New England to Florida waterway. If you don't like boats, you may not like Annapolis. But if you do, this charming Chesapeake port could be the next best thing to paradise.

BOATING. Harbor cruise, Severn River and Spa Creek tours, day cruise to St. Michaels on the Eastern shore. The only company that operates out of City Dock is Chesapeake Marine Tours, Box 3350, Annapolis, MD 21403, 268–7600.

SAILING CHARTERS. Charters available with or without a captain. Chesapeake and Coastal Charters, Box 3322, Annapolis, MD 21403, (800) 636–SAIL or (301) 268–0068. Sailing yachts and trawlers, captained; 27-foot to 52-foot, hour, day, or weekend; Annapolis Bay Charter, Inc., 7074 Bembe Beach Road, Annapolis, MD 21403. Phone 269–1776.

SAILING SCHOOLS. If you've ever had a hankering to sail, the Bay's the place to learn. Sailing schools in the Annapolis area include Annapolis Sailing School, 601 6th St., 267–7205; Chesapeake Sailing School (charters available), 7074 Bembe Beach Rd., 269–1594; and Severn Sailing Associations, Box 1463, Annapolis (ages 10–16 only), 269–6744.

SEASONAL EVENTS. U.S. Sailboat Show and U.S. Powerboat Show, held back-to-back during first two weeks in October. Largest in-water boat shows in the world, with hundreds of domestic and foreign manufacturers represented, displays of nautical equipment and services. Admission fee. Call 268–8828.

TOURS. U.S. Naval Academy. Tourist information at Visitors' Gate #1 Rickett's Hall; guided tour recommended. (There are dull academic places that have no interest for a visitor.) Tours are perhaps somewhat long for senior citizens and the handicapped. Arrangements for bus transport between major stops can be made (one week in advance). Among points of interest are the crypt of John Paul Jones, Bancroft Hall (world's largest dormitory), and the Naval Museum. Naval Academy Tour Guide Service, Annapolis, MD 21402, 263–6933.

HISTORIC ANNAPOLIS. Several agencies conduct walking tours of old houses, inns, and governmental buildings: Historic Annapolis Tours, Inc., 267–8149; Three Centuries Tour, 263–5401; Town Crier (pedicab, summer only), 263–7330.

Waterfront. City Dock is the center of the Annapolis waterfront. Strolling areas, easy distances between restaurants, hotels, marinas, specialty shops, galleries, the Market House, and such scheduled attractions as the Maryland Clam Festival every August.

OTHER ATTRACTIONS. Banneker-Douglass Museum. 84 Franklin St., off Church Circle. Afro-American history, with emphasis on Maryland and Tidewater. Open 10 A.M. to 3 P.M. Tuesday through Friday, noon to 4 P.M. Saturday. 974–2893. Donations accepted.

Helen A. Tawes Garden. State Dept. of Natural Resources Building, Taylor Ave. and Rowe Blvd. Living showcase of "Maryland in miniature"—varied natural environments on six acres of small-scale streams, ponds, marshes, mountainsides, and forests. Open to the public during daylight hours. 974–3717.

Maryland State House (1772–79). Oldest U.S. State House in continuous legislative use, and **Old Treasury Building** (1735), oldest public building in Maryland; both on State Circle. The Old Treasury Building now houses Historic Annapolis tour office. Open Monday–Friday 9–4:30, and weekends June–Labor Day. Phone 267–8149.

Tobacco Prise House. 4 Pinkney St. Exhibits of implements used in Maryland's tobacco industry. Weekends, April–October; phone 268–9784.

William Paca Garden. Two-acre terraced 18th-century garden at 1 Martin St. off East St. Open daily except Thanksgiving and Christmas. Adults $2, senior citizens $1.75, children $1; half-price in winter. Phone 267–6656.

Londontown Publik House. Seven miles south in Edgewater. Open 10 A.M. to 4 P.M. Tuesday through Saturday, 1 P.M. to 4 P.M. Sunday. Closed January–February. 956–4900. Impressively restored 18th-century tavern and extensive gardens overlooking South River.

Victualling Warehouse. 77 Main St. Local maritime history and archaeological artifacts from 17th- and 18th-century port. Open 11 A.M. to 4:30 P.M. daily. 268–5576; adults $1, children 50¢.

STATE PARK. Sandy Point State Park, 800 Revell Hwy., near the Bay Bridge. Boating, camping, fishing, and picnicking beside Chesapeake Bay. Call 757–1841 for information.

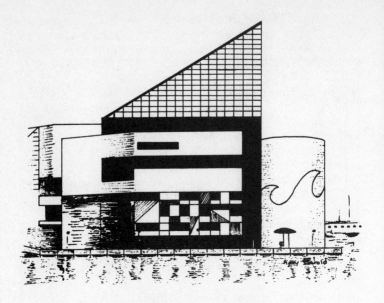

BALTIMORE

by
ERIC SMITH

Baltimore is a city that took everyone by surprise in the early 1980s.

Its spectacular downtown renaissance, barely more than a dream in the 1970s, has turned the old port city at the top of the Chesapeake Bay into a modern miracle of urban revival and a major tourist destination on the east coast.

Today Baltimore fairly hums with cultural and commercial life. It is the twelfth largest city in the U.S. and the second busiest container port on the Atlantic seaboard. It is the home of one of the country's foremost universities, Johns Hopkins, as well as the largest aquarium, the oldest academy of arts and sciences, and an internationally renowned music conservatory. Its seafood restaurants, ethnic festivals, nightlife, and historical attractions are celebrated throughout the Tidewater region.

Despite all this activity and growth, Baltimore hasn't given up its fundamental character as a city of quiet, tightly-knit neighborhoods and low-key charm. *Life* magazine calls it "the most downright liveable major city in the U.S." Over the years, this friendly city on the Upper Bay has been home to such diverse citizens as Babe Ruth, Edgar Allan Poe, Billie Holiday, Wallis Warfield Simp-

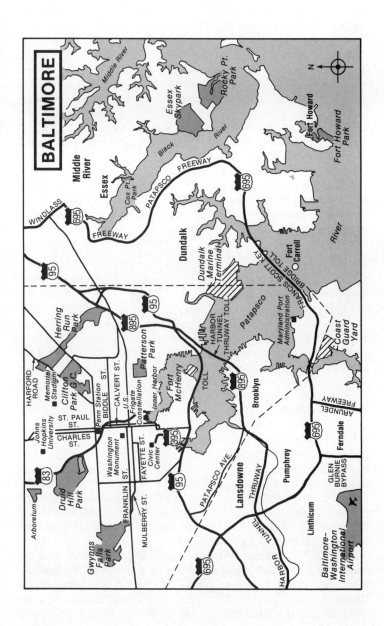

son, Ogden Nash, Thurgood Marshall, F. Scott Fitzgerald, H.L. Mencken, Johnny Unitas, Brooks Robinson, and Jim Palmer. Baltimore is a unique blending of North and South, an amicable mix of various ethnic strains. Visitors will sense the city's "liveability" and experience its charm as they tour outwards from the bustle and excitement of Harborplace to any of seven historic markets or colorful districts—such as Little Italy, Fell's Point, or Federal Hill. With its neat blocks of red brick rowhouses fronted by white marble stoops, Baltimore is a big town on a human scale.

The showcase of the city's rebirth is at the Inner Harbor, a glittering collection of glass high-rises, malls, pavilions, plazas, and shops overlooking the Patapsco River. (That's "Tapsico" in "Bawlamer's" distinctive accent.) Here, at the water's edge, a venerable old warship coexists in quiet dignity with the splendor of a glittering Harborplace. Inner Harbor is the city's focal point; many of its major attractions are clustered here or are within an easy stroll back from the shore.

Union of Two Hamlets

In some ways Baltimore's current boom is a return to the dominance it enjoyed in the past. Named for the Lords Baltimore of the Calvert family, whose members founded the Maryland colony in 1634, it began as a pair of settlements on opposite banks of a creek now known as Jones Falls, not far from the present harbor. These hamlets were joined in 1745 to create the town of Baltimore, 16 years after it had been established by law. For a long time it was overshadowed commercially by the capital city, Annapolis, 30 miles to the south.

After the Revolution, however, business started to pick up fast. By 1790 Baltimore's population had doubled, and ten years later it had doubled again. As the 19th century began, the boom was on, fueled by the fortunes of geography that placed the city close to a great tidal bay and beside the swiftly-flowing Fall Line streams that drop off the Piedmont plateau to the fertile and gentle coastal plains. It was here that mills could be constructed to grind the wheat coming in from the region's outlying farmlands, and it was from the city's deep natural harbor that an enormously profitable overseas trade could be launched.

William Fell, the early American equivalent of a real estate developer, had meanwhile laid out the waterfront lots on Fell's Point, which became the hub of Baltimore's shipbuilding industry. Rum, slaves, and sugar poured in from the Caribbean Islands while grain and local goods poured out—mostly on Baltimore-built or -owned ships.

Privateers aboard nimble *Baltimore Clippers* so angered the British during the War of 1812 that a force led by Admiral Sir George Cockburn attacked their home port in the autumn of 1814, shortly after burning Washington, D.C. Francis Scott Key wrote "The

Star-Spangled Banner" to commemorate Fort McHenry's survival of a punishing bombardment from the harbor, but the unsung Baltimore militia deserves equal credit for saving the city by stopping the British advance at the Battle of North Point a few miles away.

Harvesting the Bay's Bounty

As the century wore on, the bounty of the bay replaced grain as the key to the city's prosperity. Advancing technology made it possible for seafood, especially juicy bay oysters, to be purchased and packed fresh in Baltimore and then transported out by sail, rail, and road to seafood-hungry customers hundreds of miles from the sea.

A disastrous downtown fire in 1904 slowed progress in the early years of the 20th century, and the Great Depression of the '30s further eroded the city's manufacturing base. After World War II many people left to join the "suburban flight" that was taking place all over the northeast. By the late 1960s, Baltimore's luster was fading fast and few believed that better days were just a few years ahead.

Few "Bawlamerians" will deny that one man sparked the rebirth of their beloved but decaying city. That man was the energetic William Donald Schaefer, now the governor of Maryland, who was elected mayor in 1971. Days after he assumed office, Mayor Schaefer began applying his "Do it now" philosophy toward reversing the city's failing fortunes. Mixing public revenues, private venture capital, and a generous measure of local pride, Baltimore has reversed its downward spiral and thoroughly revitalized itself as a good place to live as well as a thriving center for commerce and culture.

EXPLORING BALTIMORE

The Inner Harbor

Begin, where the city's renewal itself began, at the Inner Harbor, 95 acres of dazzling development along the water's edge that not too long ago boasted little except decayed docks and shabby warehouses. The undisputed centerpiece of the area is Harborplace at Pratt and Light Streets, a prizewinning project by James Rouse that has served as a model for many other inner-city sites.

Here is an irresistible shopping and dining complex that houses more than 140 restaurants, boutiques, bistros, cafes, specialty stores, and gourmet markets in two glass-enclosed pavilions. While both buildings offer a mixture of places to eat and browse, retail shops are concentrated in the Pratt Street Pavilion while the Light Street Pavilion across the way specializes in food outlets. And when it comes to food, you might as well accept the fact that you should be dieting for days before and after you sample the almost overwhelming variety of eateries in Harborplace. All three meals and snacks are served for eating on the go, standing up, or sitting down—from Baltimore's famous crabcakes and Maryland cheese bread to exotic ethnic fare, tempting tidbits, and outrageously rich sweets.

Between bites you can shop for gifts, crafts, clothing, collectibles, housewares, books, toys, nautical items, accessories, and even kites on both levels of the two pavilions.

Conveniently gathered around the Inner Harbor are a number of other places of interest worth visiting, and you can see them all on foot—no hiking boots necessary.

Right outside the tall windows of the Light Street Pavilion is the U.S. Frigate *Constellation,* a lovingly preserved American warship dating back to the days of sailing ships. Launched from nearby Fell's Point in 1797, the *Constellation* went on to become the first U.S. Navy ship to win a battle on the high seas and today is among the world's oldest vessels still afloat. More ships are on display close by at the Baltimore Maritime Museum, where you can take guided tours of the submarine *Torsk* and the lightship *Chesapeake.*

Step across Pratt Street to see The Gallery, a multi-level complex of upscale stores with the prettiest atrium lobby in Baltimore, and then over to Top of the World for a bird's-eye view of the city from the 27th floor observation deck of the World Trade Center.

Down at the end of Pier 3 is the futuristic building that houses the National Aquarium, the biggest and most technically advanced aquarium in the U.S.—8,000 specimens of 600 varieties of fish, mammals, plants, birds, reptiles, and amphibians living in recreations of their natural environments. After you've seen the main tank, with its coral reef, shark ring, and astonishing varieties of marine life, don't fail to visit the tropical rain forest on the roof.

If you want to explore even higher than that, the Maryland Science Center and Davis Planetarium on the other side of the harbor offers filmed flights of imagination through the heavens, scores of instructional displays, and hands-on learning experiences. This is also the home of the Maryland Academy of Sciences, the oldest such institution in the U.S.

Federal Hill, Little Italy, and Fells Point

Behind the Science Center is the steep, green slope of Federal Hill, which overlooks the harbor. Early Baltimoreans learned of approaching ships from a signal station here, and Union cannons were placed where a park is today to dominate the pro-Southern city of 1862. This south Baltimore neighborhood is the site of a successful homesteading program, and new specialty shops and pubs are opening all the time.

A few blocks to the east of the Inner Harbor is Little Italy, a temptingly delicious concentration of restaurants that are devoted to authentic northern or tomato-rich southern Italian cuisine. Generations of Baltimoreans—and some savvy visitors—have been dining heartily here for years. Continue for a mile or so on to Fell's Point, where the old waterfront, cobbled streets, and Colonial townhouses have come back to life, and where the seafood restaurant business is booming. Despite its rehabilitation (Fell's Pointers brag that it will someday rival the Inner Harbor), the area still retains much of its raffish maritime flavor.

On your way back to the harbor, you might want to look in at the Star-Spangled Banner Flag House on East Pratt Street, a little jewel of Federal-style architecture that was the home of the woman who made the flag seen "by the dawn's early light" over Fort McHenry.

Fort McHenry itself, set on a peninsula in southeast Baltimore, is worth a special trip. Fully restored to its War of 1812 condition by the National Park Service, this silent, solid structure is an awe-inspiring reminder of a crucial time in American history; once you have climbed its brick ramparts and walked its 43 acres of carefully groomed grounds, our national anthem should take on a deeper, more personal meaning.

Back from the Harbor

As you move away from the harbor area and through the surrounding communities, be prepared to encounter some street trash, the din of heavy construction (renewal is an ongoing process, after all), and a shortage of trees on the urban landscape (although more trees are being planted each year). Baltimore is not yet a city of great beauty, but you should also watch for the treasure trove of unchanged architectural details on its Colonial and Victorian buildings.

Outside the Inner Harbor tourist complex there is still plenty to see and do. Baltimore boasts more than a dozen museums that feature everything from industrial machinery to prehistoric Indian pottery. One of the most fascinating collections is at the Baltimore & Ohio Railroad Museum at Pratt and Poppleton Streets, a mile west of the downtown center. Here, inside the huge roundhouse erected in 1884, are dozens of originals and replicas of many of the most famous steam and diesel locomotives in American history. The museum also has on display a wonderful array of freight and passenger cars from all eras of railroading, including Pullman sleepers and a luxurious 1930 Imperial Salon coach. (See the following Practical Information section for details about this and other attractions.)

Historic house museums are another Baltimore specialty. Edgar Allan Poe lived and wrote in the tiny rowhouse on North Amity Street and was later buried on the grounds of Westminster Church

off Paca Street. A few blocks south, Babe Ruth's birthplace is open
to fans of this baseball legend. Farther out of town at Monroe
Street and Washington Boulevard is Mount Clare Mansion, the
oldest and most elegant Georgian house in the city.

The H.L. Mencken House on Union Square in west Baltimore
may not be fancy, but it is certainly one of the most interesting
writers' shrines in the country. It was from this modest but pleasant rowhouse that "the Sage of Baltimore" ruled American letters
from the 1920s to the 1940s. As author, editor, and columnist,
Mencken lashed out with biting wit against ignorance and censor-
ship wherever he found it. His home on Hollins Street, always open
to fellow writers, remains open today, lovingly restored to its De-
pression-era appearance (even his L.C. Smith typewriter has been
repaired). By Mencken's own wish, visitors are invited to sit on
the furniture and wander through the rooms with almost unre-
stricted freedom.

A Warm and Casual Place

Baltimore, like its favorite son, H.L. Mencken, is a refreshingly
casual, unstuffy place. It is a city of warm neighborhoods where
different ethnic groups have long been accustomed to getting along
socially and politically, and of bustling public marketplaces where
the buying and selling of food is an art form.

But at the same time, Baltimore is a cultural capital of extraordi-
nary quality and breadth. Within a mile radius of the celebrated
Lexington Market off Eutaw Street, where shirtsleeved merchants
hawk fresh oysters and Polish sausage, you can attend a recital at
the world-renowned Peabody Conservatory, view great paintings
at the Walters Art Gallery, and see a touring Broadway hit at the
Morris Mechanic Theater. If you feel like making a short side trip
to "Antique Row" in the 700 block of North Howard Street, you
can enjoy world-class browsing among the rare prints, rugs,
bronzes, glassware, jewelry, and furniture in Maryland's oldest antique district. Prices are high, but shop owners love to bargain as
much as their customers. Not far away, on West 25th Street, is
the Kelmscott Book Store, possibly the finest rare and used book
dealer on the east coast and another reason Baltimore has a growing reputation as a literary focal point for the region.

Baltimore's incredible downtown renaissance and a retained former charm have transformed it into a new city with old-fashioned
appeal—a touch of the past, a place of the future, and something
here for everyone.

PRACTICAL INFORMATION FOR BALTIMORE

Note: The area code for all Maryland is 301.

PLACES TO STAY

HOTELS, INNS, AND B&BS. Once there were only a few slightly decrepit hotels in the downtown area, but in the wake of Baltimore's business and tourist boom new hotels have sprouted up at a fast rate, mostly in the Inner Harbor. Many have special less expensive weekend or vacation rates; call for details. The following selection also includes some bed-and-breakfast establishments and inns, which usually provide continental breakfast, antique-filled rooms, and other homelike amenities. B&Bs are being added all the time. Contact B&B Reservations Service, Box 2277, Annapolis, MD 21404; 269–6232, for information and reservations.

The following categories pertain to double occupancy at regular rates: *Deluxe,* $100 and up; *Expensive,* $75 to $100; *Moderate,* $45 to $75; and *Inexpensive,* $45 and under.

The Brookshire Hotel. *Deluxe.* 120 E. Lombard St.; 625–1300. 90 suites in a 12-story luxury hotel. Close to the Inner Harbor. Two restaurants, bar, and concierge. AE, CB, DC, MC, V.

Hyatt Regency. *Deluxe.* 300 Light St.; 528–1234. An all-glass front that overlooks the Inner Harbor. Three restaurants and an indoor pool. Easy access to the Convention Center. 487 rooms. AE, DC, MC, V.

International Hotel. *Deluxe.* Baltimore-Washington International Airport, just off MD 170N; 859–3300 or (800) 638–5858. 196 rooms, with an excellent restaurant, pool and poolside service, bar, and meeting rooms. Free airport transportation. Major credit cards.

Lord Baltimore Radisson Plaza. *Deluxe.* Baltimore and Hanover Sts.; 539–8400 or (800) 333–3333. 440 rooms, 59 suites in a 23-story hotel. Restaurant, bar, and convention facilities. 56 rooms on concierge floors. Built in 1928, a renovated landmark hotel. AE, DC, MC, V.

Marriott Inner Harbor. *Deluxe.* Pratt and Eutaw Sts.; 962–0202. 352 rooms in a 10-story hotel. Restaurant, bar, pool, and convention facilities. 37 rooms on the concierge floor. Private lounge and free breakfast. AE, CB, DC, MC, V.

Omni Inner Harbor. *Deluxe.* 101 W. Fayette St.; 752–1100. Shops, restaurant, and piano bar. In the heart of downtown. 714 rooms in a deluxe 27-story hotel. Pool. AE, DC, MC, V.

Peabody Court. *Deluxe.* 612 Cathedral St.; 727–7101. A European-style luxury hotel with a brasserie, top-floor gourmet restaurant, marbled baths, and international telex services. 104 rooms, 20 suites in 14 stories. Bar and concierge.

Sheraton Inner Harbor. *Deluxe.* 300 S. Charles St.; 962–8300. 339 rooms in a 14-story hotel. Restaurant, bar, room service, and concierge. Meeting rooms. Gift shop. AE, CB, DC, MC, V.

Tremont Baltimore. *Deluxe.* 8 E. Pleasant St.; 576–1200. Restaurant, lounge, admission to athletic club, all luxury appointments. 59 suites with kitchens. Concierge. AE, CB, DC, MC, V.

Admiral Fell Inn. *Expensive to Deluxe.* 888 S. Broadway; 522–7377. A B&B in Fell's Point with all the amenities and a van to take you to the city center and Inner Harbor. 40 rooms in a 4-story inn. Concierge. AE, MC, V.

Cross Keys Inn. *Expensive to Deluxe.* 5100 Falls Rd.; 532–6900. 148 rooms, with an excellent restaurant, bar, pool, and shopping arcade. Some patios and balconies. AE, CB, DC, MC, V.

Belvedere Hotel. *Expensive to Deluxe.* 1 E. Chase St.; 332–1000 or (800) 692–2700. Overlooking Mount Vernon and most of the rest of the city. Top-floor bar, restaurant, and shops. 180 rooms. AE, DC, MC, V.

Tremont Plaza. *Expensive to Deluxe.* 222 St. Paul Place; 727–2222. Restaurant and pool. 236 suites in a wide variety of sizes and plans. AE, CB, DC, MC, V.

Days Inn Inner Harbor. *Expensive.* 100 Hopkins Pl.; 576–1000 or (800) 325–2525. 251 rooms on 9 floors. Restaurant, bar, garage, and pool. Concierge. AE, DC, MC, V.

Holiday Inn-Inner Harbor. *Moderate to Expensive.* Howard and Lombard Sts.; 685–3500 or (800) 465–4329. One of the first new hotels in Baltimore; rooftop restaurant and lounge. 371 rooms in an 11-story Inner Harbor hotel. Opposite Civic Center. AE, DC, MC, V.

Sheraton Johns Hopkins Inn. *Expensive.* 400 N. Broadway; 675–6800. 145 rooms. Restaurant. AE, DC, MC, V.

Best Western Hallmark Inner Harbor. *Moderate.* 8 N. Howard St.; 539–1188 or (800) 528–1234. 93 rooms in 7 stories. Restaurant, but no room service. Garage parking. AE, CB, DC, MC, V.

Comfort Inn. *Moderate.* 24 W. Franklin St.; 727–2000 or (800) 228–5150. 194 rooms on 9 floors. Restaurant, bar, and room service. Meeting rooms. AE, CB, DC, MC, V.

PLACES TO EAT

RESTAURANTS AND RAW BARS. Since the first settler gazed upon a plump oyster, Baltimoreans have had a wonderful time eating. A Baltimorean is perhaps happiest when the Orioles are winning, tomatoes are in season, and the table is covered with spicy steamed crabs and pitchers of cold beer.

A good starting place to join the native in epicurean bliss is a raw bar, found at the city's large markets, Harborplace, and many bars. Clams and oysters on the half shell, steamed shrimp, and mussels are slurped and gobbled amid a pleasant din of chatter and a cross-section of the city's populace. Crab houses, listed below, provide the pleasure of the area's renowned steamed crabs.

But Baltimore eating is not just seafood. The downtown area is increasingly dotted with first-rate steak houses, continental restaurants, and ethnic eateries. A stroll around the harbor area—Fell's Point, Little Italy, Federal Hill, or Harborplace—will reveal many worthy restaurants. Mount Vernon's restaurant row has something for every taste and pocketbook. Remember, our listing is merely a selection; Fodor's editors would appreciate hearing of your personal discoveries.

As a general rule our price categories are based on dinner for one person, excluding wine, cocktails, and tip. They are: *Deluxe,* over $30; *Expensive,* $20–$30; *Moderate,* $10–$20; *Inexpensive,* under $10.

The Conservatory. *Deluxe.* In the Peabody Court hotel, 612 Cathedral St.; 727–7101. Just plain elegant, with a French gourmet menu and a rooftop view of Mount Vernon. Reservations recommended. Dinner only. Closed Sun. Jacket required. AE, CB, DC, MC, V.

The Brass Elephant. *Expensive.* 924 N. Charles St.; 547–8480. Northern Italian fare in an elegant setting. Homemade tasty desserts. Also moderately priced meals. Lunch and dinner, Mon.–Fri.; dinner only weekends. Bar and five dining rooms. Jacket and tie. AE, CB, DC, MC, V.

Cafe des Artistes. *Expensive.* 1501 Sulgrave Ave.; 664–2200. A superb French menu that includes Dover sole. The cafe has a bar and a good wine list. Decorated with original artwork. No lunch Sun. Closed in late August in the French style. Major credit cards.

Cappriccio. *Expensive.* 846 Fawn St.; 685–2710. Northern Italian cuisine, featuring veal, seafood, and chicken. Bar. No lunch Sat., Sun. Closed Thanksgiving and Christmas. Weekends are busy, so reservations are a must. Major credit cards.

Chart House. *Expensive.* 601 E. Pratt St.; 539–6616. Perhaps the best view of the harbor from an eatery. Wide ranging menu with a raw bar. Open daily, lunch and dinner; dinner only Sunday. Bar. Major credit cards.

Crossroads. *Expensive.* 5100 Falls Rd., in the Cross Keys Inn; 532–6900. Maryland crab cakes and rack of lamb in an airy setting. Outdoor dining in season. No lunch Sat. Closed Christmas. Bar. Major credit cards.

Danny's. *Expensive.* 1201 N. Charles St., 539–1393. One of Baltimore's most famous, with a wide range of seafood and meat dishes. If you see a sign on the outside saying "Whales," don't worry. It's just announcing the presence of soft-shelled crabs, a Maryland treat if there ever was one. No lunch Sat. Closed Sun. and some holidays. Bar and wine list. Jackets required at dinner. AE, CB, DC, MC, V.

Jean Claude's Cafe. *Moderate to Expensive.* Light Street Pavilion, Harborplace; 332–0950. This waterside cafe's French menu features seafood and beef. Outdoor luncheon dining in season. Lunch and dinner daily. Bar. AE, MC, V.

John Eagar Howard Room. *Expensive.* Charles and Chase Sts., in the Belvedere Hotel; 332–1000. Fancy, old-fashioned setting, with veal and beef specialties as well as lighter continental fare. A trip back to the opulence of turn-of-the-century Baltimore. Some dinners in *Deluxe* range. No dinner Mon., no lunch Sat.

La Provence. *Moderate to Expensive.* 9 Hopkins Plaza; 837–6600. Maryland seafood with a French flair. Outdoor dining in season. Lunch and dinner. Closed Sun. and major holidays. Bar and wine list. AE, MC, V.

Mariner's Pier One. *Moderate to Expensive.* 201 E. Pratt St.; 962–5050. This Harborplace seafood restaurant offers three dining areas—the formal Commodore Room, a tavern, and an outdoor cafe with a good view of the harbor. Open daily, lunch, and dinner. Closed New Year's Day, Thanksgiving, and Christmas. Bar. AE, DC, MC, V.

The Prime Rib. *Expensive.* 1101 N. Calvert St.; 539–1804. A taste of New York in the Mount Vernon area, with a piano bar, lush setting, juicy beef, and seafood. Where the natives go to really treat themselves. Dinner only. Bar and wine list. Closed some holidays. Jacket required.

Tio Pepe's. *Expensive.* 10 E. Franklin St.; 539–4675. The boneless duck, the shrimp with garlic, and the whole array of Spanish dishes make this a very popular spot, which in turn means it can be hard to get reservations. No lunch Sat., Sun. Wine cellar and bar. Jackets required at dinner. AE, MC, V.

Water Street Exchange. *Moderate to Expensive.* 110 Water St.; 332–4060. Seafood and veal in a Victorian setting. Outdoor dining in season. Lunch and dinner, Mon.–Sat. Closed Christmas and Christmas Eve. Reservations suggested for weekends. AE, MC, V.

Bertha's. *Moderate.* 734 S. Broadway; 327–5795. Famous for its mussels, done up in several ways, its soups and its paella, Bertha's has long been a Fell's Point landmark and watering hole. Open daily, lunch and dinner. MC, V.

Haussner's. *Moderate.* 3244 Eastern Ave.; 327–8365. A Baltimore landmark because of its art-covered walls and relatively simple, solid and tasty American and German food. *Inexpensive* dinners available. Lunch and dinner. Closed Sun., Mon., and Christmas. Bar. AE, CB, DC, MC, V.

Little Italy, a few blocks east of the Inner Harbor. Even if it weren't for the restaurants, this area of rowhouses and thick dialect is a fine place for a stroll. If the walking has made you hungry, there's plenty to choose from, including: **Chiapparelli's,** 237 S. High St., 837–0309; **Sabatino's,** 901 Fawn St., 727–9414; and **Velleggia's,** 829 E. Pratt St., 685–2620. All are known for their salads and veal, and have extensive menus. And each is a gathering place for local politicians and other well-knowns. Moderate prices at all three.

Maison Marconi's. *Moderate to Expensive.* 106 W. Saratoga St.; 727–9522. A long-time favorite among locals for genteel dining. They pour your drinks at the table and change the menu frequently to incorporate the latest fresh catch or harvest. Lunch and dinner. Closed Sun. and Mon. and major holidays. Jacket required. MC, V.

Martick's. *Moderate.* 214 W. Mulberry St.; 752–5155. A former speakeasy and longtime hangout for artists, this tin-plated room is the setting for tasty and original French food. Veal dishes, duck, and homemade pâté are popular. Reservations recommended. Closed Sun. and Mon. Dinner only Sat. MC, V.

The Museum Cafe. *Moderate.* 10 Art Museum Drive, in the Baltimore Museum of Art; 235–3930. With a view of the sculpture garden and a menu that is fresh and inventive. Museum hours. Closed Mon. Known for its pesto. AE, MC, V.

Olde Obrycki's Crab House. *Moderate.* 1727 E. Pratt St.; 732–6399. A local favorite for years for its steamed crabs and crab dishes. The crab cocktail is much in demand. Summer season only. No lunch Sat., Sun. AE, CB, DC, MC, V.

Phillips Harbor Place. *Moderate.* 301 Light St.; 685–6600. Seafood at the Light Street Pavilion, Inner Harbor. Jazz band and outdoor dining. *Inexpensive-Expensive* dishes also available. Crab imperial a specialty. Bar. Lunch and dinner. Closed Thanksgiving and Christmas. AE, CB, DC, MC, V.

Zingaro's. *Moderate.* 400 E. Pratt St.; 837–3535. Changing menus as well as always reliable standards, including its homemade tomato sauce and pasta, make this one of the city's most popular Italian restaurants. No lunch Sat. Closed Sun. AE, MC, V.

2110. *Moderate.* 2110 N. Charles St.; 727–6692. Fresh pâtés and a simple setting have made this one of Baltimore's more enjoyable French restaurants. Closed Mon. MC, V.

Ikaros. *Inexpensive to Moderate.* 4805 Eastern Ave.; 633–3750. A pleasant blending of Greek and American cooking that features fresh seafood and lamb. Lunch and dinner daily. Closed Tues. and some holidays. Bar. Major credit cards.

Akbar. *Inexpensive to Moderate.* 823 N. Charles St.; 539–0944. Indian food. From mild to outrageously hot, Akbar has something interesting for just about everyone. Its rogan josh, marinated lamb, is particularly popular. No lunch Sat. AE, DC, MC, V.

The American Cafe. *Inexpensive to Moderate.* Light Street Pavillon, Harborplace; 962–8800. Light gourmet food, soups, and drinks, all with a harbor view. Open daily, lunch and dinner. AE, DC, MC, V.

Gunning's Crab House. *Inexpensive to Moderate.* 3901 S. Hanover St.; 354–0085. A traditional South Baltimore crab house, with

globs of spicy sauce on the hard-shelled, steamed crabs. Open daily
for lunch and dinner. AE, MC, V.

Louie's Bookstore and Cafe. *Inexpensive to Moderate.* 518 N.
Charles St.; 962–1224. A great place for tasty salads, pastries, and
cappucino. The art on the wall is an ever-changing display by local
artists. Lunch and dinner daily except major holidays and Christmas Eve. Bar. MC, V.

THINGS TO SEE AND DO

TOURING INFORMATION. Complete and up-to-date touring
information about events, attractions, dining, and lodging is available from: Baltimore Visitors Information Center, 600 Water St.,
837–4636 (Open daily, 9–5); or in advance from Baltimore Office
of Promotion & Tourism, 34 Market Pl., Suite 310, Baltimore, MD
21202, (301) 752–8632 or (301) 837–INFO (24-hour information).
For Baltimore County information, write or call: Baltimore County Office of Economic Development, 400 Washington Ave., Towson, MD 21204, (301) 887–3648.

HOW TO GET AROUND. From the airport. Airport limo service, located on the ground floor of the Baltimore-Washington International Airport, about 10 miles from city center, provides
transportation to the city's major hotels for a reasonable fee.

By subway. Baltimore's new subway operates between Owings
Mills (at Painter's Mill Rd. and I–795) and the downtown area,
with stops in between, Mon.–Fri. 5 A.M. to midnight, Sat. 8 A.M.
to midnight.

By bus. The Mass Transit Administration (539–5000) runs the
citywide bus system. The base fare is 90¢. Call for point-to-point
instructions.

By trolley. The newest addition to Baltimore's transit system is
a small fleet of replica trolley cars that travel around the Inner Harbor and up Charles Street to historic and beautiful Mount Vernon.
The trolley routes provide an easy, pleasant, and cheap way to get
around downtown. The Inner Harbor route runs daily, 11 A.M. to
7 P.M., and includes Little Italy, the Aquarium, and Harborplace
shopping pavilions. The Charles Street trolley operates from 11
A.M. to 7 P.M., Monday through Saturday. Stops are marked by special
"Trolley" signs. The trolleys can also be chartered for private
groups. Call 396–4259. The fare is 25¢.

By water. There is daily water taxi service between major harbor
points, mid-April through mid-October. The taxi is based near the
Constellation in the Inner Harbor.

BOATING. Docking and anchorage facilities are expanding in
the harbor area. Free anchorage is available in Fell's Point and the
Inner Harbor, as space permits, and docking fees start at 50¢ per

boat foot. In the Inner Harbor, contact the city dockmaster (396–3174, Channel 68) or Inner Harbor Marina (837–5339, Channel 68). Baltimore's Anchorage Marina in Fell's Point can be reached at 522–7200 or Channel 16.

Harbor Boating, in the Inner Harbor near the *Constellation* (547–0090), rents sailboats and paddle boats from spring to fall.

SAILING SCHOOL. Learn to sail on the Bay in day or week-long sessions. Sailing School of Baltimore, 1700 Bowleys Quarter Rd., Middle River, 335–7555.

HARBORPLACE. Two glass-enclosed shopping and dining pavilions at Light and Pratt Sts. are symbolic of Baltimore's revitalized Inner Harbor. The two pavilions house more than 140 shops, restaurants, and cafes—most with views of the water. Open Mon.–Thurs., 10 A.M.–9:30 P.M.; Fri. and Sat., 10–10 P.M.; Sun., noon–6. Closed Thanksgiving, Christmas, and New Year's Day. See Places to Eat, above, for a selection of eateries in the area.

HISTORIC SITES AND HOMES. Basilica of the Assumption of the Blessed Virgin Mary. Cathedral and Mulberry Sts. (727–3564). The first Roman Catholic cathedral in the U.S. Open daily, 7–6 P.M. Tours available. Free.

Carroll Mansion and the 1840 House. 800 E. Lombard St. (396–3523). Restored last home of Charles Carroll, signer of the Declaration of Independence, with period furniture and art. Adjacent house restored to show how people lived in early Baltimore. Free.

The U.S. Constellation. Constellation Dock, Pratt and Light Sts. (539–1797). Built in Baltimore in 1797, the restored "Yankee Racehorse" was the first commissioned ship in the U.S. Navy. Open daily, seasonal hours. Adults $2, senior citizens $1.50, children $1.

Davidge Hall. (1812) 522 W. Lombard St. (328–7454). Oldest building in continuous use in the teaching of medicine. Tues.–Thurs., 8:30–4:30, by appointment only. Free.

Evergreen House. 4545 N. Charles St. (338–7641). A classic mid-1800 revival structure on 26 wooded acres. Rare book library and fine arts museum. Reopening after renovations in Spring 1990. Appointments recommended.

Federal Hill. Warren Ave. near Key Hwy. Civil War observation point. Ratification of U.S. Constitution celebrated here.

Fells Point. Located east of Fayette St. to Broadway and right on Broadway to the water. Old seaport area with 350 original Federal-period residential structures.

Flag House and 1812 Museum. 844 E. Pratt St. (837–1793). Home of Mary Pickersgill, who made the flag that flew over Fort McHenry. Mon.–Sat. 10–4; Sun. 1–4. Closed Sun., Nov.–Mar. Adults $1.50, senior citizens and teenagers $1, children 50¢.

Fort McHenry. Fort Ave. off Key Highway (962–4299). Birthplace of "The Star Spangled Banner" and historic military site. Open daily. Adults $1, senior citizens and children free.

H.L. Mencken House. 1524 Hollins St. (396–7997). Wed.–Sun. 10–5. Admission $1.75.

Minnie V. Pier 1, Pratt St. (685–3750). A working oyster boat, the *Minnie V* visits Baltimore for harbor tours with guest lecturers, light snacks. Tues. and Thur. 6–8 P.M. $15 per person.

Mount Clare Mansion. Monroe St. and Washington Blvd. (837–3262). Built in 1769, this is the restored home of Barrister Charles Carroll. Tues.–Fri., 10–4:30; Sat.–Sun., noon–4:30. Adults $3, senior citizens and students $2, children 50¢.

Peabody Institute. 1 E. Mount Vernon Pl. (659–8100). The nation's oldest music school with a beautiful library where Dos Passos once worked. Library is open Mon.–Sat., 9–5. Free Tuesday concerts at noon during the school year.

Poe House. 203 N. Amity St. (396–7932). Contains the cold, tiny garret where Edgar Allan Poe wove his dark tales from 1832–35. Wed.–Sat., noon–3:45. Adults $1, children 50¢. Poe is buried nearby at the Westminster Burying Ground.

Shot Tower. 801 E. Fayette St. (837–5424). This 234-foot brick tower was used in the 1800s to make shot by pouring lead from the top into a vat of cold water at the bottom. Daily 10–4. Free.

Washington Monument. 700 N. Charles St. (396–3523). In the heart of Mount Vernon, this is the first architectural monument to George Washington. Occasionally open for visitors to climb to the top of the 178-foot marble column.

PARKS AND GARDENS. Mt. Vernon Place. Four parks with statues and fountains and a backdrop of elegant town houses and churches. **Sherwood Gardens.** Seven acres of gardens at Highfield Rd. and Greenway. **Conservatory** (1888), Gwynns Falls Pkwy. and McCulloh St., Druid Hill Park (396–0180). Elegant Victorian greenhouse, featuring tropical plants and special holiday displays. Daily. **Bufano Sculpture Garden.** The Johns Hopkins University Dunning Park, Charles and 33rd Sts. Outdoor retreat with seven life-size animals sculpted by Beiamino Bufano. **Cylburn Arboretum.** 4915 Greenspring Ave. (367–2217). 176 acres with wildflower trails, display and test gardens, and a 19th-century mansion with a nature and bird museum. Grounds open daily. Museum and horticultural library open Thurs., 1–3 P.M., except city holidays.

LIVELY ARTS. The crown jewel of the music scene is the **Baltimore Symphony Orchestra,** whose home base is the Meyerhoff Symphony Hall, 1212 Cathedral St. (783–8000). The Meyerhoff also regularly has special programs. Other choices include the Baltimore Choral Arts Society (523–7070), the Baltimore Opera Company (685–0692), Johns Hopkins University's concert series (338–7164), and the Peabody Conservatory of Music (659–8124).

A healthy mix of stage performances, including classical works, experimental pieces and pre-Broadway tryouts, are available at: the **Lyric Opera House** in Mount Vernon (685–5086); the **Morris A. Mechanic Theater** in Hopkins Plaza (625–4230); **Center Stage,** 700 N. Calvert St. (332–0033); the **Theater Project,** 45 W. Preston St. (539–3091); and the Arena Players, 801 McCulloh St. (728–6500).

MARKETS. Baltimore prides itself on its large and lively public markets. They are gathering places for the natives and offer seafood, meat—fancy veal to hamhocks—and local vegetables. **Lexington Market,** Lexington and Paca Sts., the oldest continuously operating market in the United States, has been there since 1782. Others include the **Broadway Market** at Broadway and Fleet Sts. in Fells Point; **Hollins Market,** in H.L. Mencken's neighborhood, Carrolton St.; **Cross Street Market** in Federal Hill; **Belair,** Gay and Forest Sts.; **Lafayette,** Penn and Eutaw Sts.; and **Northeast,** Monument and Chester Sts. Lazing at a market's raw bar is perhaps the best way to get to see Baltimoreans in their most natural state.

MUSEUMS AND GALLERIES. Babe Ruth Birthplace/Maryland Baseball Hall of Fame. 216 Emory St. (727–1539). Includes documentaries and exhibits on the Babe and Baltimore Orioles. Daily except Easter, Thanksgiving, Christmas, New Year's. Adults $2.50, senior citizens $2, children $1.25.

Baltimore Art Museum. N. Charles and 33rd Sts., Wyman Park (396–7101). Rodin's "Thinker," largest Matisse collection in U.S., sculpture garden with cafe, and American and African art. Tues.–Fri., 10–4; Sat. and Sun. 11–6. Adults $2. Thursdays free.

B & O Railroad Museum. 901 Pratt St. (237–2387). Birthplace of American railroading, the museum features the nation's first freight and passenger station, an 1884 roundhouse and tracks, and an engine called Tom Thumb. Closed Mon. and Tues. Adults $3.50, senior citizens and children $2.50.

Baltimore Maritime Museum. Pier 3, Pratt St. (396–3854). Includes the USS *Torsk,* a World War II submarine that sank the last four Japanese ships at the end of the war, and the Lightship *Chesapeake.* Daily 9:30 A.M.–5 P.M. Adults $2.50, senior citizens $2, children $1.

B. Olive Cole Pharmacy Museum. 650 W. Lombard St. (727–0746). An extensive collection of pharmacy artifacts, turn-of-the-century pharmacy, and library. Weekdays 10–4. Closed major holidays.

Life of Maryland Gallery. 901 N. Howard St. (539–7900). Baltimore's only corporately sponsored gallery, featuring well-known artists and changing exhibits. Weekdays 8–5.

Maryland Science Center. 601 Light St. (685–5225). Hands-on exhibits, IMAX ultrawide-screen films, and planetarium. Hours vary. Adults $6.50, senior citizens, children, military $5.50.

Museum and Library of Maryland History. 201 W. Monument St. (685–3750). Collections of furniture, prints, maps, the original manuscript of "The Star Spangled Banner," early Maryland artifacts. Tues.–Fri. 11–4:30. Sat. 9–4:30. Adults $2.50, senior citizens $1, children 75¢.

Museum of Industry. 1415 Key Highway (727–4808). Recreations of early industrial jobs and machines. Thur.–Fri. noon–5, Sat. 10–5, Sun. noon–5. Adults $2, senior citizens and students $1.

The Peale Museum. 225 Holliday St. (396–1149). This, the first Baltimore City Hall, includes exhibits of early Baltimore life. Tues.–Sat. 10–5, Sun. noon–5. Adults $1.75, senior citizens $1.25, children 75¢.

The Star-Spangled Banner Flag House and Museum. 844 E. Pratt St. (837–1793). The 1793 home of Mary Pickersgill, who sewed the flag that inspired Francis Scott Key to write "The Star-Spangled Banner." Mon.–Sat. 10–4, Sun. 1–4. Adults $1.50, senior citizens and teenagers $1, children 50¢.

Streetcar Museum. 1901 Falls Rd. (547–0264). Exhibits and a trolley ride on a one-mile track. Sun. noon–5 year-round; Sat. noon–4 June–Oct. only. Museum free; trolley fares, adults $1, children 50¢.

Walters Art Gallery. 600 N. Charles St. (547–9000). One of the country's most famous, its exhibits span 6,000 years. Stained glass, Mesopotamian and Egyptian art, manuscripts, sculpture. Tues.–Sun., 11–5. Adults $2, senior citizens and students $1. Wednesdays free.

World Trade Center. (837–4515). Next to Harborplace, the Center offers a marvelous view from its 27th-floor observatory as well as exhibits of the city's history. Open Mon.–Sat. 10–5, Sun. noon–5. Adults $2, senior citizens and children 75¢.

SHOPPING. The most interesting shopping plan in Baltimore is to browse by area. Charles St., from Lombard to Eager Sts., is lined with art and craft galleries that include works by nationally known and local artists.

Harborplace. In addition to a mouth-watering and satisfying array of Places to Eat (in all price ranges), the two pavilions at Harborplace (see above) house more than 100 gourmet food stalls, crafts shops, and well-known clothing stores. Open daily except Thanksgiving, Christmas, and New Year's Day.

Fells Point. Fells Point is crowded with intriguing antique and maritime stores. Antique Row, on Howard St. in **Mount Vernon,** has more than 35 shops ranging from the posh to knickknack collections.

SPECTATOR SPORTS. The Orioles play baseball at Memorial Stadium; the Skipjacks play hockey and the Blast play indoor soccer at the Baltimore Arena.

Pimlico Race Track opens its gates at 1 P.M. during its spring and summer seasons. The Preakness, middle leg of the Triple Crown, is run at Pimlico on the third Saturday in May.

Baltimore is the mecca of lacrosse, and local colleges, including Johns Hopkins (338–8197) and Loyola College (323–1010), have home games in the spring. A **Lacrosse Hall of Fame** is located at the Johns Hopkins University, Charles and 34th Sts. (235–6882). Open before and after home games.

For more information: Orioles, 338–1300; Skipjacks, 727–0703; Blast, 528–0100; Pimlico, 542–9400.

TOURS AND CRUISES. Baltimore offers many tours, several by water, of the harbor and the Chesapeake shore, as well as tours of downtown Baltimore and outlying areas. Walking tours have become popular and besides being fun are easily managed in a city of Baltimore's compact size. Walking tour information is available at many hotels, the Women's Civic League (837–5424), and at the city's Office of Tourism, 752–8632.

Other tours and cruises include: About Town Tours Unlimited (592–7770) and American Tours and Tour Guides (235–6484) offer personalized tours of Baltimore and other areas. American Cruise Lines (800–556–7450), with 7-day bay cruises. Baltimore Rent-a-Tour (653–2998) sightseeing, walking and insomniac tours. Clipper City, tall ship touring (575–7930). Defender and Guardian (685–4288), between the harbor, Fells Pt. and Fort McHenry. Harbor Cruises (727–3113) offers lunch, dinner, and charter packages. Maryland Tours (685–4288) offers daily harbor tours. Minnie V Skipjack (522–4214) has harbor and charter tours. Minnie Tours (256–4384) includes theme tours. Tours of Mount Vernon and other neighborhoods are available from Shoe Leather Safaris at 764–8067. Total Picture Tours (325–1978) offers helicopter, water, and bus-limousine tours throughout the area. Tour Tapes of Baltimore (837–4636 or 800–282–6632) provides three car tapes ($9.95 each, $25 for three) that direct you to and explain major sights in the city.

NIGHTLIFE. Once boringly sedate, the town is now starting to jump, with bars and clubs offering jazz, rock, new wave, and Irish music. Besides those spots listed below, there are many night entertainments to be found just by strolling in the Inner Harbor, Federal Hill, and Fell's Point areas.

Blues Alley (1225 Cathedral St., 837–2288). Opened by the proprietors of the successful D.C. spot of the same name, this club has a regular schedule of top-name jazz stars.

8×10 (10 E. Cross St., 625–2000) provides some of the best in local and national blues and rock.

The Thirteenth Floor in the Belvedere Hotel (Charles and Chase Sts., 332–1000) is a piano bar with great views.

The Lounge at the top of the Peabody Court Hotel (612 Cathedral St., 727–7101) is sedate and elegant and also offers fine views.

The Fishmarket (34 Market Place, 576–2222), a virtual theme park of nightclubs, has a 1920s Harlem jazz club and an Olde English Pub, all in a restored fish market next door to the Inner Harbor.

ZOOS. Baltimore Zoo (Druid Hill Park, Druid Hill Lake Drive, 366–5466). More than 1,200 animals, birds, and reptiles inhabit this 150-acre zoo, including lions, giraffes, and baby animals for petting. Open daily, 10–4:20, 10–5:20 on summer Sundays. Adults $4, senior citizens and children $2.

THE NATIONAL AQUARIUM. Located at Pier 3, Inner Harbor (576–3810), the Aquarium boasts more than 5,000 creatures, a rain forest, ocean tank of sharks, and a coral reef. Summer and winter hours. Access for the handicapped. Adults $7.75, senior citizens and students $6, children $4.75.

STATE PARK. Gunpowder Falls State Park, 10815 Harford Rd., Glen Arm, MD 21057, a dozen or so miles northeast of the city on Rte. 147 or US 1. The park offers boating, canoeing, fishing, windsurfing, picnicking, and hiking. Call 592–2897 for information.

RAIN OR SHINE? Baltimore's climate is very mild, averaging 41 inches of rain and 23 inches of snow per year. Summer temperatures average 77 degrees, with winter at an average 37. The city is freeze-free 232 days out of each 365. Call 936–1212 for up-to-date weather reports.

THE UPPER BAY

by
JAMES DAY

It is difficult to understand why the Upper Bay is often ignored in tours of the Chesapeake region. True, it lacks the bustle and relative sophistication of Baltimore or the sunstruck pleasures of the Atlantic resorts. But the Upper Bay, where the mighty Susquehanna empties and the wild goose flies, is one of the most lush, bountiful, and historic parts of the Bay area.

The pace here is easy. The eastern shore of the Upper Bay, easily reached but still furthest away from major highways and cities, is perfect for a relaxed drive through its farmland and towns, or a cruise up its many creeks and rivers. It is a trip to a quieter time with simpler pleasures. The land and water provide a cornucopia of corn, tomatoes, fish, clams, and other seafood, all available at homegrown prices. Some, of course, are there for the catching. The area lies within the Atlantic Flyway and is renowned for its hunting opportunities. In the spring the region is crazy with dogwood and forsythia, and in the fall it becomes, except for the honking of geese, quiet and crisp, a Thanksgiving tableau. To all of this the Upper Bay's western shore adds its Bay-related commercial towns, the Susquehanna, and a history that dates back to the founding of the colonies.

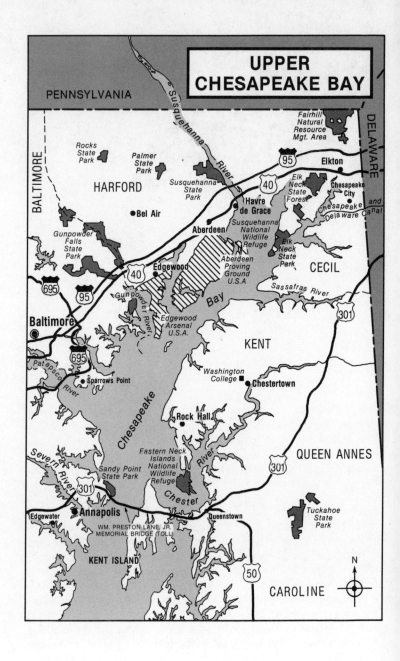

UPPER
CHESAPEAKE BAY

PENNSYLVANIA

DELAWARE

Fairhill
Natural
Resource
Mgt. Area

Rocks
State
Park

Palmer
State
Park

95 Elkton

Elk
Neck
State
Forest

Chesapeake
City

HARFORD

Susquehanna
State
Park

40

Bel Air

Havre
de Grace

Chesapeake and
Delaware Canal

BALTIMORE

Aberdeen

Susquehanna
National
Wildlife
Refuge

Elk
Neck
State
Park

CECIL

Gunpowder
Falls State
Park

40 Edgewood

Aberdeen
Proving
Ground
U.S.A

Sassafras River

695

Gunpowder River

95

Bay

301

Baltimore

Edgewood
Arsenal
U.S.A.

KENT

695

Patapsco
River

Sparrows Point

Washington
College   Chestertown

Chesapeake

Rock Hall

QUEEN ANNES

Severn
River

Fastern Neck
Islands
National
Wildlife
Refuge

301

Sandy Point
State Park

River

Tuckahoe
State
Park

301

Annapolis

Chester

Edgewater

Queenstown

WM. PRESTON LANE, JR.
MEMORIAL BRIDGE (TOLL)

N

KENT ISLAND

50

CAROLINE

Both shores boast numerous marinas and are close by Baltimore, Washington, and Interstate 95.

The clearest introduction to the Upper Bay is by county, which is also how the natives often identify themselves.

Baltimore County

The county, only part of which is directly connected to the water, surrounds Baltimore City in a crablike grip. It was founded in 1659. Its Bay side, the lower eastern side of the country, is ribboned with inlets, rivers, creeks, marinas, and Bay-related industries. Oncemighty Sparrows Point, site of steel producing and shipbuilding, juts into the Bay. Farther north and inland, the county provides Baltimore with some of its busiest and most populous suburbs. As the county stretches north to the Pennsylvania line, it becomes a place of rolling fields, genteel mansions, and cross-country horse racing.

Harford County

To the northeast of Baltimore County, Harford begins, especially in its more northern reaches, to show the country air of the Upper Bay. It changes from marsh to piedmont as one travels north and has long been known for its love of horses and country-style horse racing. It is home of the U.S. Army's Aberdeen Proving Ground, complete with a museum of weapons, and the historic towns of Bel Air and Havre de Grace. Its state parks offer an uncluttered view of the land as it was when the first settlers arrived, and the county has made an effort to provide exhibits and museums of how people lived and worked. Its shore is known for its marinas and its easy access to deeper water.

Cecil County

Cecil sits on the uppermost reaches of the Bay and is bordered by both Pennsylvania and Delaware. It is, in effect, the first or most northern of the Eastern Shore counties. Bordered by the Susquehanna and traversed by the Chesapeake and Delaware Canal and I-95, much of its commercial life is linked with the north. Captain John Smith first visited what is now the county in 1608. Elkton, the county seat, was for years a nortorious place for out-of-staters to come to be married in haste. But the county's place in history goes back much further. Lying along a main north-south route of travel Cecil County saw a busy time and many troops in the Revolutionary War. Restored taverns and homes now mark the routes. The county soon became one of the young nation's busiest grain and paper producers. Chesapeake City is a quiet and charming town that is increasingly popular with sightseers.

Kent County

The oldest county on the Eastern Shore, Kent County lies south of Cecil and is the epitome—in terms of gently rolling land, restored buildings, and a myriad of inlets to the Bay—of the Upper Bay. Chestertown, a bustling port in the 18th century, is now the beautifully preserved and restored home of Washington College. The Sassafras River in the north is one of the most enchanting streams in the Bay country.

PRACTICAL INFORMATION FOR
THE UPPER BAY

Note: The area code for all Maryland is 301.

PLACES TO STAY

HOTELS AND MOTELS. Though slightly higher in cost than its country cousins, Baltimore City's hotels provide the most accessible and most plentiful accommodations in the lower western section of the Upper Bay. (See the Baltimore section of this guide.) Accommodations in the rest of the Upper Bay range from small roadside motels to charming restored historic hotels in some of the towns. Off-season rates, weekend rates, and special package deals are sometimes available, and the general rates are clearly less than city-center prices. Bed and breakfast establishments, more common in Kent than in the other counties, are included in this list, and up-to-date information on the ever-expanding B&B industry can be had by contacting The Traveler, Box 2277, Annapolis, MD 21404 (269–6232) or Amanada's Bed and Breakfast, Ltd., 1428 Park Ave., Baltimore, MD 21217 (225–0001).

Many of the towns are so small and what they offer so obvious that the addresses are simply a route number. Don't be discouraged. The route inside a town is often only a block or so long and the establishment is easily found. The following rates are based on double-occupancy during the usual tourist season: *Deluxe,* over $100; *Expensive,* $75–$100; *Moderate,* $45–$75; *Inexpensive,* under $45.

Harford County

Best Western Red Coach Motor Inn. *Moderate.* 783 W. Bel Air Ave., Aberdeen; 272–8500. Pool. Near Aberdeen Proving Ground and weapons museum. 49 rooms. AE, DC, MC, V.

Holiday Inn. There are two Holiday Inns in the area, one in the *Moderate* range: 793 W. Belair Rd., 272–6000; and the *Expensive*

Holiday Inn **Chesapeake House,** 1007 Beards Hill Rd., 272–8100. The former has 124 rooms, the latter 122. AE, DC, MC, V.

Sheraton Aberdeen. *Moderate.* I–95 (exit 85) and Rte. 22; 273–6300. Restaurant, pool, nightclub, and game room. 131 rooms. AE, DC, MC, V.

EconoLodge. There are two EconoLodges (*Inexpensive*) in the Aberdeen area, each with a restaurant and lounge: Rte. 22 and I–95 (exit 85), 272–5500; and close by on Rte. 22, 679–3133. AE, DC, MC, V.

Cecil County

Inn at the Canal. *Moderate to Expensive.* 104 Bohemia Ave., Chesapeake City; 885–5995. 6 rooms with private baths. Restaurants nearby. AE, MC, V.

Sutton Motel. *Inexpensive.* 405 E. Pulaski Hwy., Elkton; 398–3830. This small motel, with 11 rooms, is one of the few motels along this stretch of US 40. Restaurant nearby. For additional accommodations in the area, see Harford County above.

Kent County

The Imperial Hotel. *Deluxe.* High near Queen St., Chestertown (778–5000. Victorian decor, rather lavish appointments. 11 rooms, 2 suites. No credit cards.

White Swan Tavern. *Expensive to Deluxe.* 231 High St, Chestertown; 778–2300. B&B with restaurant nearby and museum. 6 rooms. No credit cards.

Inn at Mitchell House. *Expensive.* Rte. 21 south of Chestertown; 778–6500. Antiques, B&B format with full breakfast, on a 10-acre site. 6 rooms, 5 with private bath. MC, V.

Rolph's Wharf Inn. *Expensive.* Rolph's Wharf Road, Chestertown; 778–1988. Bed and breakfast style with homemade cakes and live entertainment at night. Restaurant next door. 6 rooms, each with private bath. AE, MC, V.

Great Oak Landing Resort and Conference Center. *Expensive.* Handy Point Rd., Chestertown; 778–2100. Tennis, restaurant, marina, beach, and golf course available. 29 rooms. AE, MC, V.

Lantern Inn. *Moderate.* Ericsson Avenue, Betterton; 348–5809. Beach nearby. 7 B & B rooms, 2 with private baths. MC, V.

PLACES TO EAT

RESTAURANTS. There is no place better to get the best in Chesapeake Bay than around the Upper Bay. The land provides sweet corn and other vegetables, while the water provides clams, oysters, numerous varieties of fish, and crabs. The food is simply prepared, but the tastes are exquisite and usually moderately priced. Waterfront dining along the rivers and canals is especially enjoyable. Price categories, as elsewhere in the guide, are for dinner for one, excluding drinks and tip: *Deluxe,* over $30; *Expensive,* $20–$30; *Moderate,* $10–$20; *Inexpensive,* under $10.

Harford County

Andy Wargo's. *Moderate.* 308 E. Jarrettsville Rd., Forest Hill; 879–9747. Reliable selection of steak and seafood with interesting sandwich options. Lunch daily, dinner Wed.–Sun. MC, V.

Bayou. *Moderate.* US 40, 927 Pulaski Hwy.; 939–3565. Italian-American menu, specializing in seafood. AE, DC, MC, V.

Georgetown North. *Moderate.* 12 S. Main St., Bel Air; 838–8666. Daily seafood specials in the heart of town. AE, DC, MC, V.

Colonel's Choice. *Inexpensive to Moderate.* US 40 and S. Philadelphia Blvd., Aberdeen; 272–6500. Italian and lobster dishes. A spot frequented by the locals. AE, DC, MC, V.

Campus Cafe. *Inexpensive.* 2436 Churchville Rd., Bel Air; 836–2077. Surf and turf for lunch and dinner daily. MC, V.

Hickory Inn. *Inexpensive.* 2119 Conowingo Rd., Bel Air; 838–3686. Chinese and American cuisines, with special buffets on weekends. MC, V.

Cecil County

Fair Hill Inn. *Moderate to Expensive.* 3370 Singerly Rd., Fair Hill; 398–4187. Historic country inn. Sunday brunch. Closed Mon. AE, MC, V.

Bayard House. *Moderate.* 11 Bohemia Ave., Chesapeake City; 885–5040. Waterfront dining on the C&D Canal. Open daily, lunch and dinner. All major credit cards.

Conowingo Inn. *Moderate.* 373 Conowingo Rd., Rte. 1, Conowingo; 378–4692. Crab specialties. Open daily, lunch and dinner. No credit cards.

Dockside Yacht Club. *Moderate.* 605 Second St., Chesapeake City; 885–5016. Waterfront dining, late March through October. AE, V.

Island Inn *Moderate.* 648 Broad St., Perryville; 642–3448. Seafood. No dinner Tues. AE, MC, V.

North East Harbor House. *Moderate.* 200 Cherry St., North East; 287–6800. Waterfront dining, docking available. Lunch and dinner daily. CB, DC, MC, V.

Schaefer's Canal House. *Moderate.* Bank Street, Chesapeake City; 885–2200. Canalside dining. Open daily, lunch and dinner. Breakfast on Sunday, with dinner at noon. AE, MC, V.

Archway Inn. *Inexpensive.* 2835 Crystal Beach Rd., Earleville; 275–8609. Italian and seafood offerings. Open daily. No credit cards.

Kent County

Imperial Hotel Dining Room. *Expensive.* 208 High St., Chestertown; 778–5000. French specialties in a Victorian setting. No credit cards.

Fin, Fur, Feather Inn. *Moderate.* 424 Bayside, Rock Hall; 639–7454. As the name implies, a little of everything. Crab cakes and chowder from the catch of the day are the house's pride. Open daily, breakfast through dinner. No credit cards.

Old Wharf Inn. *Moderate.* Foot of Cabin St., Chestertown; 778–3055. Catch of the day specialties. MC, V.

THINGS TO SEE AND DO

TOURING INFORMATION. Advance touring information for the Upper Bay area may be obtained for the Upper Bay area may be obtained from the following: **Harford County,** Harford County Office of Economic Development, 29 W. Courtland St., Bel Air 21014, (301) 838–6000, Ext. 339; **Cecil County,** Cecil County Office of Planning and Economic Development, Co. Office Bldg., Room 300, Elkton 21921, (301) 398–0200, Ext. 144; **Kent County,** Kent County Chamber of Commerce, Box 146, 118 N. Cross St., Chestertown 21620, (301) 778–0416.

GETTING AROUND THE UPPER BAY. Baltimore-Washington International Airport, south of Baltimore, is little more than an hour and a half, at the most, from most parts of the Upper Bay. Other nearby airports include Philadelphia International, the Greater Wilmington Airport, the Cecil County Airpark near Elkton, and the Scheeler Field-Gill Airport near Chestertown.

The Upper Bay is very convenient to major highways. Interstate 95 and US 40 run along the western shore, while US 301, a major route for tobacco and farm produce, bisects the eastern portion of the Upper Bay. The two-span Bay Bridge ($1.25 each way) is easily reached from the Baltimore-Washington area.

BOATING. The Upper Bay is a boating paradise. With several major rivers flowing into the bay and countless streams, inlets, and creeks, boating in the area can range from a lazy, slow meander up a backwater creek to gaze at the cattails and wildlife to a full-fledged Chesapeake cruise. There are too many Bay marinas to list here, but after selecting the area you wish to visit, you can call the following numbers for more information: Baltimore County, 887–3648; Harford County, 838–6000; Cecil County, 398–0200; or Kent County, 778–0416. Most marinas in the area monitor Channel 16.

CRUISES AND TOURS. Tours and cruises can be arranged through these groups: Tourism Council of the Upper Chesapeake, 208 N. Commerce St., Centreville, MD 21617 (758–2300); The Touring Machine, Box 5686, Baltimore, MD 21210 (889–7633); or Three Centuries Tours, Box 29, 48 Maryland Ave., Annapolis, MD 21404 (263–5401). The Kent County Chamber of Commerce (118 N. Cross St., Chestertown, MD 21620, 778–0416) provides a detailed and interesting driving guide for the county and its towns.

SIGHTS AND MUSEUMS. The Upper Bay is one of the most historic parts of the Chesapeake area. In addition to historic sights and homes, you can find interesting specialized museums.

Harford County

Concord Point Lighthouse. Lafayette Street, Havre de Grace. Built in 1829, one of the oldest continuously used lighthouses on the East Coast. Spectacular view of the Upper Bay.

Eden Mill. Off Rte. 136, Fawn Grove. This 1805 mill is surrounded by a 56-acre park with nature trails, a ski lift, and skating pond. Daylight hours. Free.

Havre de Grace Decoy Museum. Giles and Market Sts., Havre de Grace; 939–3739. A complete collection of Madison Mitchell, Paul Gibson, and Charlie "Speed" Joiner decoys. Wetland displays, a working decoy shop, and recreations in wax. Open Tues.–Sun., 1–5 P.M.

Ladew Topiary Gardens and Manor House. Rte. 146, 5 miles north of Jacksonville (557–9466). The 22-acre world-famous garden features sculptured trees and shrubs. The mansion houses a collection of antiques, hunting memorabilia, and an extensive library. The house and gardens are on the National Register of Historic Places. Open mid-April through Oct., Tues.–Fri. 10–4, Sat.–Sun. noon–5. Adults $5, senior citizens and students $4, children $1.

Steppingstone Museum. 463 Quaker Bottom Rd., Havre de Grace (939–2299). Farmhouse and shops exhibit the trades and skills of rural life in the late 1800s. Small admission fee.

Susquehanna Museum. Lock House, Erie and Conesto Sts., Havre de Grace (939–5780). Exhibits are housed in the first lock of the old Susquehanna and Tidewater Canal. Hours vary. Donations accepted.

U.S. Army Ordnance Museum. Aberdeen Proving Ground, US 40 and Rte. 715, Aberdeen. An extensive collection of small arms, artillery, tanks, and ammunition. Also houses captured German long-range railway gun nicknamed "Anzio Annie." Tues.–Fri. noon–4:45, Sat.–Sun. 10–4:45. Free.

Cecil County

Chesapeake City Historical District. Once the center of canal-related commerce, the area is now being restored.

107 House/Tory House. Market and Cecil Sts., Charlestown (287–8793). Restored Colonial kitchen and tavern. Open Sun. 11–4, mid-May–Sept., other times by appointment. Free.

Mount Harmon Plantation. Grove Neck Road, Earleville (275–2721). This restored 18th-century plantation sits on the banks of the Sassafras River and provides a detailed look at the elegance of plantation life, at least as the owners knew it. Includes main house, boxwood garden, tobacco house, and wharf. Hours vary. Small admission fee.

There are a number of restored houses that can be seen but not entered. A detailed "Historic Tour Guide," which includes a map of Revolutionary War marches by various armies, is available at the Cecil County office building in Elkton (398–0200).

C & D Canal Museum. Second St. and Bethel Rd., Chesapeake City (885–5621). The Old Lock pump house is a National Register site. Shows the history of the Chesapeake and Delaware Canal, which links the Upper Bay with Delaware Bay. Daily 8–4, Sun. 10–6. Closed Sun., Oct.–Easter. Free.

Historical Society Museum. 135 East Main St., Elkton (398–1790). Exhibits include a country store and the first local schoolhouse. By appointment only.

Rogers Tavern. Rte. 7, Perryville. (no phone) This restored 18th-century tavern on Old Post Rd. was a favorite stopping place between Baltimore and Philadelphia for George Washington, Thomas Jefferson, and other Colonial founding fathers. Open May–Oct., 2nd Sun., 2–4 P.M.

Upper Bay Museum. Walnut St., North East (287–5718). Includes exhibits of decoy making, duck hunting devices, guns, boats, and fishing tools—all native to the region. Summer Sundays, 9–4 and by appointment.

Kent County

Many of the historically interesting homes and sites are private but can be found in walking tours of the county's towns. The Kent County Historical Society, on Church Alley near Queen St., and the Chamber of Commerce at 118 N. Cross St. (778–0416), provide tours, open-house events, and guides for walking tours of Chestertown and other areas.

There is also a detailed and interesting driving tour of the county provided by the Chamber of Commerce.

Betterton. On the Sassafras River, Betterton was once a busy beach resort. Nearby is Still Pond, where women first voted in Maryland in 1908.

Buck-Bacchus Store Museum. High and Queen Sts., Chestertown. (778–0416) Exhibits of early Americana in a restored general store. May–Oct., Sat. 1–4 P.M. Admission.

Kent Museum. Rte. 448, Turners Creek Public Landing, near Kennedyville. (348–5855) This museum features antique farm equipment. Apr.–Sept., 1st and 3rd Sats., 10–4 P.M. Admission.

Rock Hall. A small town (1,600) with a deep harbor, Rock Hall is a fine example of many Kent County fishing communities.

The Historical Society's Geddes-Piper House. Church Alley near Queen St. (778–3499). The Society continues to develop its museum and library of early regional art and furnishings, written records, and photographs. May through Oct., Sat. and Sun., 1–4.

Rock Hall Museum. Municipal Building, South Main St., Rock Hall (639–7611). Exhibits include paintings, boat models, and the country's first X-ray machines. Wed.–Sun. 2–4:30. Free.

Washington College. Washington and Campus Aves., Chestertown. Includes the Middle, East, and West Halls, dating from 1845 and standing on the site of the original college, which started in 1782 and where Washington received a law degree in 1784. Washington is the nation's tenth oldest college and Maryland's first.

White Swan Tavern. 231 High St., Chestertown. (778–2300) Afternoon tea between 3–5 P.M. in this restored Colonial inn is a pleasant experience when touring historic and picturesque Chestertown. The White Swan is now a B&B. Charges for tour and tea.

HUNTING AND FISHING. The Upper Bay is a fisherman's paradise, a hunter's dream, and a sailor's fantasy. For more information on licensing and regulations, see the Eastern Shore section of this guide. Native and transient wildlife may be seen but not harmed at **Remington Farms,** Route 20 north of Rock Hall. Remington Farms is a 2,000-acre wildlife research area that includes nature trails for self-guide tours. Another wildlife viewing and learning center is the **Eastern Neck National Wildlife Refuge,** Route 445, south of Rock Hall. This area includes marshes, coves, and ponds, with fall and winter feeding grounds for migrating Canada geese.

SAILING SCHOOL. Learn to sail while you're vacationing or touring the Upper Bay. Capt. Phineas McHenry, Ltd., 24 S. Main St., North East, 287–2028.

SHOPPING. Antiques and water-related native crafts—decoys, hunting boats, etc.—are the most interesting and ubiquitous items for sale in the Upper Bay. Many of the restored sections of the region's small towns include at least one antique and crafts shop. Shops include: **Flyway Gallery,** 955 Blueball Rd., Elkton (398–7500). Wildlife and Bay art. Local and original art works. **Gallery 5,** Cannon and Cross Streets, Chestertown, Kent County (778–

3483). Original arts and crafts. The **Day Basket Factory,** West
High St. in North East, has handmade oak baskets. Open weekdays
8–4, Sat. 10–4. Call 287–6100.

LIVELY ARTS. Local production companies include the **Covered Bridge Theater,** 105 Railroad Ave., Elkton, Cecil County
(392–3780); the **Edwin Booth Theater,** Harford Community College, Bel Air (836–4211).

OUTDOOR RECREATION. State Parks and Forests in the
Upper Bay area include: **Gunpowder Falls State Park,** Baltimore
and Harford Counties (592–2897), off Rte. 155, 5 mi. north of
Havre de Grace; **Rocks State Park,** Harford County (557–7994),
Rte. 24, 8 mi. northwest of Bel Air; **Susquehanna State Park,** Harford and Cecil Counties (939–0643), off Rte. 155, 5 mi. north of
Havre de Grace; **Elk Neck State Forest** and **Elk Neck State Park,**
Cecil County (287–5777 and 287–5333), south of North East, Rte.
272.

MARYLAND'S EASTERN SHORE

by
JAMES DAY

Everywhere you look on Maryland's Eastern Shore there is a point jutting out into the Bay, a marshy creek providing a home to geese and ducks, old Southern mansions, wildflowers, and piney woods. This is pure Chesapeake Bay country and it is fascinating and relaxing to explore.

It is a particularly quiet place, removed geographically and historically from the motion of the Upper Bay and the Baltimore region but retaining its own history, which in fact predates much of its better-known neighbors to the west and north. Its flat terrain and sandy soil, its pace, and its woods, remind one of the South, as do its many small towns and fishing communities. It can be a hard place for those who live there, and there are the problems of poverty in some Eastern Shore rural areas. But the area is making a comeback, and tourism—with all the amenities for tourists and boating afficionados—is increasingly an important part of the region's economy.

The Bay has created a dramatic but gentle coastline, leaving a scattering of islands—many of which can be visited and explored—

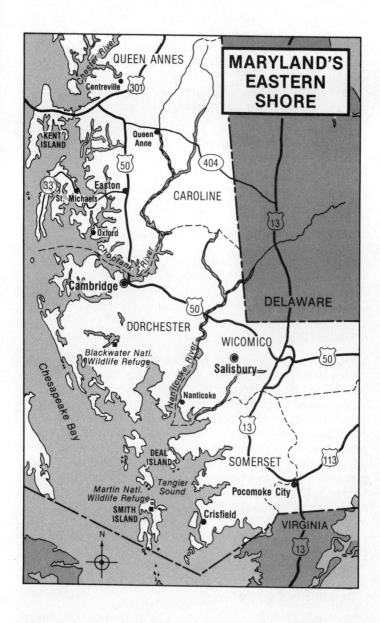

MARYLAND'S
EASTERN
SHORE

Chester River
QUEEN ANNES
Centreville
301
KENT
ISLAND
Queen
Anne
50
404
CAROLINE
33
Easton
St. Michaels
13
Oxford
Choptank River
Cambridge
50
DELAWARE
DORCHESTER
WICOMICO
Blackwater Natl.
Wildlife Refuge
Salisbury
50
Nanticoke River
Nanticoke
Chesapeake Bay
13
DEAL
ISLAND
SOMERSET
113
Tangier
Sound
Martin Natl.
Wildlife Refuge
Pocomoke City
SMITH
ISLAND
Crisfield
VIRGINIA
N
13

and a ragged mass of quiet inlets and wet marshes, many of which can be sailed or fished or hunted. Crabbing and fresh- or salt-water fishing are easily learned and the end result, especially a Bay crab smothered in hot sauce and steamed until a fiery red, is delicious. This place is the home of Maryland's grandest tree—the 95-foot Wye Oak—and its most noble canine, the Chesapeake Bay retriever, Maryland's state dog.

As in the Upper Bay, the clearest guide to the Eastern Shore is by county, and it is county by county that we will explore Maryland's Eastern Shore.

Queen Annes County

The Bay Bridge slopes gently into Queen Annes County and travelers to seashore resorts in Maryland and Delaware whiz past. But away from the main highways a visitor can find a simple and relaxing county with an unusually unbroken view of the sky and with an almost constant breeze from the Bay.

The southern end of Kent Island was the site of the first settlement in Maryland. This is where William Claiborne established his fort and trading post in 1631. Centreville, the county seat, remains a good example of the sleepy Southern village/county seat, complete with a statue of Queen Anne on the green.

Talbot County

Talbot is a much busier but no less attractive county than Queen Annes, its neighbor to the north. Its county seat, Easton, toots its horn as the "shopping center for the entire Eastern Shore." St. Michaels, a natural harbor and haven for boats, is becoming a popular stopover point for cruising boaters and motoring tourists. St. Michaels has a number of good restaurants. While the harbor, Chesapeake Bay Maritime Museum, and its restaurants attract increasing numbers of visitors each year, this old Bay port has managed to retain—even enhance—much of its former charm. The county's historic and deeply felt connection with the Bay is understandable since it claims that Talbot's 602 miles of waterfront is the most of any county in continental United States.

Tidal streams have created a long series of "necks," and most every neck is the site of an old mansion, a picturesque village, or more recently, a busy marina.

Dorchester County

South of Talbot, Dorchester, like the other Eastern Shore counties, is steeped in its own quiet history. It is home to the oldest Episcopal church in continous use in the United States. Cambridge is an attractive town that has links to the earliest settlers in the colonies. The county has numerous and longstanding fishing communities, and shares with Talbot County the Choptank River, setting for much of James Michener's *Chesapeake*. Indian lore has always been part of the county's heritage and many of its geographical names can be traced to the tribes that once hunted, fished, and lived on and around these shores. Dorchester is the largest county on the Eastern Shore, and probably has more marsh than any other. The county's marshland includes the Blackwater National Wildlife Refuge, which is nestled among wetland marshes such as Kentuck Swamp and Raccoon Creek and is home during the fall migrations to an estimated 80,000 Canada geese and 30,000 ducks.

Caroline County

Caroline has been referred to as the "inland county," although this is not totally accurate since the Choptank runs through it to the Bay. But, with its back against the Delaware state line, it does lack frontage on the Bay. While its commerce is therefore not particularly water-related, it does boast good bass fishing in the Choptank. Caroline's strength lies in being "a green place," and so it calls itself. This is a farming county that is blessed with good soil. The county is known for its tomatoes, canteloupes, and watermelon. It is proud of its simple way of life, its lack of great amusement parks or major tourist areas, even its lack of spectacular geography. It does, however, stress its large number of parks, campgrounds, and fishing and canoeing locations.

Wicomico County

Also linked closely with the Indians—its name comes from the tribe that once lived there—Wicomico County is the youngest of Maryland's counties, having been created in 1867. But Salisbury, the county's and the entire lower Shore's major center of commerce, was founded in 1732. Salisbury has restored many of its historic homes and other sites while retaining its place as a hub of the poultry, farming, and finance industries of the Shore.

Somerset County

Resting on the Virginia line, Somerset County and the nearby Bay islands remain as tightly involved with the Bay as they did when John Smith first visited and admired this part of the Bay in 1608. Workboats, including the Chesapeake's famous skipjacks— oyster boats powered by sail—still ply the waters, and Crisfield is known, and not just by its local boosters, as the "Seafood Capital of the World." Princess Anne, the county seat, is considered one of the most charming towns on the Shore. Life can be tough in a county that is so closely tied to the vagaries of the weather and water, but the people who live in Somerset have long been known to be a sturdy and persistent group. Nearby Smith and Deal Islands, perfect examples of fishing towns and life on the water, can be visited.

PRACTICAL INFORMATION FOR
MARYLAND'S EASTERN SHORE

Note: The area code for all Maryland is 301.

PLACES TO STAY

HOTELS, MOTELS, AND INNS. Lodging on the Eastern Shore ranges from the small roadside motel—not always charming but usually clean and reasonable in price—to restored historic hotels and inns in some of the towns. Off-season rates, weekend rates, and special package deals are sometimes available. Bed and breakfast establishments are included in this list. There are several registries of accommodations in homes, yachts, and inns: Amanada's Bed and Breakfast, Ltd., 1428 Park Ave., Baltimore, MD 21217, 225–0001; The Traveler, Box 2277, Annapolis, MD 21404, 269–6232.

The following rates are based on double occupancy during the usual tourist season: *Expensive,* over $75; *Moderate,* $45–$75; *Inexpensive,* under $45.

Queen Annes County

Holly's Restaurant and Motel. *Inexpensive.* US 301 and US 50; 827–8711. 22 rooms. Restaurant. A good location for visitors heading south. No credit cards.

Talbot County

1876 House. *Expensive.* 110 North Morris St., Oxford; 226–5496. A B&B with 3 rooms, tennis, boating, and golf. Restaurant nearby. No credit cards.

The Inn at Perry Cabin. *Expensive.* Rte. 33, St. Michaels; 745–5178. 6 rooms, with private baths. Five dining rooms with good view of Miles River. Includes Continental breakfast. Closed Christmas. AE, DC, MC, V.

Robert Morris Inn. *Moderate to Expensive.* A gracious and attractive old inn 32 rooms, 29 with private baths. The Strand at Morris St., Oxford; 226–5111. Excellent restaurant, no TV or phones. AE, MC, V.

Kemp House Smithton Inn. *Moderate.* 412 Talbot St., St. Michaels; 745–2243. A B&B, with restaurant nearby and bikes for rent. MC, V.

Martingham Harbourtowne Inn. *Expensive.* St. Michaels; 745–9066. 77 rooms, including villas. Outdoor pool, tennis, golf, and restaurant. AE, DC, MC, V.

The Tidewater Inn. *Moderate to Expensive.* Dover and Harrison Sts., Easton; 822–1300. 120 rooms in a genteel 4-story tidewater inn. Excellent restaurant, room service, and pool. AE, CB, DC, MC, V.

EconoLodge. *Moderate.* US 50 in Easton; 822–6330 or (800) 446–6900. 48 rooms. Restaurant nearby. AE, DC, MC, V.

St. Michaels Motor Inn. *Moderate.* Rte. 33 and Peaneck Road, St. Michaels; 745–3333. 93 rooms and restaurant for breakfast. AE, DC, MC, V.

Dorchester County

The Governors Ordinary. *Moderate to Expensive.* Water and Church Sts., Vienna; 376–3530. A five-room B&B with tennis and boat ramp nearby. MC, V.

Quality Inn. *Moderate.* US 50, 1 mile east of town, Cambridge; 228–6900 or (800) 228–5150. Outdoor pool and restaurant. Bar. 60 rooms in a 2-story motel. AE, DC, MC, V.

Sarke Plantation. *Moderate.* 6033 Todd Point Rd., Cambridge; 228–7020. A five-room B&B in a country home with pool room. AE.

Caroline County

The Sophie Kerr House. *Inexpensive.* 5th St. and Kerr Ave., Denton; 479–3421. A B&B-style establishment with indoor pool, biking, badminton, and croquet. Its 5 rooms make it not only the *largest* inn in the county, but the *only* inn in Caroline County. Personal checks, no credit cards.

Wicomico County

Sheraton Salisbury Inn. *Expensive.* 300 S. Salisbury Blvd. (US 13), Salisbury; 546–4400. 158 rooms. Live entertainment, indoor pool, restaurant, and gym. Bar. AE, CD, DC, MC, V.

Best Western Statesman. *Moderate.* 712 N. Salisbury Blvd. US 13 Bus.; 749–7155 or (800) 528–1234. Pool. Refreshments in lobby. AE, DC, MC, V.

Howard Johnson. *Moderate.* 3 miles north of Salisbury on US 13; 742–5195. 56 rooms, with a pool and a 24-hour restaurant next door. AE, CB, DC, MC, V.

Lord Salisbury. *Moderate.* Four and a half miles north of Salisbury on US 13; 742–3251. 50 rooms. Pool. Restaurant adjacent. AE, CB, DC, MC, V.

Somerset County

The Pines Motel. *Moderate.* Somerset Ave., Crisfield; 968–0900. 40 rooms. Outdoor pool. Restaurant within 3 blocks. No credit cards.

Washington Hotel Inn. *Inexpensive to Moderate.* Somerset Ave., Princess Anne; 651–2525. 12 rooms, each with private bath. Two large dining rooms and coffee shop. Restaurant closed Sun. MC, V.

PLACES TO EAT

RESTAURANTS. Expect lots of crab dishes, fish, and fresh vegetables, all done in the simple but extremely tasty Eastern Shore manner. From the water to the kitchen is only a short distance, and much of the menu will vary with the catch of the day. Crab cakes and Imperial crab—a rich mixture of crabs, mayonnaise, and spices—are available at most eateries. Eating hardshelled crabs is messy—mounds of the tasty creatures on a newspaper on the table, accompanied by a pitcher of beer and cole slaw. Locals will sometimes race to see who can dismantle a crab the quickest, a wonder to behold as you slowly crack and claw your way through the meal. But don't fret. This is all part of the fun, and the taste of freshly steamed crab, grilled oysters, or steamed clams, is worth the time and trouble.

Our price categories are based on dinner for one, excluding drinks and tip. They are: *Deluxe,* over $30; *Expensive,* $20–$30; *Moderate,* $10–$20; *Inexpensive,* under $10.

Queen Annes County

The Narrows. *Moderate to Expensive.* US 50, a short distance south of Bay Bridge; 827–8113. Lunch and dinner, with Sun. brunch. Maryland seafood recipes, including crab. Children's portions and outdoor dining in season. CB, DC, MC, V.

Hemingway's. *Moderate to Expensive.* At the eastern foot of the Bay Bridge off US 50, MD 8 south 1 block, then toward the Bay on Pier 1 Rd.; 643–2196. Comfortable setting with a good view of the bridge and a professionally done menu of seafood, beef, and locally made desserts. AE, DC, MC, V.

Talbot County

The Inn at Perry Cabin. *Expensive.* Rte. 33, St. Michaels; 745–5178. Seafood, veal, steak, and lamb in a pleasant, water setting at Fogg Cove. Oyster bisque and crab cakes are house specialties. AE, MC, V.

Robert Morris Inn. *Expensive.* 314 Morris St., Oxford; 226–5111. Gracious dining in a charming old inn. You'll write postcards home about the Maryland crab cakes and prime rib. AE, MC, V.

Tidewater Inn. *Moderate to Expensive.* Dover and Harrison Sts., Easton; 822–1300. Long known by locals and regular visitors for its solid and tasty fare, ranging from seafood to poultry and beef. Open daily, lunch through dinner. Bar. AE, CB, DC, MC, V.

Harbour Watch. *Moderate.* 3 mi west of St. Michaels on MD 33, Harbourtowne Resort; 745–9066. Breakfast, lunch, and dinner, with a Sun. brunch. Bar. Wine list. Full menu, with the accent on seafood and chicken. AE, MC, V.

The Crab Claw Restaurant. *Moderate.* Navy Point, St. Michaels; 745–2900. Steamed crabs ("if he don't kick we don't cook"— meaning they're *fresh*), cold beer and mixed drinks and a full menu besides. Oysters and clams in all sorts of ways—steamed, fried, and casinoed. No credit cards.

Longfellow's. *Moderate.* 125 Mulberry St., St. Michaels; 745–2624. Friendly restaurant in a harbor setting frequented by the boating crowd. Fried oysters, crab dishes, and catch of the day. Also beef. No breakfast during winter months. MC, V.

Dorchester County

Clayton's. *Moderate.* On the creek at 108 Commerce St., Cambridge; 228–7200. Steamed crabs as well as other seafood and meat dishes. Open daily, lunch and dinner. AE, MC, V.

East Side Seafood Co. *Moderate.* At the foot of the bridge on Maryland Ave., Cambridge; 228–9007. As the name implies, fresh seafood dishes done in the Eastern Shore manner. Bar. No lunch Sun.–Fri. No credit cards.

Caroline County

Melvin House. *Moderate to Expensive.* 106 Market St., Denton; 479–1513. Family-run Continental restaurant with a menu that uses the local vegetables and fish. Bar and wine list. Dinner only. Closed Sun. and Mon. AE, MC, V.

Wicomico County

Argyll's. *Moderate.* Downtown Plaza, Salisbury; 546–3104. Tableside cooking, surf and turf, veal and steaks. Bar. Lunch and dinner. Closed Sun. AE, MC, V.

Royal Exchange Pub. *Moderate.* Rte. 13, Salisbury; 749–1263. Continental-style dining and menu plus freshly baked desserts and bread. 2 bars, one with dancing. Open daily, lunch and dinner. Dinner only Sun. AE, CB, DC, MC, V.

Johnny and Sammy's. *Inexpensive to Expensive.* 670 S. Salisbury Blvd., US 13, Salisbury; 742–1116. Varied menu, featuring seafood and beef. Breakfast, lunch, dinner. Bar. MC, V.

Somerset County

Auntem's. *Inexpensive.* Richardson Ave., Crisfield; 968–0353. Known for its crab cakes, done in the meaty Eastern Shore style, and other seafood. Bar service. Open daily, breakfast through dinner. No credit cards.

THINGS TO SEE AND DO

TOURING INFORMATION. A **Maryland Visitor Information Center** is located on US 13, just north of the Virginia state line. Closed Thanksgiving, Christmas, New Year's Day, and Easter. Advance touring information may be obtained from the following county offices: **Queen Annes** County Tourism Coordinator, 208 N. Commerce St., Centreville 21617, (301) 758–2300; **Caroline** County Tourism Coordinator, Box 207, Denton 21629, (301) 479–0660; **Dorchester** County Tourism, Box 307, Cambridge 21613, (301) 228–3234; **Wicomico** Convention & Visitors Bureau, Civic Center, Glen Ave. Ext., Salisbury 21801 (301) 548–4914; **Somerset** County Tourism, Box 243, Princess Anne 21853, (301) 651–2968.

HOW TO GET AROUND. Baltimore-Washington International Airport, south of Baltimore, is little more than an hour and a half, at the most, from most parts of the Eastern Shore. The Easton Airport is linked by regular flights to BWI. Also, Washington's National Airport is about an hour's drive from the Bay Bridge via US 50.

The Eastern Shore begins at the Bay Bridge (toll: $1.25 each way) and shortly after the bridge you may choose US 50, which swings south and parallels the Bay before turning east toward the ocean; US 301, which runs northeast into the farmland of the Upper Bay; or State Rte. 404, which cuts through the heart of the Eastern Shore on the way to the Delaware ocean resorts.

BOATING. Perhaps most popular among Chesapeake boaters, the Eastern Shore of the Bay offers countless inlets and rivers to sail and explore. "Boating" is spoken here by just about everyone, and the area is a favorite for cross-Bay trips out of Annapolis or Baltimore.

There are simply too many marinas and rental/charter companies to list, but after selecting the area you wish to visit, you can call the following numbers for more extensive information: Queen Annes, Caroline, and Talbot, 758–2300; Talbot County, 822–4606; Dorchester, 228–3234; Caroline, 479–0660; Wicomico, 548–4914; or Somerset, 651–2968.

Most marinas in the area monitor Channel 16.

CRUISES AND TOURS. Walking and driving tours are available at most of the county tourism offices: **Queen Annes, Caroline,** and **Talbot:** Tourism Council of the Upper Chesapeake, 208 N. Commerce St., Centreville, MD 21617, 758–2300; **Dorchester,** Dorchester County Tourism, Box 307, Cambridge, MD 21613, 228–3234; **Wicomico,** Convention and Visitors Bureau, Civic Center, Glen Ave. Extended, Salisbury, MD 21801, 548–4914; **Somerset,** Somerset County Tourism Commission, Box 243, Princess Anne, MD 21853, 651–2968.

Cruises include Chesapeake Travel and Tours, a wide variety of land and water tours, 822–4383; Capt. Jason, Crisfield to Smith Island, 425–4471; Capt. Tyler, Crisfield to Smith Island, can include lunch and bus tour, 425–4271; *Island Belle II,* Crisfield to Smith Island, 425–4271; *The Patriot,* Bay cruises, 745–3100; Tangier Island, VA, Crisfield, 968–2338; Smith Island Cruises, *Capt. Evans* and *Spirit of Chesapeake,* Bay cruises from Reedville, VA, 804–453–3430. Most towns have local rental agencies for small boats and stores for a visitor's nautical needs.

SIGHTS AND MUSEUMS. The six counties of Maryland's Eastern Shore offer a number of exploring opportunities—historic sights, museums, fishing towns, wildlife refuges, zoos, and more.

Queen Annes County

Queen Annes Courthouse and **Statute of Queen Anne,** 122 N. Commerce St., Centreville. One of two 18th-century courthouses in Maryland, with a statute of the queen on the green. Mon.–Fri. 8:30–4:30. Free.

Queen Annes Courthouse, at Queenstown, Rte. 18 off US 301. Old courthouse and jail, dating back to 1708. Open summer, Sat. and Sun. 1–4. Free.

Tucker House, 124 S. Commerce St., Centreville (758–1208). Houses local historical society museum. By appointment.

Wright's Chance, 119 S. Commerce St., Centreville (758–0658). Noted for its original wood paneling, dating from 1681. By appointment.

Talbot County

Academy of the Arts. Harrison and South Sts., Easton. Center for the arts for Talbot and surrounding counties. Exhibits can be seen Mon.–Fri., 10–4 P.M. Phone 822–0455 or 822–ARTS.

Customs House, Morris St. and the Strand, Oxford (226–5122). Replica of first U.S. Customs House. Sat.–Sun. 2:30–4:30. Free.

Chesapeake Bay Maritime Museum. Maritime Rd., St. Michaels Harbor (745–2916). Floating collection of Chesapeake Bay working boats, and Bay and nautical history. Hooper Straight Lighthouse is a focal point. Gift shop. Summer hours: Sun.–Fri. 10–5, Sat. 10–7. Other seasons: daily 10–4. Adults $4, children $1.50.

Historical Society of Talbot County Museum. 25 S. Washington St., Easton (822–0773). Several changing exhibits, Federal townhouse (1810) and frame cottage (1795). Gardens and tours. Tues.–Sat. 10–4. Sun. 1–4. Adults $2.

Oxford Museum. Morris and Market Sts., Oxford (226–5122). Local exhibits on this charming old maritime town. Hours vary.

St. Marys Square Museum. At "The Green" in St. Michaels (745–9561). Local exhibits. Sat.–Sun. 10–4, May–Oct. Free.

St. Michaels. Known as the birthplace of the Baltimore Clipper sailing sloop, this town—now spruced up and an increasingly popular stopover for tourists—provides lodging, restaurants, and historical exhibits. A pleasant harbor town for browsing.

Third Haven Meeting House. 405 S. Washington St., Easton (822–0293). This may be the oldest (1682) frame building for religious services in the United States. William Penn preached there and Lord Baltimore attended services. See caretaker for tour. Free.

Tilghman Island. On Rte. 33. Typical Chesapeake fishing town and home port to large portion of state's skipjack fleet.

Tred Avon (Oxford-Bellevue) Ferry. Oxford and Bellevue, (226–5408). Oldest "free running" ferry in the United States. 9 A.M.–sunset (7 A.M.–sunset in summer). Car and driver $3.75, passengers 25¢; bike and rider $1.50.

Wye Church, Wye Mill, and Wye Oak. Wye Mills. Wye Church is one of the oldest Episcopal churches in America (Call 827–8853 for hours. Free). The Mill (827–6909 or 438–3747) ground flour for Washington's army and still produces meal. Sat.–Sun. 11–4, Apr.–Dec. only. Contribution. The mighty Wye Oak is the state's official state tree and is more than 450 years old. Free.

Dorchester County

Becky Phipps Cannon, Taylor's Island. During the War of 1812, the British blockaded the Bay, captured Maryland ships, and seized livestock and crops. But when the ice jammed a British ship in the Choptank, the island militia seized a British landing party and this 12-pound cannon.

Blackwater National Wildlife Refuge. Key Wallace Dr. off Rte. 335, Church Creek (228–2677). Massive and beautiful flocks of Canada geese rest and feed here in the late fall. Mid-October to mid-March is considered the best time to observe the birds that winter in these marshes. Besides the geese, the birds include whistling swans and more than 20 species of duck. Resident birds include some geese, ducks, the great blue heron, and the bald eagle, for whom the area ranks second only to Florida as a nesting place in the eastern United States. The mammals of Blackwater include the red fox, muskrat, deer, and several varieties of squirrel. Facilities offered include a visitor center with exhibits, a "wildlife drive" along the marshes, walking trails, a bike route, and fishing and boating. Visitor center is open Mon.–Fri. 8–4, Sat.–Sun. 9–5;

closed weekends in June, July, and August. Outdoors accessible dawn to dusk all year.

Cambridge. This old Eastern Shore tidewater town provides walking tours (guides available at the county office building at the foot of Court Lane, 228–3234). The tours take you among some of the oldest homes and streets on the Shore, while the guide explains the various architectural styles.

Dorchester Heritage Museum. Horn Point (228–5530 or 943–8201). Contains maritime, aircraft, farming, and naturalist exhibits. Also contains exhibits of Indian life. Sat.–Sun., 1–4:30. Free.

East New Market. Rte. 14 off Rte. 392. This community was settled in 1660. It includes many old homes, and a tour guide is available to explain the history of the houses and the town. East New Market was a supply center for the Continental Army. For information: 228–3234 or 228–3575.

Meredith House. LaGrange Ave., Cambridge (228–7953 or 228–3234). Exhibits of seven Maryland governors, a farm museum, and a smoke house from the early 1700s. Thurs.–Sat. 10–4 and by appointment. Free.

Old Trinity Church. Rte. 16 near Church Creek (228–2940). Dating from 1675, it is said to be the oldest Protestant church still in active use in the United States. Hours vary. Free.

South Dorchester County. Take Rte. 16 off US 50 to Rtes. 335 and 336. This part of Dorchester has been called "the Cape Cod of the South." Picturesque, with small watermen's villages.

Spocott Windmill. Rte. 343, 6 miles west of Cambridge (228–7090). The original post windmill, used for grinding grain, was built in 1850 but destroyed in the awful blizzard of 1880. The present structure was erected in 1971 and is still operated in mild winds. Visible at all times. Free.

Vienna. US 50 and the Nanticoke River. Founded in 1700, this town probably got its name from the "emperor" of the Nanticoke Indians, Vinnacokasimmon. Historic homes along Water St. include the home of Gov. Thomas Holliday Hicks, who defeated legislators who wanted to join the Confederacy.

Caroline County

Ashly Acres. Gorey Rd., off Rte. 404 just north of Denton (479–1159). On this 90-acre farm live the first miniature horses to trot in a Presidential Inaugural parade (George Bush's). Shown by appointment.

Choptank. Off Rte. 16. A small fishing town where you can fish and crab.

Mason-Dixon Crownstone. Marydel. Elaborately carved limestome post with the coats of arms of Lord Baltimore and William Penn. Free.

Pungy Wreck and George Martinak Cabin. Martinak State Park, Denton (479–1619). Skeleton of old-fashioned sailing vessel from Watts Creek. The cabin exhibits local memorabilia. Cabin seen by appointment. Free.

Wicomico County

Art Institute and Gallery. US 50 and Lemmon Hill Lane, Salisbury (546–4748). The gallery features the work of local Eastern Shore artists. Wed.–Sat. noon–4, Sun. 1–5.

Mardela Springs. US 50 at Mardela. Famous 19th-century mineral springs. Free.

Mason-Dixon Marker. Rte. 54 near Mardela Springs. Eastern end of the north-south line of the Mason and Dixon boundary. Surveyed to settle fuss between Penn and Calvert families.

Newton Historic District. Elizabeth St. and Poplar Hill Ave., Salisbury (548–4914). Includes Poplar Hill mansion, oldest building in the city, and a group of Victorian homes built after the 1886 fire.

Nutter's Museum. N. Division St., Fruitland (546–1281). Housed in the last building that was used solely as a voting house, the museum features Americana and political exhibits. Thurs., May–Sept., 10–4 P.M.

Pemberton Hall. Pemberton Dr., Salisbury (548–4914). Built in 1741 by Isaac Handy, the founder of Salisbury. Historic park on its 61 acres. Sun. 1–4, May–Oct. Donation.

Poplar Hill Mansion. 117 Elizabeth St., Salisbury (749–1776). Renowned architectural work, especially the cornices. Sun. 1–4.

Salisbury Zoo. S. Park Dr., Salisbury (548–3188). More than 400 reptiles, birds, and mammals, including Spectacled Bears, jaguars, and bison. Daily 8:30–7:30, Memorial Day to Labor Day; daily 8:30–4:30 at other times.

Whitehaven and Whitehaven Ferry. Off Rte. 352. Oldest town on Wicomico River and once an important port and shipbuilding center. Washington's grandmother is believed to have lived here. The ferry carries passengers and cars across river during daylight hours. Free.

Wildfowl Carving and Art Museum. Holloway Hall, Salisbury State College, Rte. 13, Salisbury (742–4988). Works of the preeminent waterfowl artists Steve and Lem Ward are among the exhibits of bird carvings and antique decoys. Tues.–Sat. 10–5, Sun. 1–5.

Somerset County

Crisfield. Rte. 413. The self-proclaimed—not inaccurately—"Seafood Capital of the World." The city dock is the site of packing plants, oyster dredge repair shops, and a crab barrel factory.

Deal Island. Rte. 363 off US 13. Small watermen's village where skipjacks can be seen before the oystering season.

Eastern Shore Early Americana Museum. Hudsons Corner (623–8324). Old poultry house includes rural exhibits from 1750 to the present. Thurs.–Sun., 10–5. Small admission fee.

J. Miller Tawes Historical Museum. Somers Cove Marina, Crisfield (968–2501). From Indian times to the present, a full look at the history of life on and near the water. Daily 10–4, June–Sep.; Tues.–Sat. 10–4 at other times. Closed Dec.–Feb. Adults $1, children 50¢.

Princess Anne. Rte. 388. Princess Anne's historic district includes the Manokin Presbyterian Church (1765), Tunstall Cottage (1733), and St. Andrews Episcopal Church (1770). Free walking tour brochure. Phone 651–2968.

Smith Island. Tangier Sound in the Bay (651–2968). Laced with canals, this is the Eastern Shore in all its beauty and hard work. About 800 persons live on the island, which can be reached only by boat (see Cruises). The island is named for Captain John Smith, who first saw it in 1608.

Teackle Mansion. Prince William St., Princess Anne (651–1705). Replica of Scottish manor house built in 1802. Sun. 2–4 and by appointment. Adults $2, children $1.

FISHING. You don't have to be an expert fisherman or hunter to enjoy the Shore's unique and bountiful opportunities. Fishing and crabbing sites are available in almost every tidewater town off almost every bridge and along each shore. You are permitted to catch up to one bushel of crabs per day. Methods include simply dipping the net in the water and hoping you see a crab to chase and catch. Most crabbers use bait (usually chicken necks or fish heads) on the end of a line. The crab will approach the bait slowly and if you're careful can be coaxed within the range of your long-handled net. Traps are also used and are available at many local fishing stores, as are nets, steaming pots, and friendly expert advice.

Most of the purely fresh-water fishing on the Shore is in ponds and the upper reaches of the many streams and rivers. Trout and bass are stocked. Caroline County offers several fresh-water fishing sites (Tourism Council of the Upper Chesapeake, 208 N. Commerce St., Centreville, MD 21617, 758–2300).

Bay fish include black drum, channel bass, flounder, blue fish, perch, and weakfish. Tidewater rivers—the Choptank, Nanticoke, Pocomoke, and Wicomico—are home to the largemouth bass, bluegill, and other species. Licenses are required for most areas. Write the Department of Natural Resources, Licensing and Consumer Services, Box 1869, Annapolis, MD 21404 (974–3211) for information.

For information about charter boats call or write the Tourism Council of the Upper Chesapeake, 208 N. Commerce St., Centreville, MD 21617 (758–2300); or Somerset County Tourism Commission, Box 243, Princess Anne, MD 21853 (651–2968).

HUNTING. Hunting geese and ducks is a major sport on the Eastern Shore, which lies at the heart of the Atlantic Flyway. Quail

and deer are also popular targets. The regulations for hunting—as
for fishing—are strict and detailed. For more information, write
or call the Department of Natural Resources, Licensing and Consumer Services, Box 1869, Annapolis, MD 21404 (974–3211).

OUTDOOR RECREATION. State Parks in the above Eastern
Shore counties include: **Tuckahoe State Park,** Queen Annes and
Caroline Counties (634–2810), Eveland Rd. off Rte. 404, 6 mi.
north of Queen Anne; **Martinak State Park,** Caroline County
(479–1619), Deep Shore Rd. off Rte. 404, Denton; **Janes Island
State Park,** Somerset County (968–1565), Rte. 358, 1.5 mi. north
of Crisfield.

OCEAN CITY AND
WORCESTER COUNTY

by
JAMES LOUTTIT

Although Ocean City isn't actually *on* Chesapeake Bay, Maryland's Atlantic Ocean resort and the state's easternmost county lie well within the Chesapeake vacationland.

Ocean City is sun, sand, surf, and sky—a salt-air mecca of sun-washed days and soft summer nights, soaring gulls and sauntering bikinis, sandcastles, beach cottages, high-rise hotels and condominiums.

Inland from Ocean City (and Assateague Island to the south), Worcester County is a haven of rural tranquility—picturesque Snow Hill and Pokomoke City, farmland, river, and natural forest.

Most visitors will enter Worcester County by car: US 113 or Route 528 south from Delaware; US 50, east from Salisbury to Ocean City; State Route 12 between Salisbury and Snow Hill, or US 13, south from Salisbury or north from Norfolk, Virginia. But because Ocean City is the focal point, this chapter will explore Worcester County outward from the coast.

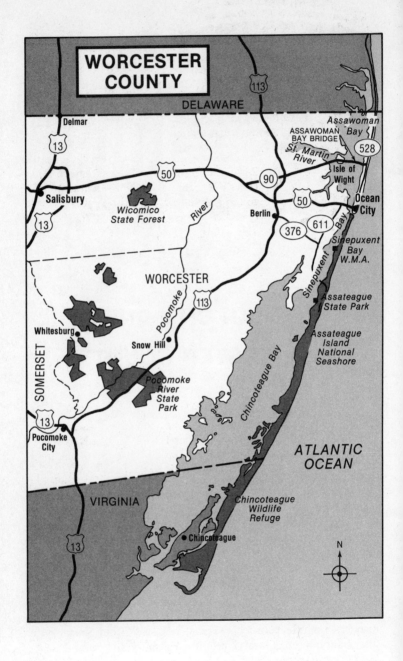

Ocean City

Built along a barrier strip of sand that is often only two blocks wide, Ocean City stretches south from the Delaware state line for more than 150 city blocks. Blessed with almost 10 miles of sandy ocean beach, the city looks eastward toward the Atlantic and westward toward the mainland over a series of picturesque and protected bays—Montego, Big Assawoman, Isle of Wight, and Sinepuxent. The bays and the city's commercial boat harbor are open to the ocean through the Inlet between Ocean City and Assateague Island to the south. The Ocean City boardwalk fronts on the ocean between the Inlet and 28th Street. Motorists enter Ocean City via the Coastal Highway (Rte. 528) from the north (Delaware), the Assawoman Bay Bridge (Rte. 90 at 62nd Street), or US 50 near the heart of Ocean City's Old Town.

Assateague Island

Assateague Island, like Ocean City, is a barrier strip of seashore and a major touring destination—but the similarity between the two stops there. Each has more than a fair share of sun, sand, and surf, but if Ocean City is a wonderland of beach bunnies and boardwalk fun, Assateague is the lovely and natural home of the Assateague pony, the tern, and the gull.

North Assateague

North Assateague is the Maryland section of the island and is easily accessible by car from Ocean City. Take US 50 west for about a mile, then turn left on Rte. 611 (south) and watch for the left turn (a short distance past Frontier Town) over the New Bridge to Assateague Island. The National Park Service has a headquarters and maintains a Visitor's Center (on your right) shortly before you cross the bridge over Sinepuxent Bay to Assateague. North Assateague is divided into three parts: six sandy miles of "wild" beach, accessible only on foot, on your left as you drive onto the island; Assateague State Park in the mid-section; and, to the south, Assateague Island National Seashore, another natural expanse of surf and sandy dunes. There is a State Park Information Center (with campground registration) on your left near the park end of Sinepuxent Bay Bridge.

And now, a word about those free spirits of the seashore—Assateague's famous ponies: They may look gentle, and usually they are, but they're also unpredictable—they kick and sometimes they bite. It's really hard to blame them, considering the fact that their forebearers swam ashore from a foundering Spanish galleon in the 16th century and they've been munching on marsh grass and bayberry leaves ever since.

There are two herds of Assateague ponies on the island, a larger group in the Virginia section to the south, and a smaller herd in Maryland. Virginia's Chincoteague Volunteer Fire Department owns the southern ponies and manages an annual July roundup and auction; the National Park Service manages Maryland's Assateague's wild pony herd.

PRACTICAL INFORMATION FOR
OCEAN CITY AND WORCESTER COUNTY

Note: The area code for all Maryland is 301.

PLACES TO STAY

HOTELS AND MOTELS. Ocean City is a seaside resort, worshiping the sun in the summer, but attracting an increasing number of visitors during the balmy days of spring, the crisp days of autumn, and even the quiet months of winter. Room rates in the following selection of accommodations will vary widely between summer and winter, and our prices, when given, are intended merely as a guide. If possible, call or write before you commit yourself. If this isn't possible, pin down the price before you sign in, perhaps even request to see the unit or room. Finally, keep in mind that this is a *selection* only, and we can't include all of the many excellent accommodations in the Ocean City resort area. As elsewhere in the guide, our general price categories, double occupancy for one night, are: *Deluxe,* over $150; *Expensive,* $90–$150; *Moderate,* $50–$90; *Inexpensive,* under $50.

Carousel Hotel. *Deluxe.* 118th St., Coastal Hwy. on the beach, 524–1000. 265 rooms, 15 suites, with June to September rates higher. Two restaurants, two cocktail lounges, open year round. Pool. AE, CB, DC, MC, V.

Sheraton Fontainbleu Inn & Spa. *Deluxe.* 101st St. and 10100 Ocean Hwy., 524–3535 or (800) 638–2100. 277 rooms, including 22 suites, most with an ocean view. Full-service restaurant and cocktail lounge. Heated indoor pool and fully equipped health spa. AE, DC, MC, V.

Holiday Inn-Ocean Front. *Expensive to Deluxe.* 67th St. and Ocean Front, 524–1600 or (800) 465–4329. 217 rooms, open year round. Indoor and outdoor pools. Restaurant and lounge. AE, DC, MC, V.

Quality Inn-Boardwalk. *Expensive to Deluxe.* Boardwalk at 17th St., 289–4401 or (800) 228–5151. 172 rooms. Most efficiencies, with honeymoon suites. Restaurant and room service. AE, DC, MC, V.

Quality Inn-Ocean Front. *Expensive to Deluxe.* On the Ocean-front and 54th St., 524–7200 or (800) 228–5151. 130 rooms. Year-round inn with 5-story plant-filled atrium. Atrium Cafe. AE, DC, MC, V.

Best Western Flagship Ocean Front. *Expensive.* Boardwalk and 26th St., 289–3384 or (800) 528–1234. 93 rooms. Jonah and the Whale Seafood Buffet. Weekends only, Jan.–early Feb. The Flag-ship is on the ocean. AE, DC, MC, V.

Castle in the Sand. *Expensive.* Oceanfront and 37th St.; 289–6846. 180 rooms in five-story motor hotel and 37 cottages. Restaurant, bar, pool, and airport transportation. Closed Nov.–mid-Apr. AE, MC, V.

Fenwick Inn. *Expensive.* 138th St. and Coastal Hwy.; 250–1100 or (800) 492–1873. 201 rooms in a year-round inn. Penthouse restaurant and lounge with nightly entertainment. Indoor heated pool. AE, DC, MC, V.

Phillips Beach Plaza Hotel. *Expensive.* Oceanfront at 13th St., 289–9121. 86 rooms. Phillips-by-the-Sea Restaurant. Cocktail lounge and Beach Plaza Cafe. Golf privileges. Shopping arcade. Open all year. AE, CB, DC, MC, V.

Safari. *Expensive.* Boardwalk at 13th St.; 289–6411. 38 rooms in 4-story oceanfront inn. All-day restaurant nearby. Balconies. Closed Nov.–Mar. AE, DC, MC, V.

Spinnaker Motel. *Expensive.* 18th St. and Oceanside, 289–5444 or (800) 638–3244. 100 rooms, all units with kitchens. Private balconies with ocean views. Heated outdoor pool with sundeck. Coffee shop. Closed Nov.–Feb. AE, MC, V.

Stardust. *Expensive.* Oceanfront at 33rd St.; 289–6444. 76 units, with kitchens, in 3-story motel. No elevator. Pool. All-day restaurant nearby. Closed Nov.–Mar. Balconies overlooking the beach. AE, DC, MC, V.

Stowaway Americana Hotel. *Expensive.* 22nd St. and Board-walk, 289–6191. 132 rooms, open year round. Pool and restaurant. AE, MC, V.

Surf and Sands Motel. *Moderate to Expensive.* 23rd St. and Boardwalk, 289–7161. 96 rooms, open Easter to October. Coffee shop, breakfast and lunch. Efficiencies available. Outdoor and heated kiddy pool. MC, V.

The Dunes Motel. *Moderate.* 27th St. and Beach, 289–4414. 104 rooms, February till October 27. Efficiency oceanfront units. Coffee shop. Outdoor pool. AE, MC, V.

Executive. *Moderate.* Baltimore Ave. and 30th St.; 289–3101. 47 rooms in a three-story motel. Balconies, but no elevator. Restaurant nearby. MC, V.

Nassau Motel. *Moderate.* 6002 Coastal Hwy.; 524–6200. 21 rooms, 41 efficiencies. April through October. Pool. MC, V.

Sahara Motel. *Moderate.* 19th St. and Oceanfront, 289–8101. 113 rooms, mid-April through September. Poolside, oceanview, and oceanfront rooms. Pool. MC, V.

Santa Maria Motor Hotel. *Moderate.* 1500 Baltimore Avenue; 289–7191. 102 rooms. Full-service restaurant. 30 rooms facing the ocean. Balconies. MC, V.

PLACES TO EAT

RESTAURANTS AND CAFES. As is true with any popular resort city, visitors to Ocean City are faced with a happy but bewildering selection of places at which to eat—fast food to fabulous food, hot dogs to chateaubriand. The following selection of restaurants is not meant to be all-inclusive. We have attempted to include eating places that will appeal to a wide variety of tastes and pocketbooks—family groups to swinging singles, the inexpensive to the wildly extravagant. The editors would appreciate hearing of that "very special place" that you discover during your stay in Ocean City. If space permits, we will try to include it in future editions. Price categories for dinner, drinks and tips excluded, are: *Deluxe,* over $30; *Expensive,* $20–$30; *Moderate,* $10–$20; *Inexpensive,* under $10.

Reflections. *Expensive.* 67th St. and Coastal Hwy.; 524–5252. French-American cuisine in the European tradition. A respectable wine list, with local seafood, beef, and veal. Year round at Holiday Inn-Ocean Front. AE, DC, MC, V.

The Garden. *Expensive.* 45th St., Village; 289–4592. A Continental menu and a good wine list in a pleasant garden setting. Seafood and duck are house specialties. Dinner only. Closed Sun.–Tues., Nov.–Mar. AE, MC, V.

Bonfire Restaurant. *Moderate to Expensive.* 71st St. and Coastal Hwy.; 524–7171. Steak, seafood, prime rib, and Chinese. A year-round favorite with locals and tourists. Dinner only, 5:30 P.M. Bar. Reservations preferred. AE, CB, DC, MC, V.

Captain Bill Bunting's Angler. *Moderate to Expensive.* Talbot St. and the Bay, 21842; 289–7424. Restaurant, patio bar, and marina, with "a free cruise with dinner." Early—5 A.M.!—breakfast for early risers. Tropical drinks. Reservations suggested. MC, V.

The Hobbit Restaurant and Bar. *Moderate to Expensive.* 81st St. and the Bay; 524–8100. Fish, fowl, and veal francaise—all entrees served with Hobbit salad and fresh-baked bread. Bar and wine list. MC, V.

Mario's. *Moderate to Expensive.* 22nd St. and Philadelphia Ave.; 289–9445. Continental menu, with a bar, and entertainment during summer season. Closed early December and Mondays during the winter. AE, MC, V.

The Wharf. *Moderate to Expensive.* 128th St. and North Coastal Hwy.; 524–1001. Seafood, veal, steaks, and chicken in a nautical atmosphere. Lounge with happy hour between 5 and 6 P.M. Adjacent to Wharf Seafood & Spirits Market. Dinner only. AE, MC, V.

Fager's Island. *Moderate to Expensive.* 60th St. in the Bay; 524–5500. Lunch and dinner, with a bar till 2 A.M. and a spacious outdoor deck. Spectacular sunsets on the quiet side of the beach. Entrees from traditional to exotic. Dinner menu includes fresh fish, lobster, veal, prime rib, and roast duckling with orange sauce. AE, CB, DC, MC, V.

B.J.'s on the Water. *Moderate.* 75th St. and the bay; 524–7575. Surf and turf daily for lunch and dinner. AE, MC, V.

Jonah & the Whale. *Moderate.* 26th St. and the Boardwalk; 524–CRAB. Billed as the Fabulous Seafood Buffet. Bar and frozen drinks. Dinner after 4 P.M. Open mid–May-mid–Sept. Whaling tavern decor. MC, V.

Kate Bunting's. *Moderate.* 10 Talbot St.; 289–1441. Steamed crabs a specialty. Dinner after 4 P.M., in a restored turn-of-the-century inn. Closed Tues. and Thur. during winter. AE, DC, MC, V.

The Marina Deck. *Moderate.* 306 Dorchester St.; 289–4411. Fresh seafood, with a raw bar. Domestic wine list, but there's always that strawberry shortcake or pecan pie. MC, V.

Paul Revere Smorgasbord. *Moderate.* Boardwalk at 2nd St.; 524–1776. Roast beef, pork chops, chicken, and 100 other home-cooked entrees, including homemade bread and desserts. Children's prices. April through October. Major credit cards.

Phillips by the Sea. *Moderate.* Boardwalk and 13th St.; 289–9121. A "seafood adventure" in Phillips Beach Plaza Hotel, featuring crab cakes, crab claws, and steamed spiced shrimp. AE, CB, DC, MC, V. Also, **Phillips Crab House,** 21st St. and Philadelphia, 289–6821, casual and relaxed. AE, MC, V; and **Phillips Seafood House,** 14101 Coastal Hwy. and 141st St., 250–1200, where seafood is a specialty. AE, MC, V.

Tony's. *Moderate.* 33rd St. and Coastal Hwy.; 289–4588. A full Italian menu, with homemade pastas. Live entertainment in the Sandbar Lounge. Open at 4 P.M. AE, MC, V.

Harrison's Harbor Watch. *Moderate.* Boardwalk South, overlooking the Inlet; 289–5121. A spectacular view and overstuffed sandwiches; fresh local seafood. Bar and wine list. Raw bar. AE, MC, V.

La Hacienda. *Moderate.* 80th St. and Coastal Hwy.; 524–8080. Mexican food and spirits, and also take out. Dinner only. Reservations for parties of 8 or more. Bar. AE, MC, V.

O.C. Sneakers. *Moderate.* On the Bay, 6103 Sea-Bay Dr. at 61st St.; 723–3463. Cajun style, seafood, beef, veal, and pasta. Deck dining. Pianist in restaurant, live entertainment in the lounge. Lunch and dinner. Reservations recommended. Closed Sun. and Mon., Dec.–Feb.

THINGS TO SEE AND DO

TOURING INFORMATION. The Ocean City Convention Center overlooks Isle of Wight Bay at 4001 Coastal Hwy. For information, contact the Convention Center at (301) 289–8311, or Ocean City Visitors and Convention Bureau, 289–8181.

THE BEACH. First there is the beach, then the Boardwalk, then the city, and finally the Bay. But it all starts at the beach, where Atlantic surf meets the shore. The beach is why it's all *there.* Ocean City's beaches, which fringe the ocean for ten sandy miles, lie totally within the city's limits, stretching northward from the Inlet to the Maryland-Delaware line. Sunbathing and swimming—or watching others sunbathe and swim—are the main beach pursuits, but designated sections of the beach have been set aside for fishing and surfboarding. If you've never splashed in salt water, ogled a bikini, listened to the racous cry of a gull, or helped a child build a sandcastle, don't worry—it's really easy; you'll catch on soon enough.

THE BOARDWALK. Ocean City is proud of its ocean boardwalk—and rightly so. Three miles long (the Inlet to 28th Street), the boardwalk is open 24 hours a day for strolling, jogging, and ocean or people watching. Bicyclists may use the boardwalk between 6 and 10 in the morning. The Boardwalk Train runs the length of the boardwalk every 20 minutes, 10 A.M.–10 P.M., Memorial Day through Labor Day. The fare is $1 each way.

Ocean City Life Saving Station Museum. Located at the south end of the boardwalk, overlooking the Inlet, the Life Saving Station Museum traces Ocean City's history from its founding as a fishing village in the 1800s to the resort it is today. Housed in the former Life Saving Station, built in 1891, the museum is open daily from 11 A.M. to 10 P.M., June through September, and weekends the rest of the year. Adults $1.25, 12 and under 50¢. Phone 289–4991.

OLD TOWN. "Downtown" Ocean City, bounded by South Second St. on the Inlet to 15th St. and the ocean to the bay, features Inlet Village with fine restaurants and shops, "the widest beach in town" on the ocean side, docks and fishing boats on the bayside, interesting shops, hotels, and restaurants throughout Old Town, and a scattering of arcades and amusement centers: Fun City, 100 S. Boardwalk at Caroline St.; Marty's Playland, Boardwalk at Worcester St.; Sportland, Boardwalk and Worcester, Photon, 401 S. Boardwalk/Pier; and Trimpers Amusements, Boardwalk at the Inlet.

CRUISES. The following is a partial listing of evening, ocean, and bay cruises out of Ocean City. Times and destinations are subject to change, so call before making your plans. Boats and cruises include *Angler,* Talbot St. at Angler Restaurant, 289–6980 or 289–7424; Tyler's Cruises, Rhodes Point, 425–4271; Tangier Island Cruises, 10th and Main Sts., Crisfield, 968–2338; and *Maryland Lady* Cruises, Salisbury, 543–2466.

SPORTFISHING. Ocean City is the White Marlin Capital of the World, and the Ocean City Marlin Club is one of the oldest fishing clubs in the country. The $30,000 White Marlin Open is held in mid-August, with the White Marlin Tournament following Labor Day weekend. Outboard motor boats may be rented from Bahia Marina, on Bay between 21st and 22nd Sts., 289–7438, and Props and Bottoms Marina at two locations on the Bay, 66th St. and 54th St., 524–5455. Fishing charters include: Captain Bill Bunting's *Angler,* 289–6980; *Taurus,* 289–2565; Ocean City Guide Service, 289–5520; and Reel Surprise Fishing and Pleasure Charters, 307 Dorchester St.

BOATING. Boat rides and sailing are available through *Therapy* Sailing Cruises, Shantytown Marina, US 50 and the Bay, 352–5195, or *Sea Rocket,* Marchita Motel Dock, Wicomico St. and the Bay.

On the Mainland—Worcester County

Frontier Town. Route 611, a short drive south of Ocean City; 289–7877. (Rte. 50, west one mile, then south a few miles on Rte. 611, Stephen Decatur Hwy.) The Wild, Wild West on the Eastern Shore—a family theme park with bank holdups, Indian dancers, gunfights, and can-can girls, plus rides on a riverboat, steam train, stagecoach, and ponies. Open daily during the summer, 10 A.M. to 6 P.M. One admission for all shows and rides: adults $7, senior citizens and children $6. Light lunches at Longhorn and Golden Nugget Saloons.

OUTDOOR PARKS AND PICNIC AREAS. Shad Landing State Park, boating and picknicking on the Pocomoke River, Route 113 south of Snow Hill; **Milburn Landing State Park,** west bank of Pocomoke, Rte. 12, west of Snow Hill; **Pocomoke State Forest,** deer hunting in season, Rte. 12, west of Snow Hill; **Byrd Park** in Snow Hill; **Stephen Decatur Park** in Berlin; **Pocomoke Cypress Swamps** (Pocomoke River State Park), accessible from Rte. 113, Pocomoke, and—of course—**Assateague Island State Park and National Seashore.** For information, phone: (301) 641–2120 (Park) or (301) 641–1441 (Seashore).

HISTORIC SITES. Snow Hill. A charming and historic hamlet—and Worcester County seat—on the Pocomoke River, Rtes. 12 and 394. Founded in 1642, Snow Hill was once a busy river port. The Julia A. Purnell Museum, 208 West Market St., is Snow Hill's showcase of Worcester County lore. The museum is open weekdays, 9 A.M. to 5 P.M., and weekends, 1 P.M. to 5 P.M.; 632–0515. The Nassawango (Iron) Furnace, one of the oldest industrial sites in Maryland, has been registered as a National Historic Place and is being restored, Rte. 12, Old Furnace Rd., near Snow Hill. Daily 11–5, Apr.–Oct. Adults $1, children 50¢. 632–2032.

Pocomoke City on US 13 and the Pocomoke River has beautifully restored homes along the waterfront. Of particular interest are Cellar House, Beverly of Worcester, and Costen House and Winter Quarters.

VIRGINIA'S EASTERN SHORE

by
RODNEY N. SMITH

Virginia's Eastern Shore, a 70-mile peninsula and secluded barrier islands, is one of the most fancifully beautiful places in America. It is a haven for herds of wild ponies. There are unspoiled beaches with rare and elaborate seashells, as well as charter boats to the islands, lazy lagoons, and quiet coves.

This is a region visited by Blackbeard the pirate and one adorned with romantic place names such as Nassawodox, Kiptopeke, and Pungoteague. Even the familiar names are colorful: Temperanceville, Birdsnest, and Modest Town.

One side of Virginia's Eastern Shore is bathed by the Atlantic and the other by the Chesapeake Bay. This favored location guarantees the visitor a continuous feast of delicious and succulent seafood. There is even an annual local festival to honor it, with fresh oysters, fried eel, steamed clams, and chowder of unmatched quality and flavor.

The attractions of this area are unique and varied. Two of America's few preserved debtor's prisons are here, one at Eastville and one at Accomack. Tiny Tangier Island, accessible only by boat, has residents who still speak Elizabethan dialect. At Chincoteague and Assateague, each summer brings the famous Wild Pony

117

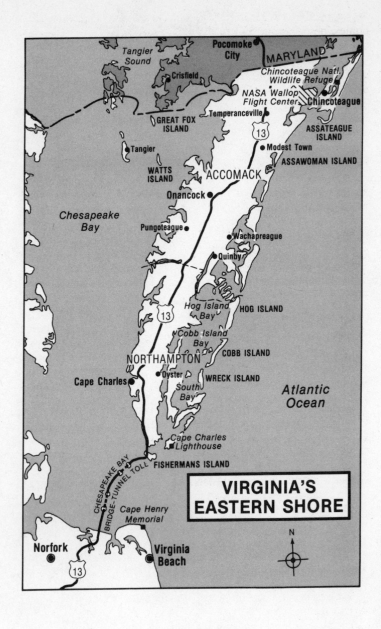

Tangier
Sound

Pocomoke
City

MARYLAND

Crisfield

Chincoteague Natl.
Wildlife Refuge

NASA Wallop
Flight Center

Chincoteague

GREAT FOX
ISLAND

Temperanceville

13

ASSATEAGUE
ISLAND

Tangier

Modest Town

WATTS
ISLAND

ACCOMACK

ASSAWOMAN ISLAND

Onancock

Chesapeake
Bay

Pungoteague

Wachapreague

Quinby

13

Hog Island
Bay

HOG ISLAND

Cobb Island
Bay

NORTHAMPTON

COBB ISLAND

Cape Charles

Oyster

WRECK ISLAND

South
Bay

Atlantic
Ocean

Cape Charles
Lighthouse

CHESAPEAKE BAY
BRIDGE-TUNNEL TOLL

FISHERMANS ISLAND

Cape Henry
Memorial

VIRGINIA'S
EASTERN SHORE

Norfork

13

Virginia
Beach

N

Roundup. This is a day of carnivals and shows, good food, and high spirits, a time to retell the fascinating legends about the island ponies, descendants of horses that swam ashore from a wrecked Spanish galleon centuries ago.

A trip to the Eastern Shore is not complete without a close look at some of the beautiful craftwork created here. Eastern Shore duck decoys, for instance, are deservedly in demand nationwide. There is also excellent saltwater fishing here, as well as canoeing in the marshes and hiking everywhere. Some particularly lovely natural areas are in the Chincoteague National Wildlife Refuge. The vigilant observer can spot numerous marsh and water birds, rabbits, raccoons, deer otters, and muskrats.

Everywhere visitors go on Virginia's Eastern Shore they are aware of being in a very special and natural world. From the isolated fishing villages to the unspoiled beaches, this is what America was like in less complicated times when nature was untouched by progress.

EXPLORING VIRGINIA'S EASTERN SHORE

The 17.6-mile Chesapeake Bay Bridge-Tunnel deposits north-bound visitors from Virginia Beach, Norfolk, and Williamsburg on the southern tip of Virginia's Eastern Shore. The views from this bridge are a delight. There is a scenic stop, restaurant, and a fishing pier with bait and tackle. Visitors can see both the Atlantic Ocean and Chesapeake Bay as they cross this engineering marvel to the quiet peninsula north of Norfolk. Dipping from the bridge into one of the tunnels and under a massive, oceangoing freighter will take some visitors' breath away.

Virginia's Eastern Shore is bounded on the east coast by the wet-lands and barrier islands of the Atlantic Ocean, and on the west by Chesapeake Bay. It was first visited by Europeans in 1608 when an exploring party lead by Captain John Smith mapped the bayside and Chesapeake Islands. In 1614, the Jamestown government obtained the land from the Indians. The English came to the peninsula to stay in 1620. The settlement was called Accomack Plantation until 1634 when it became one of the eight original counties. In 1643, the name was changed to Northampton. Then, in 1663, the county was divided to form Accomack County in the north and Northampton County in the south. The area has been able to preserve much of its early charm because of the relative isolation it enjoyed until the Bay Bridge-Tunnel opened in 1965.

The people of Accomack organized early. There was a census in 1624, listing their names and ages, and the ships on which they had arrived. In these two counties can be found the earliest continuous court records in the United States, dating from 1632.

Among other things, the records tell of the trial and acquittal in the case of a play, "The Bear and the Cub," in 1665, giving the Eastern Shore the distinction of having the first record of a dramatic performance in America. Tours of the two county seats include the Debtor's Prison in Accomack, and the Debtors Prison, Court House, and Clerk's Office in Eastville.

Eastern Shore architecture is unique. Most early dwellings now standing are of frame construction with varying roof levels and two or more chimneys. The roofs are mostly of the A-type with small dormer windows on the front and back. Other houses are two full stories, some all brick, some with brick ends, and some all frame. A house with four different roof levels is often referred to as "big house, little house, colonnade, and kitchen." These houses can be explored all over the area.

Cape Charles

Cape Charles, first major exit from the Bay Bridge-Tunnel, was established in 1884 when the New York, Philadelphia and Norfolk Railroad extended its service from Philadelphia to Norfolk. It is the largest town in Northampton County and offers excellent fishing, boating, and beaches. It is one of the few places on the East Coast where visitors can watch breathtaking sunsets over water.

Eyre Hall, for example, just south of Eastville, was built by Littleton Eyre in 1735 and has been in his family ever since. It boasts one of the oldest and loveliest boxwood gardens in America. It was enlarged by his son, Severn, in 1765 and furnished with handsome Queen Anne, Chippendale, Hepplewhite, and Chinese pieces, as well as family portraits. In the cross hall is an interesting scenic wallpaper in French block design by duFour. Throughout the house are fine woodwork and paneling.

Eastville itself was not founded until 1766, but it has the distinction that its County Court declared the Stamp Act of Parliament unconstitutional. The old Courthouse in Eastville contains the oldest court records in the United States, the first legible date being January 7, 1632. The preservation and survival of these records is all the more remarkable because they were housed in the homes of the court clerks for more than 100 years. Other sights include a Debtor's Prison (1644), the Clerk's Office (1719), the Court House (1730), and Parke Hall (1794). The nearby town of Oyster is famous for its seafood industries.

Historic Onancock

Still farther north and on the Bay, Onancock is the home of the Eastern Shore Historical Society, housed in Kerr Place, which was originally built in 1790. Onancock's large, deep harbor offers well-protected docking facilities for pleasure craft of all sizes. The public dock and boat launching ramp are used by local and visiting sportsmen and commercial boats.

Historic sights in Onancock include the site of Fowkes' Tavern, home of the first play in America, and St. George's Episcopal Church, built in 1652. Sights from the 20th-century include the Town of Willis Wharf with its seafood industries and fishing facilities and the Virginia Institute of Marine Sciences.

Within a short radius of Accomack, in the North, visitors will find more restored Colonial architecture than in any other place in the United States except Williamsburg. Individual houses, however, are not opened to the public except when advertised or for Historic Garden Week. Sights include The Glade, The Little House (circa 1767), The Haven (1794), Ailworth House (1795), Roseland (1771), Seymour House and Ice House (1791), Court House Green and the Debtor's Prison (1782).

The Eastern Shore, however, relies for income less on tourism than on agriculture, the biggest industry. The two counties together produce a bounty on the 120,000 acres of cropland. The Eastern Shore leads the state in the production of vegetables. The Irish potato is the most important crop with 30,000 acres planted annually but corn and soybeans are fast growing in importance. Sweet potatoes, snapbeans, tomatoes, cucumbers, and peppers are grown. Whether passing through or spending a vacation, visitors will want to stop at the roadside stands to sample and purchase the luscious local produce. There are also almost 150,000 acres of beautiful forestlands with loblolly pines predominating.

More and more farmers are moving into the production of broilers and two processing plants for chickens are in Accomack County.

Another important source of income for the Shore is the seafood industry. This includes oysters, hard clams, sea clams, crab, and finfish. Oyster beds are cultivated on both bayside and seaside. Hard clams or quahog are in great quantity. The largest clam packing plant in the world is located on Chincoteague. The sea clam industry is new to the Shore where both blue and soft crabs are abundant. The finfish industry is based on some 40 different species.

Chincoteague

Chincoteague Island, Virginia's only resort island, is perhaps the most beautiful of the many islands that dot Virginia's Eastern Shore. World famous for its oyster beds and clam shoals, this picturesque island is the gateway to the National Seashore and Chincoteague Wildlife Refuge. This serene fishing settlement, seven miles long and 1½ miles wide, and abounding with history and natural beauty, welcomes visitors to explore its unique heritage.

The first Colonists were humble sailors and herders who arrived in the early 1670s. With the exception of salvaging shipwrecks off Assateague Island, the economy remained primarily farming and livestock. Today, however, the surrounding waters are the main source of local income.

The island's famous salt oysters, sold since 1830, are cultivated on leased "rock" and public grounds that the watermen seed and harvest. Chincoteague is the home of many outstanding craftsmen and artists who produce some of the world's finest hand-carved duck decoys and wildfowl wood carvings.

Assateague Island

Protecting Chincoteague Island from the Atlantic Ocean, Assateague Island boasts more than 37 miles of the widest and most beautiful beaches on the East Coast. This rare beauty is protected by the Assateague Island National Seashore and Chincoteague National Wildlife Refuge. A wide variety of nature activities and many miles of unspoiled beaches and sand dunes are there to explore.

Assateague Island is well-known as a birdwatchers' paradise. Over 260 species are to be found, and as the days get colder, the arrival of the Canadian geese and snow geese and the whistling voices of the swans herald the onset of winter.

The most popular inhabitants of the Refuge, however, are the Chincoteague wild ponies, made famous in Marguerite Henry's book, *Misty of Chincoteague*. The legend has it that these island ponies are descendants of horses that swam ashore from a wrecked Spanish galleon centuries ago. The famous Wild Pony Roundup and Swim to Chincoteague is held annually in late July. It is a day of high spirits and good food.

In 1945, a launch site was established on Wallops Island by the Langley Research Center, then a field station of NASA. The site is on Route 13, the major north–south road to Chincoteague (Rte. 175 east to Chintoteague; Rte. 697 to Wallops). In the early years, research at Wallops was concentrated on obtaining aerodynamic data at transonic and low supersonic speeds. Wallops has been the launch site of over 150 unmanned spacecrafts and today is used primarily to obtain scientific data about the atmosphere and space. It continues to be an active part of the NASA unmanned space program. Tours can be arranged, and it is possible to make reservations to watch the launching of minor satellites.

The string of barrier islands running the length of the peninsula remain a natural wilderness. They are inaccessible except by boat and are privately owned by the Nature Conservancy or the Government. Smith Island, the southernmost, was discovered by Capt. John Smith and named for himself. The Cape Charles lighthouse, the most powerful in Virginia, is on the island.

Tangier Island

Tangier Island in the heart of the Chesapeake can be visited by ferry from Reedville on Virginia's Northern Neck (US 360). The island was discovered by Capt. John Smith in 1608 and settlement was permanently established in 1686. There is no industry on the island and no cars are allowed. The population is only 800. The peace and quiet of the isolated village is a tonic after the hustle and bustle of the 20th century. Transportation to the island is also possible via mail boat, leaving Crisfield, Maryland at 12:30 P.M. each day (Rte. 413 from US 13).

PRACTICAL INFORMATION FOR
VIRGINIA'S EASTERN SHORE

Note: The area code for Virginia's Eastern Shore is 804.

PLACES TO STAY

MOTELS AND INNS. There are few luxury or deluxe accommodations on this stretch of the peninsula, but neither are there many towns of any real size. This is part of the charm of Virginia's Eastern Shore. But then, of course, Norfolk isn't all that far to the south, and Salisbury, Maryland is just up US 13 to the north.

Channel Bass Inn. *Deluxe.* 100 Church Street, Chincoteague; 336–6148. Eleven rooms, many furnished with antiques, near the wildlife sanctuary. Closed Christmas and New Year's. AE, DC, MC, V.

Island Motor Inn. *Moderate to Expensive.* 711 N. Main St., Chincoteague; 336–3141. Waterfront rooms, some with balconies and boardwalk. Open all year. 48 rooms, on the waterfront. AE, DC, MC, V.

Refuge Motor Inn. *Moderate to Expensive.* One block west of Assateague Bridge Beach Rd., Chincoteague; 336–5511. 68 units with picnic tables and grills overlooking wildlife refuge. AE, MC, V.

America House. *Moderate.* On US 13 at the entrance to the Chesapeake Bay Bridge-Tunnel, Cape Charles; 331–1776. 79 rooms with balconies, a private beach, sailboats, picnic tables, and grills. Open all year. AE, CB, DC, MC, V.

The Driftwood Motor Lodge. *Moderate.* Beach Rd. at Assateague Bridge, Maddox Blvd., Chincoteague; 336–6557. 52 rooms with private patios and balconies overlooking the shore at the entrance to Assateague National Seashore. AE, DC, MC, V.

Sea Shell Motel. *Moderate.* 215 Willow St., a short block south on South Main, Chincoteague; 336–6589. 40 rooms, including efficiencies. Closed mid-Oct.–mid-Mar. Pool. AE, MC, V.

Sunrise Motor Inn. *Moderate.* Chicken City Rd., Chincoteague; 336–6671. 24 units, some with kitchens. Closed Nov.–Mar. Pool and picnic tables. Weekly seasonal rates. AE, MC, V.

Birchwood Motel. *Inexpensive to Moderate.* 573 S. Main St., turn right when entering Chincoteague; 336–6133. 40 rooms. Closed Dec.–Mar. AE, MC, V.

PLACES TO EAT

Channel Bass. *Moderate to Deluxe.* 100 Church St., Chincoteague; 336–6148. Continental menu specializing in seafood español, backfin crab souffle, and oyster souffle. Elegant Colonial atmosphere. Chef-owned. AE, DC, MC, V.

Towne House Restaurant. *Moderate to Expensive.* VA 178, Onancock; 787–2144 or 787–9620. Noted for its fine food for more than three decades; many local diners feel the Towne House is the leading restaurant on the lower peninsula. Prime rib is a speciality, but there's always fresh fish, of course. Reservations advised. MC, V.

Beachway. *Inexpensive to Expensive.* Maddox Blvd., Chincoteague; 336–5590. Breakfast, lunch, and dinner. Closed Dec.–Feb. Full American menu in an English atmosphere. Beer and wine. Closed Tues.–Wed., except in summer. AE, MC, V.

The Trawler Restaurant. *Moderate.* US 13, Exmore; 442–2092. Seafood is the house speciality, but there's also a dinner theater. Reservations advised. MC, V.

Hilda Crockett's Chesapeake House. *Inexpensive to Moderate.* On Main St., Tangier Island; 891–2331. Meals daily from April 15 through mid-October. Crab—cakes, fritters, or however you like it. Worth the ferry ride. No credit cards.

Landmark Crab House. *Inexpensive to Moderate.* Landmark Plaza, Chincoteague; 336–5552. The Landmark specializes in fresh local fish, with crabs a special delight. Casual. Children welcome. AE, DC, MC, V.

THINGS TO SEE AND DO

TOURING INFORMATION. For advance touring information about Virginia's Eastern Shore, write or phone Eastern Shore of Virginia Tourism Commission, Box 147, Accomac, VA 23301, (804) 787–2460, or Chincoteague Chamber of Commerce, Box 258, Chincoteague, VA 23336, (804) 336–6161.

MUSEUMS. NASA Wallops Visitor Center Flight Facility. Box 98, Wallops Island 23337; 824–1344. The Center features exhibits on the history of aeronautics and space flight. Thurs.–Mon. 10–4; daily 10–4 in summer. Admission free. **Oyster Museum** of Chincoteague. Shellfish farming and island history. Memorial Day–Labor Day. Phone 336–6117 for schedule. **Refuge Waterfowl Museum.** Chincoteague; 336–5800. Exhibitions of the waterman's life, featuring duck decoys, arms, and boats. Thurs.–Mon. 10–5; daily 10–5 in summer. Adults $2.50, children $1. **Hopkins & Brother Store**

Museum. 2 Market St., Onancock. (787–8220). This general store, built in 1842, is a National Historic Landmark. Cruises to Tangier Island depart from its wharf. Open Apr. 15–Jan. 1. **Debtor's Prison.** Accomac. This jailor's residence (circa 1783) also depicts the debtor's prison, 1824 to 1842. Call 787–4686 for details and reservations. There is also a **Debtor's Prison** in Eastville, where records dating back to 1632 are stored at Northampton County seat. Tours Mon.–Fri. Phone 678–5126 for schedules and details.

SHOPPING. The Decoy Factory. Stoney Point Decoys, Ltd., US 13, Oak Hall, 824–5621. Watch duck decoys being made in the world's largest decoy factory. Wildlife gifts are on sale at the factory. **Pony Tails.** Maddox Blvd., Chincoteague; 336–6688. Experience life in a saltwater taffy factory, with souvenirs and gifts from Virginia's Eastern Shore.

SPECIAL INTEREST. Chincoteague Miniature Pony Farm. 306 Pension St., Chincoteague; 336–3066. Not quite Assateague's famous miniature wild ponies, but the farm's collection of unusual horses, ponies, and donkeys is a child's delight. Daily 10–9 in summer.

NORFOLK AND VIRGINIA BEACH

by
EDGAR and PATRICIA CHEATHAM

Norfolk

Site of the world's largest naval base and NATO's Atlantic headquarters, this seafaring city now looks with pride to its waterfront.
Stunning Waterside Festival Marketplace, designed by James
Rouse Enterprises Development Corp. and boasting more than 100
boutiques, restaurants, lounges, and specialty shops, fronts on the
Elizabeth River. So popular it is being doubled in size, Waterside
has helped inspire the revitalization of downtown Norfolk. Neighboring Town Point Park is home each year to more than 230 free
"Festevents" concerts and events and features ethnic foods, games,
and live entertainment. Among Festevents: Summer's Eve Tuesday
Night Concerts, June to August; Lunchtime Concerts, May and
September; Wednesday Outdoor Movie Festival Series, June
through August; TGIF Friday After-Work Concerts, June
through October.

In downtown Norfolk, historic Selden and Monticello Arcades have been handsomely restored, as has a jewel-like landmark hotel, The Madison. Ghent and The Hague, attractive in-town neighborhoods, have been refurbished and renovated into a pleasing mix of traditional and contemporary decor.

Norfolk's waterfront also includes Ocean View, bordering Chesapeake Bay. This 14-mile stretch of sandy beaches and peaceful waters is ideal for family enjoyment. Ocean View is adjacent to the Norfolk end of the Bay Bridge-Tunnel.

Festivals have become a tradition in Norfolk. The April International Azalea Festival is followed by the May Ghent Arts Festival in Town Point Park, and the lavish three-day June Harborfest celebration with fireworks, tall ship parades, boat races, luscious seafoods, and live entertainment. In mid-October the Renaissance Faire livens the Waterside with music, dance, strolling minstrels, poetry, and Shakespeare readings.

Virginia Beach

Virginia Beach, one of the Eastern Seaboard's most popular and attractive seaside resorts, boasts 29 miles of fine sand beaches and offers superb surf swimming, waterskiing, boating, and fishing.

Atlantic Avenue, fronted by the city's famed boardwalk, has been revitalized and beautified as a pedestrian mall with greenery, benches, and public gathering spots. Free daily outdoor entertainment and Sunday fireworks are offered Memorial Day through Labor Day. Also free "Summer Sundays on the Beach" concerts are held at the Norwegian Lady statue, 25th St. and Oceanfront, and family fun is the focus of "Saturdays at the Park" at various city parks.

Popular seasonal events include the late June Annual Boardwalk Art Show, Shakespeare-by-the-Sea Festival in late August at Pavilion Convention Center, and, the last weekend in September, the Virginia Beach Neptune Festival, with parades, dances, golf and tennis tournaments, arts and crafts, and seafood feasts. Throughout the summer, anglers can participate in a series of saltwater fishing tournaments for $15,000 in collective prize money.

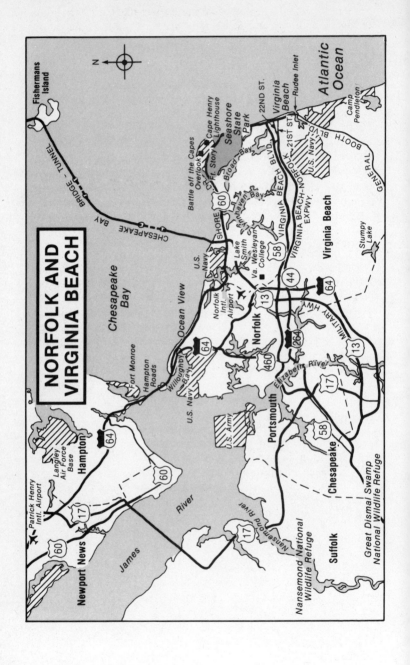

NORFOLK AND VIRGINIA BEACH

PRACTICAL INFORMATION FOR
NORFOLK AND VIRGINIA BEACH

Note: The area code for Norfolk and Virginia Beach is 804.

PLACES TO STAY

HOTELS AND MOTELS. Most accommodations in Norfolk and Virginia Beach generally offer varied rate structures on a seasonal basis. Peak summer-season rates, particularly in the popular Virginia Beach resort area, are considerably lower at other times of the year. Here are general categories based on room rates per night, double occupancy, during the peak summer season. *Deluxe,* over $100; *Expensive,* $75–$100, *Moderate,* $45–$75; *Inexpensive,* under $45.

Norfolk

Hilton-Airport. *Expensive to Deluxe.* 1500 N. Military Highway at Northampton Blvd., 466–8000 or (800) 445–8667. 250 rooms, 28 in *deluxe* tower. Color TV, outdoor pool, tennis courts, health center with indoor pool, sauna, gym, Jacuzzi, lounge, specialty restaurant, coffee shop, nightclub. AE, DC, MC, V.

Omni International Hotel. *Expensive to Deluxe,* year-round rates. 777 Waterside Dr., 622–6664 or (800) 843–6664. 442 rooms, 57 on *deluxe* classic floors. Color TV, in-room movies, pool, valet parking, lounges, live entertainment, dancing, two restaurants, concierge, harborside location, convenient to Waterside Festival Marketplace. AE, CB, DC, MC, V.

Best Western Center Inn. *Moderate to Expensive,* year-round rates. 1 Best Sq., 461–6600 or (800) 528–1234. 152 rooms. Color TV, Olympic-size pool in courtyard, spa with indoor pool, sauna, Jacuzzi, lounge, and restaurant. AE, CB, DC, MC, V.

Holiday Inn-Waterside Area, Downtown. *Moderate.* 700 Monticello Ave., 627–5555 or (800) 465–4329. Color TV with movie channel, Olympic size outdoor pool, racquetball, lounge, live entertainment, restaurant, shops, convenient to Scope Convention Center, free shuttle service to Waterside Festival Marketplace. AE, DC, MC, V.

Hotel Madison. *Moderate.* Grandy and Freemason Sts., 622–6682. 137 rooms. Color TV, sauna, steambath, hot tub, in-room Continental breakfast, valet parking, lounge, two restaurants, concierge; an elegantly restored traditional hostelry. AE, CB, DC, MC, V.

Ramada Inn—Newtown. *Moderate.* 6360 Newtown Rd.; 461–1081 or (800) 228–2828. 140 rooms in a two-story motor inn. Restaurant, bar, room service, and pool. Near Naval Base and Norfolk Airport. AE, DC, MC, V.

Days Inn—Military Circle. *Moderate.* 5701 Chambers St., I–264 (exit N. Military Hwy.); 461–0100 or (800) 325–2525. 162 rooms. Pool, playground, gift shop, restaurant, airport transportation. AE, DC, MC, V.

EconoLodge. *Moderate.* 1850 E. Little Creek Rd., 583–1561 or (800) 446–6900. 59 rooms. Color TV, pool, nonsmokers' rooms, guest laundry, and lounges. Restaurants nearby. AE, DC, MC, V.

Virginia Beach

Best Western Oceanfront. *Deluxe.* Atlantic Ave. and 11th St., 422–5000 or (800) 528–1234. Color TV, in-room movies, heated outdoor pool, laundry and dry cleaning services, golf, and off-season packages. Some suites with hot tubs and waterbeds. Restaurant, lounge, and Beach Cabaret nightclub with entertainment. 110 rooms. AE, DC, MC, V.

Hilton Inn. *Deluxe.* Atlantic Ave. at 8th St., 428–8935. 124 rooms. Color TV, heated indoor, outdoor, and kiddie pools, whirlpool, poolside cocktail and snack bars, marina, golf and tennis privileges, bridal rooms with mirrored ceilings, lounge with entertainment, and restaurant. 124 rooms. AE, DC, MC, V.

Holiday Inn on the Ocean. *Deluxe.* 3900 Atlantic Ave. at 39th St., 428–1711 or (800) 465–4329. Color TV, pool, lanai facing ocean, surfing, tennis, golf privileges, roof-top dining room, coffee shop, and lounge with entertainment; open year-round. 266 rooms. AE, DC, MC, V.

Sheraton Beach Inn & Conference Center. *Deluxe.* Oceanfront at 36th St., 425–9000. 203 rooms. Color TV, heated pool, laundry and dry cleaning service, golf, fishing and tennis nearby, recreation and game rooms, lounge with entertainment and dancing, and restaurants; open year-round. AE, DC, MC, V.

Ocean Holiday. *Deluxe.* 2417 Atlantic Ave. at 25th St., 425–6920. Color TV, indoor pool, golf and tennis privileges, lounge with entertainment and restaurant; open year-round. Convenient to golf, fishing, and tennis facilities. 105 rooms. AE, DC, MC, V.

Cavalier Hotel. *Expensive to Deluxe.* Atlantic Ave. and 42nd St., 425–8555. 408 rooms. Cavalier Oceanfront is a restored vintage hostelry dating from the early years of the century; the Oceanside Tower is contemporary. Color TV, outdoor and indoor playgrounds, platform tennis, valet parking, laundry services, family restaurant, patio dining, and lounge. Supper club for dining with entertainment. AE, CB, DC, MC, V.

Radisson Hotel Virginia Beach. *Expensive to Deluxe.* 1900 Pavilion Dr., adjacent to Virginia Beach Pavilion Convention Center, 422–8900 or (800) 333–3333. 282 rooms. Color TV, in-room movies, indoor pool, all-weather tennis courts, health spa and fitness center, and complimentary transportation to the beach. Lounge and restaurant; open year-round. AE, CB, DC, MC, V.

Princess Anne Inn. *Expensive to Deluxe.* Atlantic Ave. and 25th St. on the Ocean, 428–5611. 60 rooms. Color TV, in-room movies, heated indoor pool with automated sunroof for tanning in any weather and giant sun solarium for natural tans, enclosed walkway from rooms to pool, whirlpool baths, dry sauna, oceanfront rooms with large glass-enclosed balconies, lounge, oceanside dining, and room service for all meals; outdoor cafe; open year-round. AE, CB, DC, MC, V.

Ramada Inn Oceanside Tower. *Expensive to Deluxe.* Oceanfront at 57th St., 428–7025 or (800) 365–3032. Color TV, indoor-outdoor pool, health spa, atrium area, lounges, and restaurant; open year-round. 215 rooms. AE, CB, DC, MC, V.

Courtyard By Marriott. *Moderate to Expensive.* 5700 Greenwich Rd.; 490–2002. Restaurant, bar, heated pool, and meeting rooms. 146 rooms. AE, CB, DC, MC, V.

Sea Gull. *Expensive.* Atlantic Ave. at 27th St.; 425–5711. 38 rooms in a 3-story motel. Pool. Restaurant nearby. AE, MC, V.

Empress Motel. *Expensive.* Atlantic Ave. at 28th St.; 428–3970. 38 rooms, with a restaurant nearby. Pool. Balconies and patios. AE, DC, MC, V.

Howard Johnson's Motor Lodge. *Expensive.* 3705 Atlantic Ave. at 38th St., 428–7220. 177 rooms. Color TV, in-room movies, oceanside pool, and coin laundry. Convenient to dinner theatres, shops, golf, fishing and tennis facilities. Lounge and restaurant; open year-round. AE, CB, DC, MC, V.

Idlewhyle Motel & Efficiencies. *Moderate to Expensive.* Atlantic Ave. and 27th St., 428–9341. Color TV, in-room movies, indoor heated pool, oceanfront location, baby-sitting service. Restaurant nearby, coffee shop on premises. Open year-round. 46 rooms. AE, MC, V.

Days Inn Virginia Beach. *Moderate.* 4564 Bonney Rd.; use Exit 3B from Rte. 44 to Independence Blvd., north ¼ mile to Bonny Rd., exit east to Inn, 497–4488 or (800) 325–2525. Color TV, in-room movies, outdoor pool, lounge, and restaurant; open year-round. 144 rooms. AE, DC, MC, V.

BED & BREAKFAST. For information about bed and breakfast choices in Norfolk, Virginia Beach, and vicinity, contact Bed & Breakfast of Tidewater Virginia, Box 3343, Norfolk, VA 23514, 627–1983, or 627–9409; call anytime, answering machine in use when coordinators are away from phone.

CAMPGROUNDS. Virginia Beach campgrounds offer both seasonal and year-round facilities. Inquire about rates from individual establishments; pets on leash are accepted. Reservations advised, especially during peak summer vacation season. For further information, contact: Virginia Div. of Tourism, 202 N. Ninth St., Suite 500, Richmond, VA 23227; (804–786–4484). The following are available in the Virginia Beach area:

Best Holiday Trav-L-Park. 1075 General Booth Blvd.; Open year-round. Playground, 4 pools, 3 stores, LP (bottled) gas, showers and restrooms, dumping station, water, electricity, sewer hookups, and tent sites, (425–0249). MC, V.

KOA Campground. 1240 General Booth Blvd.; Open Mar. 1–Dec. 1. Playground, 3 pools, store, LP gas, showers and restrooms, dumping station, water, electricity, sewer hookups, and tent sites, (428–1444). AE, CB, MC, V.

North Bay Shore Campground. 3257 Colechester Rd., 23456; Open Apr.–Oct. Playground, pool, store, LP gas, showers and restrooms, dumping station, water and electricity, and tent sites, (426–7911). MC, V.

Seashore State Park. 2500 Shore Dr., 23451. Open Apr.–Nov. Store, showers, and restrooms. Dumping station, but no water or electric hookups. Cabins available, additional fee for pets; reservations through Virginia State Parks or Ticketron (481–2131). MC, V.

Seneca Campground. 144 S. Princess Anne Rd., 23457. Open year-round. Playground, pool, store, showers and restrooms, dumping station, and water and electricity hookups (426–6241). No credit cards.

PLACES TO EAT

RESTAURANTS. Fresh Chesapeake Bay seafood is the order of the day in many popular Norfolk and Virginia Beach restaurants, but steak lovers will find many seafood establishments cater to their strange tastes as well. Ask about Early Bird, daily specials, and children's plates. Estimated costs are per person excluding wine, cocktails, and tips. *Deluxe,* over $30; *Expensive,* $20–$30; *Moderate,* $10–$20; *Inexpensive,* under $10.

Norfolk

Le Charlieu. *Expensive.* 112 College Pl., 623–7202. Intimate dining with a French touch, in restored Downtown area. Lunch and dinner. Reservations. Bar. Jacket and tie requested. AE, CB, DC, MC, V.

Esplanade. *Moderate to Expensive.* Omni International Hotel, 777 Waterside Dr., 623–0333. Elegant small gourmet dining room offers impeccable service and superb American and Continental cuisine. Dinner only, Tues.–Sat. Reservations. Jacket and tie requested. Bar. AE, CB, DC, MC, V.

Lockhart's of Norfolk. *Moderate to Expensive.* 8440 Tidewater Dr., 588–0405. One of area's oldest and most popular restaurants for seafood and prime rib. Nautical decor, with antiques. Family proprietors grow their own vegetables. Bar. AE, CB, DC, MC, V.

The Ships Cabin Seafood Restaurant. *Moderate to Expensive.* 4110 E. Ocean View Ave., 480–2526. This very popular award-winning seafood restaurant serves mesquite-grilled fresh fish and choice steaks. Good choice of Virginia and California wines. Dinner only. Bar. AE, CB, DC, MC, V.

Tidewater Dinner Theatre. *Moderate to Expensive.* 6270 Northampton Blvd.; 461–2933 or 245–8304. An excellent buffet with professional theater. Wed.–Sun., cocktails at 6, dinner at 7, and an 8:30 curtain. Hours vary Sun. Reservations. MC, V.

Phillips Waterside. *Moderate.* 333 Waterside Dr., inside Waterside Festival Marketplace, 627–6600. Airy setting overlooks bustling Elizabeth River. Specialties include crab delicacies, grilled tuna, other local seafoods. Lunch and dinner. Evening piano bar, acoustic guitar, ragtime-band entertainment. Bar. AE, CB, DC, MC, V.

Il Porto of Norfolk. *Moderate.* 333 Waterside Dr., 627–4400. Taverna setting, Italian specialties; overlooks harbor. Evening ragtime piano. Bar and wine list. AE, MC, V.

Szechuan Garden Chinese Restaurant. *Inexpensive to Moderate.* 123 W. Charlotte St., 627–6130. Authentic Szechuan cuisine; friendly, personalized service; locally popular. Lunch and dinner. Reservations requested. AE, DC, MC, V.

Virginia Beach

Orion's Roof. *Deluxe.* Top of the Cavalier, Atlantic Ave. at 42nd St., 425–8555. Continental menu, live entertainment, and dancing in a sophisticated supper club. Bar and wine list. AE, DC, MC, V.

Blue Pete's. *Moderate to Expensive.* 1400 N. Muddy Creek Rd., 426–2278. Casual seafood restaurant, locally popular. Noted for sweet-potato biscuits and fresh vegetables. Dinner only. AE, MC, V, traveler's checks accepted.

Captain George's Seafood Restaurants. *Moderate to Expensive.* Three Virginia Beach locations: 1956 Laskin Rd., 428–3494; 2720 N. Lynnhaven, 431–1133; and 2272 Pungo Ferry Rd., 721–3463. All are noted for gourmet seafood and nautical decor. Mixed drinks. Children's menu. Open daily. AE, MC, V.

The Lighthouse. *Moderate to Expensive.* Rudee Inlet at 1st St. and Atlantic Ave., 428–7974. Maine lobster and Eastern Shore seafoods, with its own bakery. Bar. Outdoor dining in season. Sunday brunch. AE, DC, MC, V.

39th St. Seafood Grille. *Moderate to Expensive.* Holiday Inn-on-the-Ocean, 39th St. and Atlantic Ave., 428–1711 or 428–2411. Skytop restaurant and lounge. Seafoods, steaks, and lavish salad bar. Dinner only. AE, DC, MC, V.

Wesley's. *Moderate to Expensive.* 32nd St. and Holly Rd., 422–1511. Creole-accented steaks, and seafood; menu changes weekly. Peanut butter cheese cake a specialty. Extensive wine cellar. Bar. AE, MC, V.

Beach Seamarket. *Moderate.* 2312 Atlantic Ave., 422–3232. Surf and turf; cheesecake or carrot cake for dessert. Extensive wine list. AE, MC, V.

Channel Marker. *Moderate.* 25th St. and Atlantic Ave., 428–6186. All manner of fresh seafood. Home baked desserts. AE, CB, DC, MC, V.

Sir Richard's. *Inexpensive to Moderate.* 21st St. and Atlantic Ave., 428–1926. Prime rib, steaks, and seafoods; daily specials. Live entertainment. AE, MC, V.

Fogg's. *Inexpensive to Expensive.* 415 Atlantic Ave.; 426–3644. Seafood and prime beef in four dining areas. Bar, wine list. Oceanside dining, with children's plates. Reserve for dinner. Open daily, lunch and dinner. Closed Christmas. Major credit cards.

THINGS TO SEE AND DO

Norfolk

TOURING INFORMATION. Most of Norfolk's attractions are located on or near the water. This is a seaport town that has rediscovered its nautical heritage. The tours below reflect a renewed interest in Norfolk's magnificent harbor.

By Auto: Follow Norfolk Tour signs to attractions.

By Boat: Various seasonal excursions aboard *Carrie B* (393–4735) riverboat replica; *New Spirit* launch (627–7771); *American Rover* topsail schooner (627–SAIL).

By Bus: Tours of world's largest naval base, Mar.–Nov. Tickets, departure at The Waterside or the Naval Base Tour Office (444–7955).

By Guided Tour: For list of companies, also complete sightseeing information, contact Norfolk Convention & Visitors Bureau, 236 E. Plume St., Norfolk, VA 23510, 441–5266 or (800) 368–3097. Or drop by Bureau Visitor Centers: Ocean View, W. end of 4th St., off I–64, 588–0404, or The Waterside, second level, "Ask Me" booth, 588–0404.

THE WATERSIDE. Down by the water, once (not too long ago) a decaying section of a tired, old port, Norfolk's rejuvenated Waterside is a sparkling example of the way things can and should be. Waterside is the magnet—a "festival marketplace" of more than a 100 shops, restaurants, and places to stay. Things happen here, on and by The Waterside, for this is Norfolk *Today*. (See also Places to Eat and Places to Stay, above.) Located on East Branch of Elizabeth River, 333 Waterside Dr., with easy exit from I–264.

GARDENS. Norfolk Botanical Gardens (441–5386). Located on Airport Rd., Norfolk's 175-acre botanical gardens are site of International Azalea Festival and one of nation's top Rose Display Gardens. Open daily 8:30 A.M.–dusk. Seasonal boat and mini-train tours, picnicking, restaurant, and gift shop. Admission $2.

HISTORIC SITES. Moses Myers House, 323 E. Freemason St. (622–1211), classic Federal structure; **St. Paul's Episcopal Church,** St. Paul Blvd. and City Hall Ave. (627–4353), sole survivor of British bombardment of 1776, with a cannonball still embedded in one wall; **Willoughby-Baylor House,** 601 E. Freemason St. (622–1211), fine period furnishings, and charming herb and flower garden. All closed Mon., some holidays.

MUSEUMS. Chrysler Museum. Olney Rd. and Mowbray Arch (622–1211). Among the nation's top 20 museums. Notable for ancient collections, and major European and American art. Decorative Arts collection and home of Chrysler Institute of Glass. This major collection includes Tiffany and Sandwich glass. Closed Mon., major holidays. Free. Branch at Seaboard Center, 235 E. Plume St., offers several exhibits for Downtown visitors, Mon.–Fri.

The Hermitage Foundation Museum. 7637 North Shore Rd. (423–2052). English Tudor mansion on garden grounds fronting Lafayette River. Displays rare Oriental and Western art treasures. 10–5 Mon.-Sat., 1–5 Sun. Adults $3, children $1, military free. Closed major holidays.

Douglas MacArthur Memorial. Plume and Bank Sts. (441–2965) in historic City Hall. The final resting place of General MacArthur. Extensive exhibits and film chronicling his life. Open Mon.–Sat. 10–5, Sun. 11–5. Free.

Hampton Roads Naval Museum. Norfolk Naval Base (444–2243 or 444–3827). Official Naval Museum, open 9–4 daily. Free.

NATIONAL PARKS. Dismal Swamp National Wildlife Refuge (986–3705). Located approximately 24 miles southwest of Norfolk, via I–64 and US 17 S., is rare geographic area of peat bogs and thick forest, laced by manmade canals. Refuge for migratory birds, waterfowl, and black bears, Dismal Swamp was surveyed by George Washington in 1763. In its center is Lake Drummond, which can be explored by boat tours along the Dismal Swamp Canal.

ZOOS. Virginia Zoological Park. 3500 Granby St. (441–5227), on 55 wooded acres beside the Lafayette River. The zoo houses animals in natural habitat environments. Children's petting zoo. Open daily 10–5, closed major holidays. Adults $2, children $1.

SPECIAL INTEREST. Norfolk Naval Station. 9809 Hampton Blvd. (444–7955 or 623–3222). The Naval Station is home port for more than 123 ships and aircraft squadrons, plus shore-based military activities. Tours of ships every weekend, year round; base tours Apr.–Oct. (A sailor guide will ride in your car, at no charge, at other times of the year.) See **Naval Museum,** above. And, just across the river, **Portsmouth Naval Shipyard Museum,** 2 High St. (393–8591), honoring a shipyard that dates back to 1767 and the nation's naval heritage.

LIVELY ARTS. Norfolk is witnessing a cultural "boom." **Virginia Opera Assoc.** (623–1223), one of nation's top regional companies, performs at Center Theater; **Virginia Symphony Orchestra** (623–2310) appears at Chrysler Hall, next to Scope Cultural and Convention Center; **Feldman Chamber Music Society** (623–6959) offers seasonal performances in Chrysler Museum Theater; the **Virginia Stage Company** (623–1234) performs at historic **Wells Theater; Riverview Playhouse** (623–7529), community theater of Old Dominion University, presents classical, traditional, avant-garde fare; **Tidewater Dinner Theatre** (461–2933), grounds of Lake Wright Resort Complex, 6270 Northampton Blvd., offers buffet dinner and professional theater Wed.–Sun., and **Little Theatre of Norfolk** (627–8551) is one of the nation's oldest amateur groups.

WATER SPORTS. Charter Fishing, Cobbs Marina, 4524 Dunning Rd. (588–5401). **Fishing Piers,** Harrison Boathouse & Pier, 414 W. Ocean View Ave. (588–9968); and Willoughby Bay Marina, 1651 Bayville St. (583–8223). **Fresh Water Fishing**—Lakes Prince and Smith; rental boats and launching ramps.

SAILING. For charters, American Rover Marine Inc., Box 3125, Norfolk, VA 23514 (627–7245).

SPECTATOR SPORTS. Norfolk's Met Park is the scene of minor league play between the Tidewater Tides (New York Mets affiliate) and other AAA teams.

STATE PARKS. *False Cape,* accessible only by a 5-mile walk, bicycle ride, or a boat trip through Back Bay Wildlife Refuge, has maritime forests and natural dunes along the Atlantic Shore. *Seashore,* located at Cape Henry on US 60, has visitor center, guided walks, and biking over 27 miles of nature trails. The first English Colonists to the Chesapeake landed on Cape Henry in 1607.

Virginia Beach

Virginia Beach's free Boardwalk runs three and a half miles along the resort's magnificent broad and sandy beach, from Rudee Inlet at 2nd St. northward to 38th St. There are lifeguards on duty; and rental folding chairs, floats, and beach umbrellas are available. There are narrated oceanfront cruises from 200 Winston-Salem

Dr. three times daily, Memorial Day–Labor Day. Phone 422–5700 for details and schedules.

TOURING INFORMATION. Virginia Beach is an ocean resort and most of its touring attractions are located at or near the surf and the Boardwalk.

By Auto: Self-guided tour follows prominent road signs to major landmarks and attractions (see address and phone below).

By Bicycle: Rentals available along the Boardwalk for following oceanfront trail.

By Trolley: Tidewater Regional Transit Authority (TRT) vehicles run from Memorial Day to Labor Day, from Rudee Inlet to 42nd St., and Redwing Park to the Civic Center (The Dome); tel. 428–3388. Buses also run to Lynnhaven and Pembroke Malls and, in the summer, there's service to Norfolk and back via the Oceanside/Waterside Express (428–3388) that runs between The Dome and Waterside. TRT also offers tours to Norfolk Naval Station, downtown Norfolk.

By Boat: Cruises aboard *Miss Virginia Beach* from Rudee Inlet daily, Memorial Day through September. Tel. 422–5700.

For sightseeing information: Virginia Beach Visitors Information Bureau, Box 200, Virginia Beach, 23458, 425–7511 or telephone toll-free (800) 446–8038; calls are answered from 9 A.M. to 5 P.M. seven days a week. The Center provides a free continuous audiovisual presentation about the beach and the resort's attractions.

HISTORIC SITES. DeWitt Cottage (1895). The Cottage, which reflects early beach life, can be viewed from Boardwalk at 11th St.; **First Landing Cross (Cape Henry Memorial),** within Fort Story Military Reservation, marks the spot where Jamestown Colonists first touched New World shores on April 26, 1607; **Old Cape Henry Lighthouse** (1791) is adjacent to the entrance to Chesapeake Bay, open daily in summer 10–5; Adults $1, students 50¢. **Lynnhaven House** (circa 1680), tel. 460–1688, reflects fine masonry and decorative arts, open Apr.–Nov., Tues.–Sun., 12–4; Adults $2, students $1. **Adam Thoroughgood House** (1636), tel. 460–0007, is believed to be the nation's oldest brick home, open 10–5, Tues.–Sat. Apr.–Nov., 12–5 Dec.–Mar., closed holidays; **Princess Anne Courthouse** (1824), 9 miles southwest via Rtes. 615 and 149, in Princess Anne, stands beside the impressive and beautifully landscaped **Municipal Center,** open 9–5 Mon.–Fri.

MUSEUMS. Virginia Beach Arts Center (425–0000), with changing exhibits, is across from the Pavilion, off Rte. 44, Virginia Beach Expressway; **Virginia Beach Maritime Historical Museum,** 24th St. and Oceanfront (422–1587) in 1903 Seatack Lifesaving Station, houses ship models, artifacts, and shipwreck momentos;

open Mon.–Sat. 10–9, Sun. 12–5, Memorial Day–Oct.; Tues.–Sat. 10–5, Sun. 12–5, other times of year. Adults $2, senior citizens and military $1.50, children 75¢. **Virginia Marine Science Museum,** 717 General Booth Blvd. (425–3474), has unique hands-on marine exhibits, fish habitats, and a 100,000-gallon aquarium. The museum offers simulated deep ocean dives; and **Royal London Wax Museum,** 1606 Atlantic Ave. (425–3823), with over 100 life-size figures in realistic settings. Mon.–Fri. 11–6, Sat.–Sun. 11–8; daily 11–8 in Summer. Adults $4.95, children $3.75.

SPECIAL INTEREST. Association for Research and Enlightenment, Inc. (*ARE*), 67th St. and Atlantic (428–3588). ESP exploration center, offers free daily lectures, films, and tours, based on works of Edgar Cayce, history's best-documented psychic; **Little Creek Amphibious Base** (passes at Gate #5—#4 on weekends—both on Shore Dr., tel. 464–7761), welcomes visitors to museum and weekend ship open houses: **Norwegian Lady,** 9-foot bronze statue at 25th St. and Oceanfront, commemorates the 1891 sinking of the Norwegian ship *Diktator,* a gift from its sister city of Moss, Norway; **Oceana Naval Air Station,** Oceana Blvd., offers take-off and landing views of advanced Navy aircrafts; and **Wildwater Rapids,** General Booth Blvd. (425–1080), a family-oriented water park that features splashy slides, wave pools, and innertube rides.

LIVELY ARTS. The Virginia Symphony Orchestra (623–2310) presents four annual concerts at Pavilion Theater, which is also the site of performances by the **Tidewater Ballet Association.** The Symphony performs as The Pops in the Convention Center.

SPORTS. The emphasis, of course, is on the water and water-related activities, but Virginia Beach also has a full measure of fun-in-the-sun participant sports.

Boating Ramps: free at Owl Creek, General Booth Blvd.; Munden Point Park, Munden Point Rd.

Charter Boat Deep Sea Fishing: Bubba's Marina, 3323 Shore Dr. (481–3513); D&M Marina, 3311 Shore Dr. (481–7211); Virginia Beach Fishing Center, 200 Winston-Salem Ave. (425–9253 or 422–5700).

Fishing Piers: Little Island, Sandbridge, Atlantic Ocean; Lynnhaven Inlet, Starfish Rd., Chesapeake Bay; Rudee Inlet Fishing Site, south end; Sea Gull, Chesapeake Bay Bridge-Tunnel; Virginia Beach, 15th St. and Oceanfront.

Golfing: on six championship courses—challenging new Hell's Point, Red Wing, Bow Creek, Stumpy Lake, Kempsville Meadows, Lake Wright.

Scuba, Snorkeling: lessons, gear, trips from Lynnhaven Dive Center, 1413 Great Neck Rd. (481–7949); Scuba Ventures, 2247–B N. Great Neck Rd. (481–3132).

Tennis: on 14 courts, most lighted, including Owl Creek Municipal Tennis Center, considered one of nation's 200 best such complexes (928 S. Birdneck Rd. and General Booth Blvd., 422–4716).

SHOPPING. Virginia Beach has become one of the nation's fas-
test-growing centers for off-price shopping, with well over 125
stores discounting designer fashions and name-brand items. Major
centers within a 15-minute drive of the oceanfront include *Great
American Outlet Mall; Lynnhaven Mall,* with 140 stores including
six major department stores; *Pembroke Mall; Military Circle;* and
Pacific Place with quality designer wear, collector and decorative
art works, jewelry, china, and crafts. The *Virginia Beach Maritime
Historical Museum* (see above) has an outstanding gift shop featuring nautical items, clocks, brass, prints, and jewelry.

TIDEWATER VIRGINIA

by
RODNEY N. SMITH

Tidewater Virginia is the oldest part of America, a romantic land of elegant plantations and horse-drawn carriages, historic churches, and famous battlefields. It is a place of unspoiled beaches, Colonial taverns, and some of the finest nautical and space museums in the country.

In the beginning there was only Jamestown. In 1607 America's first permanent but struggling English settlement was established on Jamestown Island. The "feel" of Jamestown is recaptured today in the Old Church Tower and reconstructed church and the early foundations and unearthed streets of this first settlement. At nearby Jamestown Festival Park there are full-scale replicas of James Fort and the three tiny ships that brought those first English settlers to the shores of the New World—*Susan Constant, Godspeed,* and *Discovery.*

Tidewater Virginia is also the home of Colonial Williamsburg, the largest restored 18th-century town in America. Here visitors will find charming old taverns and Colonial homes and stately public buildings such as the Colonial Capitol and the 17th-century Wren Building on the campus of the College of William and Mary. Between the College and Colonial Williamsburg, up and down the length of Duke of Gloucester Street, every by-way thrills and delights us. A fife and drum corps marches past, a beautiful garden comes into view, or an expert artisan demonstrates his skill, producing a barrel or a basket or a candle or a silver bowl. Many of these hand-made "Colonial" wares can be bought in the charming shops about the village.

From Williamsburg, the beautiful Colonial National Parkway leads the visitor to Yorktown, where the Revolutionary War ended and a new nation had won its right to be born. Visitors should see the Yorktown Victory Center and National Park Visitors' Center, the picturesque village, and the famous battlefield. They should also try the little seafood restaurants beside the Bay, for Yorktown is home to some of America's finest fresh seafood.

Tidewater Plantations

Amid the landmarks and monuments northwest of Norfolk, nothing better recaptures early American antebellum life than the majestic plantations along the James. Tidewater Virginia has been amply blessed with some magnificent survivors. These marvelous mansions flourished along the James River from Williamsburg to Richmond and throughout the Tidewater and Northern Neck regions. Their legends are a delight. The Rolfe–Warren House stands on land given to John Rolfe by his father-in-law, Chief Powhatan. Other plantations are the ancestral or actual homes of Presidents. George Washington was born here on the banks of Pope's Creek, and Berkely Plantation is said—by Virginians—to have been the site of America's first Thanksgiving in 1619, a year before the Pilgrims *landed* at Plymouth Rock.

Tidewater Virginia is the oldest part of the state, but it also glitters brightest. Visitors can find lively golden beaches, such as world-famous Virginia Beach (see previous chapter). Popular for its sun, surf, and seafood, Virginia Beach is celebrated as one of the country's outstanding ocean resorts for fun-filled family vacations, while its neighbor, Norfolk, has rediscovered itself and its magnificent harbor.

On the Harbor

Nearby are the harbor towns, with attractions as varied as Portsmouth's Naval Shipyard Museum; Norfolk's Chrysler Museum and Scope Convention and Cultural Center; and Hampton's old St. John's Church, historic Fort Monroe, and the Hampton Coliseum.

And here too is family fun at Busch Garden's *The Old Country,* which has thrilling rides and shows, shops, and stirring oompah bands—and has something for every age.

A Tidewater vacation in the Chesapeake Vacationland can range between a visit to one of the best theme parks in the world to a

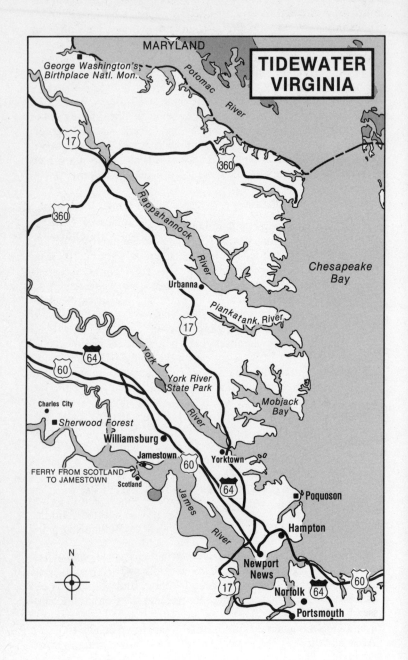

MARYLAND

George Washington's
Birthplace Natl. Mon.

Potomac River

**TIDEWATER
VIRGINIA**

17

360

360

Rappahannock River

Chesapeake
Bay

Urbanna

17

Piankatank River

64
60

York River

York River
State Park

Mobjack
Bay

Charles City

Sherwood Forest

Williamsburg

Jamestown

60

Yorktown

FERRY FROM SCOTLAND
TO JAMESTOWN

Scotland

64

Poquoson

James River

Hampton

N

Newport
News

17

60

Norfolk

64

Portsmouth

day in the sun on a wide stretch of golden sand, or from the pleasures of the moment to an appreciation of the past.

EXPLORING WILLIAMSBURG

Colonial Williamsburg is the site of one of the most extensive
restorations ever undertaken. Visitors experience life as it was lived
in George Washington's day in this small Colonial village. History
lives in Williamsburg's functioning shops, its craftspeople at work
at their specialties, and in authentic taverns serving food and drink
that would have been offered in the 18th century when this town
was the capital of English Virginia.

The 173-acre Historic Area is centered around Duke of Gloucester Street, which runs about one mile from the College of William
and Mary, where Thomas Jefferson studied, to the Capitol, where
Patrick Henry denounced King George III's stamp tax. The streets
are lined with old homes, taverns, stores, and craft shops.

In addition to the buildings open to the public and the shops,
visitors can enjoy dining in one of the village's authentic Colonial
taverns. The rich variety of food offered in the 18th century has
been carefully recreated, and is also available in the many restaurants located in and around this historic area. Shopping is another
aspect of a Williamsburg visit, and tempting souvenirs of your trip
abound in craft shops, gift shops, and stores in the Virginia Peninsula.

All this is part of the Colonial experience in Williamsburg, where
three centuries ago the town was capital of England's largest colony in America. As such, Williamsburg played a vital role in the
struggle for freedom and the representative government we now
enjoy.

Williamsburg became the second capital of Virginia in 1699. It
replaced Jamestown, the first permanent English settlement in the
New World, where Colonists had battled Indians, fire, famine, and
pestilence since 1607. The Virginia Assembly selected Middle
Plantation for the new capital and renamed it Williamsburg in
honor of their English king.

The new city was already the site of the second college in America. Six years before, in 1693, a royal charter had been granted for
an institution that would be named in honor of the British sover-
eigns, King William and Queen Mary. The royal governor and the
Assembly carefully set about raising a new and well-ordered capital, one of the first planned cities in America.

An old horseway running the length of the settlement was
straightened, widened, and renamed Duke of Gloucester Street. At
the east end, facing the handsome Wren Building a mile away, the
first government building in America to be given the dignified

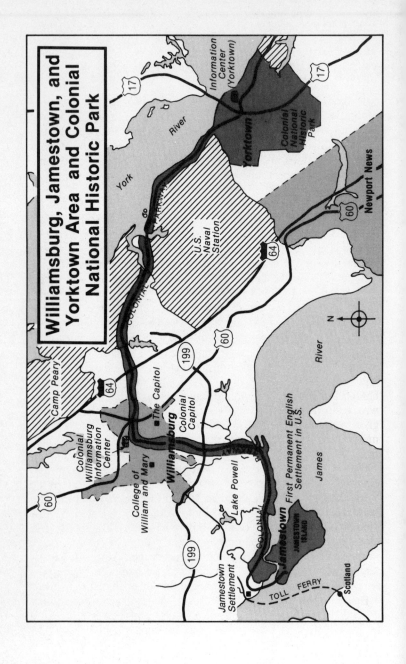

Williamsburg, Jamestown, and Yorktown Area and Colonial National Historic Park

name of Capitol was built. Midway between the College and the Capitol, a residence for the royal governor was completed in 1720. Known as the Governor's Palace, it was in time occupied by seven royal governors and the first two governors of the Commonwealth of Virginia, Patrick Henry and Thomas Jefferson (who moved the capital to Richmond in 1780 because of the threat of a British attack).

Many weathered landmarks survived to the 20th century. The Rev. W.A.R. Goodwin, then rector of Bruton Parish Church, recognized the significance of these remaining structures. Through the minister's efforts and enthusiasm, John D. Rockefeller, Jr. became interested and in 1926 the first steps were taken to preserve and restore the city's Historic Area.

The two men began a modest project to preserve a few of the more important buildings but, as the work progressed, it also expanded to include the major portion of the Colonial capital. Today, approximately 85 percent of 18th-century Williamsburg is encompassed by the undertaking. Rockefeller gave the project his personal leadership until his death in 1960, and it was his generosity and uncompromising ethic of excellence that guided and dominated its development. The old city today appears much as it did when Patrick Henry thundered his defiance of King George II, and Virginia burgesses voted their historic resolution for independence.

Carter's Grove

Nearby Carter's Grove Plantation, located seven miles from Williamsburg on the banks of the James River, has a mansion that has been called "the most beautiful house in America." Carter's Grove was the breadbasket of Williamsburg in Colonial times. One of the great plantation homes of Colonial Virginia, Carter's Grove stands majestically on 600 acres of rolling countryside. Stretching 200 feet from end to end, this Georgian mansion was completed in the 1750s. It was renovated in 1929 by Mr. and Mrs. Archibald Mc-Crea.

Remains of the 17th-century Wolstenholme Towne have also been discovered by Williamsburg archaeologists. Aided by archaeological investigations, the development of the gardens and the disclosure of Wolstenholme Towne are on-going projects that should in time enhance our understanding and appreciation of Colonial America.

Busch Gardens

Not everything about a Williamsburg visit is tied to our Colonial past; Busch Gardens, a modern theme park is 360 acres of beautiful Virginia forest, is only a few miles away. Its theme *The Old Country,* is presented in sections that recreate the romance, atmosphere, and architectural highlights of the British Isles, France, Germany, and Italy. Keyed to the four themes are live entertainment, shops, and restaurants. Among the most thrilling rides at Busch Gardens is the sensational Loch Ness Monster. Some of the biggest and brightest stars of today's entertainment world appear at Busch Gardens on special dates.

PRACTICAL INFORMATION FOR
THE WILLIAMSBURG AREA

Note: The area code for Williamsburg is 804.

PLACES TO STAY

HOTELS AND MOTELS. There is no shortage of good accommodations in the Williamsburg-Busch Gardens area, but you may not believe that if you neglect to book well ahead during the peak summer touring season. Although space limitations restrict the length of the following list, we have attempted to provide a representative *selection,* keeping convenience, personal tastes, and the traveler's pocketbook always in mind. The following price categories are based on double occupancy: *Deluxe,* over $100; *Expensive,* $75–$100; *Moderate,* $50–$75; *Inexpensive,* under $50. For full details about accommodations at Colonial Williamsburg, including the Inn, Providence Hall Wings of the Inn, Colonial houses, the Lodge, Motor House, and Cascades Wing of the last, contact Colonial Williamsburg Foundation, Box B, Williamsburg, VA 23187; 229–1000 or (800) 447–8679. Foundation accommodations require a deposit. AE, MC, V accepted.

Royce Hotel. *Deluxe.* 415 Richmond Rd., 2 blocks west of Historic Area; 229–4020. 313 rooms. Lounge, bar, restaurant, and pool. Concierge and valet parking. Golf and tennis privileges. AE, CB, DC, MC, V.

Williamsburg Inn. *Deluxe.* S. Francis St., Colonial Williamsburg; 229–1000; res. (800) 447–8679. 102 rooms, plus 85 in Colonial houses and taverns, some more than 200 years old. All in the Historic Area. The Inn is elegantly furnished in regency style; the houses are restored buildings with 18th-century decor. Restaurant, pools, golf, and tennis. AE, MC, V.

Williamsburg Hilton. *Expensive to Deluxe.* 50 Kingsmill Rd., two and a half miles east on US 60, I–64 exit Busch Gardens; 220–2500 or (800) 445–8667. 291 rooms with Williamsburg and Busch Gardens plans. Some units with private patios and balconies. Restaurants, bar, room service, and pool. AE, DC, MC, V.

Williamsburg Lodge. *Expensive to Deluxe.* S. England St., near the Inn; 229–1000 or (800) 446–8956. 314 rooms at the edge of the Historic Area. Beautiful gardens. Restaurant. AE, MC, V.

Fort Magruder Inn & Conference Center. *Expensive.* 6945 Pocahontas Trail; 220–2250 or (800) 446–4082. 304 rooms with local entertainment, lighted tennis, and golf privileges. Some rooms with private patios and balconies and some outside dining. Full convention facilities. AE, CB, DC, MC, V.

Holiday Inn—East. *Expensive.* 814 Capitol Landing Rd., a short drive east on Rte. 5; 229–0200 or (800) 465–4329. 140 rooms near the Visitors Center. Restaurant. AE, DC, MC, V.

The Motor House—Williamsburg. *Expensive.* One mile southeast of I–64, opposite the Information Center; 229–1000 or (800) 447–8679. 219 rooms with golf and tennis plans. Tennis and golf privileges, putting green, lawn games, and miniature golf. AE, MC, V.

Ramada Inn—East. *Expensive.* 351 York St., 2 blocks east on US 60E; 229–4100 or (800) 962–4743. 201 rooms in a convenient location. Restaurant and pool. AE, DC, MC, V.

Best Western Patrick Henry Inn. *Moderate to Expensive.* York and Page Sts., Rte. 60E, 2 blocks east of the Colonial Capitol; 229–9540 or (800) 528–1234. 301 rooms. Convenient location, heated pool, golf privileges. Restaurant. AE, DC, MC, V.

Quality Inn—Colony. *Moderate to Expensive.* 309 Page St., at junction of US 60E and VA 162; 229–1855. 59 rooms. Restaurant and pool. AE, DC, MC, V.

Holiday Inn Patriot. *Moderate to Expensive.* 3032 Richmond Rd., 3 miles west on US 60; 565–2600. 160 rooms Restaurant, pool. AE, DC, MC, V.

Comfort Inn—West. *Moderate.* 5611 Richmond Rd.; 565–1100 or (800) 544–7774. 80 rooms, with a restaurant and pool. AE, DC, MC, V.

Days Inn. *Moderate.* 902 Richmond Rd.; 229–5060 or (800) 325–2525. 100 rooms with golf privileges. Downtown location. Restaurant. AE, DC, MC, V.

EconoLodge—York Street. *Moderate to Expensive.* 505 York St., Rte. 60 east; 220–3100 or (800) 446–6900. 100 rooms. Pool. Morning coffee. Restaurants nearby. AE, MC, V.

George Washington Inn. *Moderate to Expensive.* 500 Merrimac Trail, a mile and a half east on Rte. 143; 220–1410. 253 rooms. AE, DC, MC, V.

Governor Spottswood Motel. *Inexpensive.* 1508 Richmond Rd, northwest about 2 miles on US 60W; 229–6444. 74 rooms. Picnic tables on a shaded lawn. AE, DC, MC, V.

Governor's Inn. *Moderate.* 506 N. Henry St., three and a half blocks north on Rte. 132; 229–1000 or (800) 447–8679. 72 rooms. Golf privileges. Pool. AE, MC, V.

Quality Inn—Lord Paget. *Moderate.* 901 Capitol Landing Rd., a mile and a half east on Rte. 5; 229–4444. 88 rooms on a resort location with a small lake. AE, DC, MC, V.

Quarterpath Inn. *Moderate.* 620 York St., a mile and a half east on US 60E; 220–0960 or (800) 446–9222. 130 rooms. Restaurant nearby. Pool. AE, CB, DC, MC, V.

Williamsburg Westpark. *Moderate.* 1600 Richmond Rd.; 229–1134. 181 rooms in 2-story motel, no elevator. Bar, restaurant, and bellhops. Room service. AE, MC, V.

King William Inn. *Inexpensive to Moderate.* 824 Capitol Landing Rd., a half mile northeast on Rte. 5; 229–4933 or (800) 446–1041. 183 rooms, some with balconies. MC, V.

Quality Inn—Mount Vernon. *Moderate.* 1700 Richmond Rd., 2 miles northwest on US 60; 229–2401 or (800) 221–2222. 65 rooms on spacious grounds. AE, DC, MC, V.

PLACES TO EAT

RESTAURANTS. Williamsburg restaurants tend to be crowded during the summer touring season, so it's a good idea to make reservations whenever possible. The following selection of restaurants has been made to appeal to a variety of tastes and pocketbooks. The general price categories, which refer to the cost of a three-course dinner for one, are: *Deluxe,* over $30; *Expensive,* $20–$30; *Moderate,* $10–$20; *Inexpensive,* under $10.

Regency Room—Williamsburg Inn. *Expensive to Deluxe.* Francis St., Historic Area; 229–1000. Fine dining in an elegant setting. Continental menu. Specialties include rack of lamb and veal with morrel sauce. Jacket and tie at dinner. AE, MC, V.

Christiana Campbell's Tavern. *Expensive.* Waller St., across the lawn from the Colonial Capitol; 229–1000. Another of the three Colonial taverns happily still in operation. Specialties include spoon bread, seafood jambalaya, and fruit sherbet. George Washington ate here often, but in the private rooms. Historic area. AE, MC, V.

Josiah Chowning's Tavern. *Expensive.* Duke of Gloucester St. at Queen St.; Historic Area; 229–1000. One of the authentic Colonial taverns of Williamsburg, featuring genuine fare such as Brunswick stew and Welsh rabbit in beer. Alehouse atmosphere. AE, MC, V.

King's Arms Tavern. *Expensive.* Duke of Gloucester St.; 229–1000. The most genteel of the 18th-century taverns. Specialties include Colonial game pies, scalloped oysters, and Sally Lunn bread. Colonial decor. Historic Area. AE, MC, V.

Riverview. *Expensive.* 100 Golf Club Rd., in the Kingsmill Resort, two and a half miles east of US 60E exit off I–64, Busch Gardens; 253–3900. Continental menu featuring escalope de veau, duck, and fresh seafood. Contemporary decor. AE, MC, V.

Layfayette. *Expensive.* 1203 Richmond Rd.; 229–3811. Continental fare specializing in rack of lamb, shrimp, and lobster. Reservations recommended. AE, DC, MC, V.

Le Yaca. *Expensive.* 1915 Pocohantas Trail in the Kingsmill Village Shops, US 60E; 220–3616. French cookery with a good wine cellar. Open-spit rack of lamb and Le Yaca's own special pastries. An elegant dining room. AE, DC, MC, V.

Trellis. *Expensive.* Duke of Gloucester St., Merchant's Square. Adjacent to Historic Area; 229–8610. Continental menu. Specialties include fresh seafood and mesquite grilling. Homemade ice cream and pasta. Dinner reservations suggested. AE, MC, V.

Aberdeen Barn. *Moderate to Expensive.* 1601 Richmond Rd.; 229–6661. Relaxed atmosphere with an open-hearth grill. Specialties in roast prime rib, steak, and seafood. AE, MC, V.

Captain George's Seafood. *Moderate to Expensive.* 5363 Richmond Rd.; 565–2323. Seafood the specialty, but also steaks and veal. Salad bar, children's portions, and bar. AE, MC, V.

The Cascades. *Moderate to Expensive.* Opposite Information Center; 229–1000. Specializes in seafood and beef. AE, MC, V.

Lobster House. *Moderate to Expensive.* 1425 Richmond Rd.; 229–7771. Lobster is a specialty. Also other seafood and steak. Salty atmosphere. AE, DC, MC, V.

Williamsburg Lodge. *Moderate to Expensive.* S. England St.; 229–1000. Offers a Chesapeake buffet Fridays and Saturdays. A pleasant garden cocktail lounge. Near Williamsburg Inn, adjacent to Historic Area. AE, MC, V.

Whaling Company. *Moderate to Expensive.* 494 McLaw Circle; 229–0275. Continental menu specializing in mesquite grilling and fresh seafood. AE, MC, V.

THINGS TO SEE AND DO

There is a lot to see and do in Williamsburg. Not all of it is in the Historic Area, but that is where most visitors start. Visitors to Colonial Williamsburg should stop first at the Visitors Center, where they can buy tickets and get sightseeing information. The Center can also help with food and lodging reservations and suggestions. There is a cafeteria and a bookstore at the Center, as well as an orientation film presentation. This is where the free buses start that take visitors around the extensive restored site.

HISTORIC AREA. The **Capitol** at the east end of Duke of Gloucester Street is probably the most important building in the Historic Area. The General Assembly met here from 1704 to 1709 and it was here that Patrick Henry delivered his fiery "Caesar-Brutus" speech in 1765.

The **Public Gaol** is north of the Capitol across Nicholson St. This is where debtors, pirates (including Blackbeard's crew), and criminals were jailed.

A few steps west and back on Duke of Gloucester Street is **Raleigh Tavern.** The Tavern was a frequent meeting place for Washington, Jefferson, Henry, and other Revolutionary patriots and was for a time the social center of the Virginia Colony. It is open to the public, but no longer offers food or lodging. Wetherburn's Tavern, one of the most popular of the period, is directly across the street.

The **Governor's Palace and gardens** at the north end of the **Palace Green** was the home of seven royal governors and Virginia's first two governors, Henry and Jefferson. One of the most elegant buildings in Colonial America, it is set in 10 acres of beautifully restored formal gardens.

Just southeast of the Palace is **Brush-Everard House,** the home of one of the early mayors. It has a hand-carved staircase and beautiful boxwood gardens. The **Peyton Randolph House** (1716) is just to its southeast. This was the home of the President of the First Continental Congress and headquarters of General Rochambeau prior to the Battle of Yorktown.

Southwest of that is the **James Geddy House,** once the home of a prominent silversmith. The site includes a working silver shop and pewter foundry. Across Palace Green at the corner of Prince George Street is **Wythe House,** the home of George Wythe, America's first law professor. Wythe taught Jefferson, Clay, and Marshall. Wythe House served as Washington's headquarters before the seige of Yorktown, and Rochambeau's later. The house, dependencies, and gardens form a miniature plantation layout.

Back on Duke of Gloucester Street, a block east of the Palace is **The Magazine,** the arsenal of the colony. Authentic arms are exhibited and demonstrated there today.

James Anderson House contains extensive exhibits on Williamsburg archeology and gives visitors a more thorough understanding of what has been accomplished here. And **Basset Hall** on York Street, southeast of the Capital, is an 18th-century house that served as local residence of Mr. and Mrs. John D. Rockefeller, Jr.

The **Bruton Parish Church** on Duke of Gloucester Street, just west of Palace Green, is one of America's oldest Episcopal churches. It has been in continuous use since 1715. Nearby is the **Public Hospital,** the first public institution in the English Colonies devoted exclusively to the treatment of mental illness. The **DeWitt Wallace Decorative Arts Gallery,** adjoining the Hospital, is a modern museum that features decorative arts of 18th-century America.

INFORMATION STATION. Located at Bus Stop 8, corner of Duke of Gloucester and S. Henry Sts., west end of Historic Area and across from Merchants Square. Tickets, rest rooms, and information available.

TOURS. Tickets to various tours can be brought at the Courthouse of 1770. The carriage ride through the Historic Area is one of the most popular. The 2½-hour Tricorner Hat Tour for children ages 7 to 11 is also popular. The Once Upon a Town Tour is designed for children 4 to 6. The Townsteader Program offers an opportunity for 8 to 14-year-olds to try 18th-century domestic crafts. The Lanthorn Tour offers guided tours of craft shops by candlelight. The Escorted Tour, a 2-hour guided tour through the Historic Area, is the most popular in Williamsburg.

College of William and Mary. Outside the Historic Area, visitors will want to take in the College of William and Mary (1693) at the west end of Duke of Gloucester Street. It is the second oldest college in America, and it initiated the honor system, an elective system of studies, and a school of law and of modern languages. It was the second American institution to have a school of medicine. The Phi Beta Kappa Society was founded here in 1776.

The oldest and most commanding building on the campus is the Wren Building (1695, restored 1928). It is the oldest academic building in America. The Earl Gregg Swem Library, housing the College Museum and Gallery of Colonial Art, and the Prsident's House (1734), the oldest such residence in continuous use in the U.S., are also both on the William and Mary campus.

Also nearby but outside the Historic Area are the Abby Aldrich Rockefeller Folk Art Center (307 S. England St.), which houses American folk painting, sculpture, decorative useful wares, and gardens; and the Craft House, the sales center for approved Williamsburg reproductions. These are located at the Williamsburg Inn and at Merchants Square.

Carter's Grove Plantation is 6 miles southeast of Williamsburg via S. England St. and the "Country Road." The focal point is a 15-room Georgian Mansion (circa 1750, restored 1927) on a bluff overlooking the James River. It is said that Washington and Jefferson both proposed marriage in this house and were turned down. This is also the site of Wolstenholme Town, an early 17th-century English Colonial settlement.

FOLK ART CENTER. Abby Aldrich Rockefeller. Located between Williamsburg Inn and Lodge, just off S. England St. American folk art in oil, watercolor, ink, and needlepoint. This outstanding collection was donated to Colonial Williamsburg by Mrs. Rockefeller and is housed in a museum that was built in her memory by her husband, John D. Rockefeller, Jr. Ticket required.

STATE PARK. York River State Park has another flavor. Eight miles northwest of Williamsburg on I–64 at the Croaker exit, and north one mile along VA 607 to VA 606E, York River State Park is a 2,491-acre natural preserve along the river and its marshes. It offers fishing, canoe trips, boat launch, hiking trails, picnicking, and nature walks.

THEME PARK. And then there is Busch Gardens—*The Old Country*. Located 3 miles east of Williamsburg on US 60, Busch

Gardens is a theme park on 360 acres. The Old Country features an "Oktoberfest" in a recreated German village, plus English, French, Italian, and Scottish villages. Each area has rides, shows, live entertainment, and national restaurants. There is transportation around the grounds by monorail, sky lift, paddleboat, and steam train. Attractions include animal acts, musical reviews, and magic shows, a reproduction of the Globe Theatre, 30 rides (including the super-thrill "Loch Ness Monster" and "da Vinci's Cradle"), arcade, antique carousel, concerts, brewery tour by monorail, miniature of LeMans racetrack, "Rhine River" boat ride, and the "Grimm's Hollow" ride for small children. For further information, call 253–3350.

SHOPPING (HISTORIC AREA). Craft House, near Williamsburg Inn, official display and sales center for Williamsburg reproductions, gifts, and souvenirs; **Tarpley's, Prentis,** and **Greenhow** — general stores on Duke of Gloucester St.; **Geddy Shop** and the **Golden Ball,** jewelry and silver on Duke of Gloucester St.; the **Colonial Post Office,** featuring maps and prints, and the **Grocer's Shop,** both on Duke of Gloucester St.; **McKenzie's Apothecary,** offering herbs, spices, and candles, on Palace St., and the **Bake Shop,** behind Raleigh Tavern, north side of Duke of Gloucester St., between Botetourt St. and the Capitol. There is a large bookshop, featuring Colonial Williamsburg publications at the Visitor Center (Merchants Square). A pleasant, shaded shopping area between the College of William and Mary and Colonial Williamsburg, bisected eastwest by Duke of Gloucester St. More than 50 shops and services, from ice cream and handcrafted sweets to pewter, old prints, and antique furniture. Places to eat include Berret's seafood restaurant and raw bar, Boundary and Francis Sts.; and A Good Place To Eat and The Trellis, a restaurant and a cafe, both on Duke of Gloucester St. Shops include Alley Antiques, The Book House, and The Bookpress, Ltd., all on Prince George St.; The Golden Touch, a jeweler, also on Prince George St.; Master Craftsmen Shop, near Boundary St.; Prince George Graphics, prints and framing, Prince George St.; Scotland House, Ltd., tartan gifts, Duke of Gloucester St.; Sign of the Rooster, folk art and furniture, Henry St.; Shirley Pewter Shop, and the Scribner Book Store, both on Duke of Gloucester St.

COLONIAL PARKWAY. An attraction in its own right, this 23-mile scenic drive links Jamestown with Williamsburg and Yorktown. Access at either end, Williamsburg, or Rte. 199, east and west of Williamsburg. There are no service stations along the parkway, which curves gently through wooded hills and skirts the James River to the west and York River to the east. Markers, overlooks, and picnic areas at Great Neck (south of Williamsburg) and Ringfield (midway between Williamsburg and Yorktown). Speed limit: 45 mph.

THE HISTORIC TRIANGLE. Colonial Williamsburg is the star, but a visit to the Virginia Peninsula should also include side trips to Jamestown and Yorktown. Any one of the three is worth a separate visit, but the *total* experience is far greater than the sum of the three separate parts. Jamestown, Williamsburg, and Yorktown are a trilogy—the beginning, middle, and end of America's Colonial experience. Here, in a lopsided triangle that measures scarcely more than a dozen miles across its base, is the nation's heritage on one small stage—the 175-year period between the landing at Jamestown in 1607 and the climactic battle at Yorktown in 1781.

EXPLORING JAMESTOWN

In mid-May, 1607 a small band of apprehensive English settlers landed on a swampy peninsula near the Bay and founded the first permanent English settlement in the New World. Three small ships, *Susan Constant, Godspeed,* and *Discovery,* brought those first Colonists to the place that is Jamestown after landing briefly at Cape Henry near the mouth of the Chesapeake. (The three vessels were re-created and put on display at Jamestown in 1959. *Godspeed* was built again in 1985 after the first replica rotted.)

Jamestown in those early years was anything but an English rose garden. Hostile Indians and voracious mosquitoes plagued the settlers, and there was seldom enough to eat. This was "The Starving Time." Much credit is given to Captain John Smith for holding it all together during those early bad years; if the London Company, patron of the colony, was stubborn but inept, Smith was stubborn and capable. Most historians acknowledge his efforts, for although only a few score settlers survived the first dreadful winter, Jamestown, like Roanoke, North Carolina, might have become another Lost Colony if the remarkable Smith hadn't been there.

But survive it did, and by 1612 Jamestown was producing commercial crops of tobacco, and the Colonists were soon producing glass, bricks, and clapboards, fishing nets, pottery, and a variety of implements and tools. The New World's first representative legislative body was established in Jamestown in 1619, only nine years after Lord De la Warre visited the dispirited Colonists and persuaded them to hang on. That same year—1619—the first African blacks in the Western Hemisphere arrived aboard a Dutch warship. Like many new white arrivals, they were probably indentured servants who paid for their passage with their labor. Although the English arrived first and established the colony, they were followed in later years by Dutch, French, Scots, Germans, Irish, Welsh, and Italians. Each newcomer brought to the New World a "national" character that would in time be woven into the fabric of Virginia.

When Jamestown became a Royal Colony in 1624, its Colonists were already feeling the first stirrings of a new and fierce independence. There was open revolt in 1676 and the village was burned. It was partly rebuilt, but decline was inevitable because of the damp, unhealthy climate. The statehouse was burned in 1698 and the government moved to Williamsburg the following year. By the time of the American Redvolution, Jamestown was no longer an active community. At about the same time, the James River eroded the sandy isthmus, and the peninsula became an island.

Nothing of the 17th-century settlement remains above ground except for the Old Church Tower. However, archaeological exploration by the National Park Service since 1934 has made the outline of the old town clear. Further careful excavation has uncovered foundations, streets, ditches, hedgerows, and fences. Markers, monuments, and recorded messages have been strategically placed to guide Jamestown visitors.

PRACTICAL INFORMATION FOR
JAMESTOWN

Note: The area code for Jamestown is 804.

HOW TO GET THERE. Jamestown Island in the James River is located about 5 miles southwest of Colonial Williamsburg as the crow flies, approximately 10 miles by car (via Colonial Parkway). Use Rte. 199 off I–64 if you're driving north from Norfolk. There is also a toll ferry from Scotland on the south bank of the James River to Jamestown Festival Park, adjacent to the old town, on Powhatan Creek.

THINGS TO SEE AND DO

TOURING JAMESTOWN. There is a Visitor Center just past the Entrance Station. From there it is possible to walk to all the sights. Starting with "New Towne," the area where Jamestown expanded about 1620, visitors walk along "Back Street" and other original streets. In this area are the sites of Country House and Governor's House, and the homesites of Richard Kemp (builder of one of the first brick houses in America), Henry Hartwell (a founder of William and Mary), and Dr. John Pott and William Pierce (who led the "thrusting out" of Gov. John Harvey in 1635).

Visitors can also take in the place that has been fixed by tradition as the point on the James that was the First Landing Site. It was also probably the site of the first fort. The Old Church Tower is the only standing ruin of the 17th-century town. The Tower is believed to be part of the first brick church in America (1636). Memorial Church adjoins the tower. This church was built in 1907 by the Colonial Dames of America over the foundations of the original. Within are foundations said to be those of the earlier church. The foundations of a brick building have also been discovered near the river. These are believed to have been those of the First Statehouse.

There is the Tercentenary Monument near the Jamestown Visitor Center, built in 1907 to commemorate the 300th anniversary of the colony's founding. Other monuments include the Captain John Smith statue, Pocahontas Monument, and Houses of Burgesses Monument (listing members of the first representative legislative body).

There is also a Confederate Fort, built in 1861, near the Old Church Tower. It was one of several Civil War fortifications on the island. Visitors can enjoy a five-mile trail that makes the entire area easily accessible. Finally, visitors can see the Glasshouse, where Colonists first made glass in 1608. There are glassblowing demonstrations daily.

Jamestown is open to visitors daily from mid-June through Labor Day, 9 to 7; after Labor Day through October and from April till mid-June to 5:30, and November through March till 5. Closed Christmas. Admission $5 per car; pedestrian or cyclist $2. 229–1733.

FESTIVAL PARK. Jamestown Settlement, formerly known as Jamestown Festival Park, was built in 1957 adjacent to Jamestown to commemorate the 300th birthday of the first permanent English settlement in the New World. Its recreation of early 17th-century Jamestown includes full-scale replicas of the *Susan Constant, Godspeed,* and *Discovery;* wattle-and-daub buildings in reconstructed James Fort of 1607; and Powhatan's "Indian Village," which has a pottery-making exhibit. The Old World Pavilion presents Virginia's English heritage, while the New World pavilion traces Virginia's history as a colony and later as a state. Both feature audiovisual displays and costumed guides. A Settlement Celebration commemorates the arrival of the first settlers each year on May 12. An indoor museum was scheduled to open in 1989. For information, call 229–1607.

EXPLORING YORKTOWN

The third treasure of American heritage on the 15-mile wide strip of land known as the Virginia Peninsula is Yorktown. Here, in 1782, American independence was won. Yorktown was first settled in 1630 when free land on the south bank of York was offered those adventurous enough to move out of Jamestown. The Assembly authorized a York River port in 1691 and the town grew quickly, soon becoming a major Colonial shipping center. Its prosperity peaked about 1750 and the port declined when Tidewater Virginia's tobacco trade declined.

Yorktown is most famous as the site of the British surrender in 1781, ending the American Revolution. British commander Cornwallis, after raiding the Virginia countryside almost without resistance, was ordered to establish a port for the winter. The French fleet, lying off the Capes, blocked the British fleet, however, while Washington's troops bottled up the British army on land. The Americans shelled the British from October 9 to October 17, when Cornwallis requested terms. He surrendered two days later while his pipers played "The World Turned Upside Down."

Yorktown today is still an active peninsula community, but many surviving and reconstructed Colonial structures effect an air of 18th-century America. Yorktown Battlefield, the third point of the Colonial National Historical Park triangle, surrounds this Virginia town.

PRACTICAL INFORMATION
FOR YORKTOWN

Note: The area code for Yorktown is 804.

HOW TO GET THERE. Yorktown is easily accessible by car from Williamsburg, Newport News, or Norfolk. The Colonial Parkway curves east along the York River from Williamsburg, while I–64, then Rte. 238, comes north from Norfolk, and US 17 crosses the York (north-south) close to town and the battlefield.

PLACES TO STAY

MOTELS. Visitors to Yorktown, one of the three major historical sites in Colonial National Historical Park, may very well base themselves in or around Williamsburg, or perhaps across the harbor in Norfolk. Here is a brief list of "local" Yorktown accommodations:

Duke of York. *Moderate.* 508 Water Street on Rte. 238, one block east of the bridge; 898–3232. 57 rooms with balconies. The Duke of York is opposite a beach and overlooks the York river. MC, V.

Thomas Nelson Motel. *Inexpensive to Moderate.* 7833 George Washington Highway, US 17, 3 miles south of Yorktown; 898–5436. 26 units with kitchenette. Pool. AE, MC, V.

Tidewater Motel. *Inexpensive to Moderate.* Four miles north of Yorktown (over York River Bridge, Rte. 17); 642–2155 or 642–6604. 33 rooms. Pool. Restaurants nearby. Picnic area. AE, CB, DC, MC, V.

Yorktown Motor Lodge. *Inexpensive to Moderate.* Two miles south of the bridge on US 17; 898–5451. 42 rooms, some with private patios. AE, DC, MC, V.

PLACES TO EAT

Nick's Seafood Pavilion. *Moderate.* Rte. 238 and Water St. at the Bridge; 887–5269. Wide variety of excellent fresh seafood, but also beef and chicken. Open daily 11 A.M.–10 P.M. No reservations, so join the queue. Closed Christmas. AE, CB, DC, MC, V.

Duke's Den Dining Lounge. *Inexpensive to Moderate.* 100 Water St., Duke of York Motor Hotel; 898–3232. Modest dining room with superb view of the York River. Breakfast, lunch, dinner. MC, V.

THINGS TO SEE AND DO

TOURIST INFORMATION. First-time visitors to Yorktown should stop first at the modern and spacious Yorktown Victory Center. In one entertaining hour you can experience the entire spectacle of the Revolutionary War and the decisive victory at Yorktown by George Washington and our French allies over Lord Cornwallis. The Center is open daily 9–7, mid-June to mid-August; daily 9–5 at other times. Closed Christmas.

A strikingly realistic film sets the stage for visitors by showing the American Colonies just before the Revolution. A stunning series of multimedia exhibits and artifact displays recreate the sights and sounds of the Revolution from Bunker Hill through Saratoga, Trenton, and Valley Forge, and finally to Yorktown. A dramatic, award-winning film, "The Road to Yorktown," concludes the presentation. Phone 887–1776.

HISTORIC SITES. In town visitors will discover the **Monument to Alliance and Victory** at the east end of Main Street. It is an elaborately ornamented 95-foot granite column memorializing the American-French alliance in the Revolution.

Swan Tavern at Main and Ballard Sts. is a reconstructed 18th-century tavern, now an antique shop. The original was destroyed by a gunpowder explosion in 1863. The **York County Courthouse,** across the street from the tavern, was reconstructed in 1955 to resemble the original 1733 courthouse. The town clerk's office has records dating from 1633.

The **Nelson House** at Nelson and Main Sts. is an original restored mansion built by "Scotch Tom" Nelson in the early 1700s. It was the home of his grandson, Thomas Nelson, Jr., one of the signers of the Declaration of Independence. It is an impressive example of Georgian architecture.

Grace Episcopal Church at Church St. was originally built in 1697. Although the church was gutted by fire in the 18th century, the original Communion service is still in use.

YORKTOWN BATTLEFIELD AND ENCAMPMENT TOURS.
Located on the bluffs above the York River at the eastern end of Colonial Parkway, about 13 miles from Colonial Williamsburg and 23 miles from Jamestown. Access from Colonial Parkway, Rte. 238 (Williamsburg Rd.), or US 17, which spans the York River from Yorktown to Gloucester Point. Battlefield and Encampment tours begin at the National Park Service Visitor Center (extreme eastern terminus of the Parkway), but those touring the *total* area are advised to first visit the Yorktown Victory Center (see above.) There are walking tours and 7-mile and 9-mile loop drives of the Battlefield and Encampment area, respectively. The *Visitor* Center, not

to be confused with the Yorktown *Victory* Center, features Revolutionary War artifacts and exhibits, and an outdoor terrace overlooking the Battlefield. For a full appreciation of one of the most stirring events in American history, visit **Moore House,** where the "Articles of Capitulation" were drafted, and **Surrender Field,** where a once-haughty British army surrendered and laid down its arms. Open daily 8:30–5:30. Closed Christmas. Phone 898–3400.

ARCHAEOLOGY EXHIBIT. Visitors may also want to see the **Virginia Research Center for Archaeology** at the Victory Center. It is conducting one of the most ambitious archaeological projects in North America under the York River, just 3 blocks from the Victory Center. There lies one of General Cornwallis' ships, sunk during the Battle of Yorktown. Ultimately, a specially constructed pier will allow visitors to walk from the shore to watch divers as they carefully excavate the hull and bring its contents to the center. The artifacts will then be placed on exhibit in the **Gallery of the American Revolution** at the Victory Center. The gallery already offers a growing collection that includes the table used by Cornwallis on this southern campaign in America, along with art works and loaned exhibits.

EXPLORING HAMPTON AND NEWPORT NEWS

Hampton claims to be the oldest English-settled community in the United States. (Jamestown is a park, not a town.) The settlement began in 1610 at a place called Kecoughtan with the building of two stockades as protection against the Kecoughtan Indians. In the late 18th century, Hamptonians were harassed by pirates until the notorious "Blackbeard" was killed by Captain Henry Maynard. Piracy came to an end here when Blackbeard's crew was jailed in Williamsburg.

Hampton was shelled in the Revolution, burned by the British in the War of 1812, and by its own citizens in 1861 to prevent occupation by the Union. Just five houses survived the last conflagration. Commercial fishing and defense are now the major industries.

Newport News, adjacent to Hampton and closer to Williamsburg, is one of three cities that make up the Port of Hampton Roads. The third is Norfolk. Settled in 1619, Newport News has the world's largest shipbuilding firm, the Newport News Shipbuilding Company, which employs 25,000 workers. Hampton Roads, 14 miles long and 40 feet deep, is formed by the James, York, Elizabeth, and Nansemond Rivers as they pass into the Chesapeake Bay. It is one of the world's finest natural harbors. It sits at the inland end of the historic Virginia Peninsula.

PRACTICAL INFORMATION
FOR HAMPTON AND NEWPORT NEWS

Note: The area code for Hampton and Newport News is 804.

PLACES TO STAY

MOTELS. Visitors to Colonial National Park sometimes find it advantageous to seek accommodations in Hampton or Newport News. The two cities, across Hampton Roads from Norfolk are convenient to most of the peninsula's Colonial sites and are easily accessible from I–64, Norfolk to Richmond. In general, accommodations in the area may be slightly less expensive than those closer to Colonial Williamsburg or to the south in Norfolk.

Hampton

Radisson. *Expensive to Deluxe.* 700 Settlers Landing; 727–9700 or (800) 333–3333. 174 rooms in a new 9-story hotel. Valet parking, pool, restaurant, bar, room service, and concierge. Shopping arcade. Airport transportation. AE, DC, MC, V.

Sheraton Inn—Coliseum. *Moderate to Expensive.* 1215 W. Mercury Blvd., Exit 8 off I–64; 838–5011. 200 rooms in an 8-story inn. Indoor pool and cafe-bar with entertainment. Meeting rooms. Suites in the *Deluxe* category. AE, DC, MC, V.

Holiday Inn. *Moderate.* 1815 W. Mercury Blvd., Exit 8 off I–64; 838–0200 or (800) 465–4329. 325 rooms in a 2-story inn. Pool, bar, and room service. Some suites and meeting rooms. Game room. Golf privileges. AE, DC, MC, V.

Newport News

Holiday Inn. *Moderate.* 6128 Jefferson Ave.; 826–4500. 162 rooms in a 5-story inn. Playground and restaurant. Room service. Bar entertainment. AE, DC, MC, V.

Best Western King James Motor Hotel. *Inexpensive to Moderate.* 6045 Jefferson Ave., Intersection US 17 and Rtes. 258 and 143; 245–2801 or (800) 528–1234. 214 rooms, outdoor pool, Beefeater restaurant, and Fox Den lounge. AE, DC, MC, V.

Ramada Inn. *Moderate.* 950 J. Clyde Morris Blvd., Jct. US 17, I–64; 599–4460. 180 rooms with lighted tennis. Restaurant open 24 hours on weekends. AE, DC, MC, V.

Econo Lodge. *Inexpensive.* 15237 Warwick Blvd.; 874–9244 or (800) 446–6900. 74 rooms, TV and sundries. AE, DC, MC, V.

Regency Inn Motel. *Inexpensive.* 13700 Warwick Blvd.; 874–4100. 48 rooms. AE, CB, DC, MC, V.

Econo Lodge Oyster Point. *Inexpensive to Moderate.* 11845 Jefferson Ave., Rte. 143 between I–64 and US 17; 599–3237. 105 rooms and efficiencies. AE, MC, V.

PLACES TO EAT

Port Arthur. *Moderate to Expensive.* 11137 Warwick Blvd., Newport News; 599–6474. Chinese-American menu, lunch and dinner. Bar and wine list. Closed Thanksgiving and Christmas. Most major credit cards.

TOURING INFORMATION. Advance information for the Virginia Peninsula may be obtained from Virginia Peninsula Tourism and Conference Bureau, 8 San Jose Dr., Suite 3B, Newport News, VA 23606, (804) 873–0092 or (800) 333–7787; or Williamsburg Area Tourism & Conference Bureau, Drawer GB, Williamsburg, VA 23187, (804) 253–0192.

THINGS TO SEE AND DO

Hampton

HISTORIC SITES. In Hampton, **Hampton Monument,** a half mile south on the grounds of the VA Medical Center, marks the approximate spot where it is believed the first settlers landed in 1607. **St. John's Church and Parish Museum** on W. Queen's Way and Court St. dates to 1728. Its Bible dates to 1599.

Hampton Institute, east end of Queen St., was founded in 1866 by Union General Samuel Champion, chief of the Freeman's Bureau, to prepare the youth of the South, regardless of color, for the work of organizing school teaching in the South. Many blacks and Indians were educated here.

SPECIAL-INTEREST TOURS. NASA has a major presence in Virginia; its **Langley Research Center** is 3 miles north of Hampton on VA 134. It offers a self-guided tour of the history of flight, aeronautics research, and space exploration. Space artifacts include a moon rock, the Apollo Command Module, and a space suit worn on the moon. Call 864–6000 for information.

The Big Bethel Battlefield commemorates the first "regular" battle of the Civil War. The Sums-Eaton Museum at 418 W. Mercury Blvd. exhibits Hampton's history. The **Kecoughtan Indian Village** at 418 W. Mercury Blvd. is a reproduction of an early Indian village. **Bluebird Gap Farm** at 60 Pine Chapel Rd. is a 60-acre farm with a barnyard zoo; indigenous wildlife including black bears, deer, wolves; and antique and modern farm equipment. It offers picnic and play areas. The **Air Power Park and Museum,** 413 W. Mercury Blvd. (727–6781), has authentic vintage jets, missiles, and rockets, historical exhibits, a playground, and picnic sites. Open daily 9–5. Closed major holidays. **Fort Monroe,** 3 miles southeast of Hampton, near I–64, stands on the site of a 1609 stockade. The **Casemate Museum** is at the fort, which was completed about 1834. For Hampton touring information, call 727–3391.

BEACHES. Buckroe Beach on Rte. 351 offers swimming, boating, and fishing on the Chesapeake Bay. Call 727–6347 for information.

Newport News

MUSEUMS. The premier attraction in Newport News is the **Mariners Museum** at the junction of US 60 and Clyde Morris Blvd. (595–0368). It features a collection of international scope devoted to maritime history in the broadest sense, including inland navigation. Exhibits include the Hall of Steamships, Chesapeake Bay Gallery, Gibbs Gallery, small craft, ships' carvings, models of commercial and fighting ships, Crabtree Collection of Miniature Ships, marine decorative arts, marine paintings, and temporary special exhibits. There is a research library and a 550-acre park with a 167-acre fishing lake and picnic area.

Since the beginning of time, the sea has captured the imagination of men. The many who were inspired to explore her waters could not have done so were it not for the craftsmen who built their vessels. It is to these craftsmen that the Mariners Museum is dedicated. Mon.–Sat. 9–5, Sun. noon–5. Adults $3, senior citizens $2.50, children $1.50.

The War Memorial Museum of Virginia at 9285 Warwick Blvd. offers a comprehensive display of more than 30,000 artifacts, including weapons, uniforms, vehicles, posters, insignia, and accoutrements relating to every major American military involvement from the Revolution to Vietnam.

HARBOR CRUISE. *Wharton's Wharf Harbor Cruise* aboard the *Ocean Patriot* leaves the boat harbor, south end of Jefferson Ave. at 12th street for a 2-hour narrated cruise on Hampton Roads, the world's largest natural harbor. Four cruises daily in summer; one cruise at 2 P.M. in other seasons. Also Intercoastal Waterway and evening cruises in summer. Call 245–1533 or (800) 877–6114 in VA for prices and schedules.

OTHER ATTRACTIONS. The **Virginia Living Museum** maintains simulated wild habitats for animals indigenous to the region, with daily shows in the planetarium. I–64 exit 62A. Summer: Mon.–Sat. 9–6, Sun. 10–6; other seasons: Mon.–Sat. 9–5, Sun. 1–5. Call 595–1900. Fort Eustis on Mulberry Island (northwest end of the city on James River) is the headquarters of the U.S. Army

Transportation Center, and includes a miniature Army port and
the *Army Transportation Museum* depicting the development of
army transportation from 1776 to the present. Open daily except
New Year's Day and Christmas. Call 878–1182. The **Peninsula
Fine Arts Center** on Museum Drive exhibits the Tidewater's and
Virginia's artists and craftsmen. Tues.–Sat. 10–4, Sun. 1–4. Call
596–8175. Free.

PARK. Newport News Park, more than 8,000 acres located a
mile north of Rtes. 105 and 143, has canoes, paddleboats, and rental boats, nature trails, rental bikes, freshwater fishing, golf, and su-
pervised camp sites. Open year-round. Call 247–8451 for park information, or Virginia Peninsula Tourism Council, 873–0092 or
(800) 333–7787, for general area information.

EXPLORING JAMES RIVER PLANTATIONS

Historic plantations dot the banks of the James River from Williamsburg to Richmond. Three of the most important along Rte.
5 begin with **Sherwood Forest,** 20 miles from Williamsburg, the
plantation home of John Tyler, tenth President of the United
States. It was also owned by William Henry Harrison, the ninth
President. This is the longest frame house in America, the same
length as a football field. Still in the Tyler family, it includes magnificent furnishings and stands on 12 acres of grounds with 80 varieties of trees. Sherwood Forest dates from 1720.

Berkeley, three miles from Shirley (below), has no peer among
the James River plantations as a center of historic interest. It is
a beautifully restored example of the mansions that graced Virginia's "Golden Age." This was the site of what Virginians say was
the first official Thanksgiving in 1619. It was also the birthplace
of Benjamin Harrison, a signer of the Declaration of Independence,
and William Henry Harrison, the ninth President. It was the ancestral home of President Benjamin Harrison and the headquarters
for General McClellan. "Taps" was written there in 1862. It was
built in 1726, and today it is in outstanding condition with excep-
tionally fine period antiques.

Finally, **Shirley** (1723), 20 miles from Richmond, has no rival
in Queen Anne architectural style. A complete set of 18th-century
brick buildings form a Queen Anne forecourt, unique in this country. The mansion, on the banks of the James River, has been the
home of the Hill and Carter families since 1660. The family portraits, silver, furnishings, superb paneling, and carved walnut staircase are all original. Shirley was the Home of Anne Hill Carter,
mother of Robert E. Lee, and is owned and operated by the ninth
generation of Carters.

Plantations that may be visited by the public are well marked
along Rte. 5, a pleasant 51-mile drive along the James River between Williamsburg and Richmond. For information, fees, and vis-

iting times, phone Sherwood Forest (829–5377), Berkeley (795–2453), or Shirley (829–5121). There are fees for these and other plantation tours. (See also **Carter's Grove** in the Williamsburg section, above.)

VIRGINIA'S NORTHERN NECK

by
RODNEY N. SMITH

Surrounded by natural waterways and laced with creeks and inlets, Virginia's Northern Neck is a boating and fishing paradise. Wherever you go on the Neck, visitors are never far from a marina or a boat landing. You can sail the Bay and the rivers, spend a day cruising in a powerboat, paddle a canoe on quiet ponds or creeks, or engage one of the friendly and experienced charter tour boat captains for a day of saltwater excitement. Northern Neck explorers shouldn't miss the daily guided cruises to historic Tangier and Smith Islands.

At the end of the day, there is nothing better than a Northern Neck seafood feast. Visitors will find fresh fish, crabs, and oysters served everywhere on the Neck, along with vegetables from local gardens and hush puppies. It is all part of the "Chesapeake Bay Lifestyle."

Peace and quiet are the Northern Neck's most precious assets, but there is also plenty to see and do. Visitors can loosen up with golf or tennis or unwind on secluded campsites or peaceful nature trails. Water skiing, swimming, and wind-surfing are all at their doorsteps.

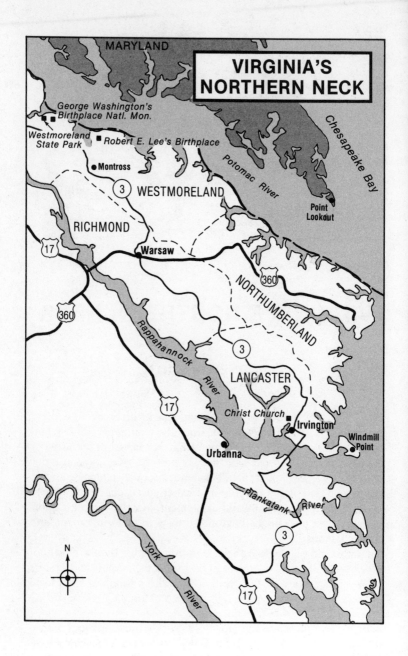

MARYLAND

VIRGINIA'S
NORTHERN NECK

*George Washington's
Birthplace Natl. Mon.*

*Westmoreland
State Park*   ● *Robert E. Lee's Birthplace*

● Montross

③ WESTMORELAND

Potomac River

Chesapeake Bay

RICHMOND

⑰

Warsaw

Point
Lookout

NORTHUMBERLAND

③⑥⓪

③⑥⓪

Rappahannock River

③

LANCASTER

⑰

Christ Church

● Irvington

Windmill
Point

● Urbanna

Plankatank River

③

N

York River

⑰

The Neck is also rich with the early history of the Republic. At the upper end of the Neck, visitors can find the birthplace of George Washington and the ancestral home of the rich and powerful Lee family of Virginia. At the lower end are historic Christ Church and the tomb of Robert "King" Carter of Carter's Grove outside Williamsburg. In between are working plantations, Colonial churches, and quaint villages dating back 300 years. Just reading historic markers can take a full day in the Neck.

And if visitors are captivated by the past, there is no need to break the spell at the end of the day. Fine resorts, historic inns, and pleasant motels offer gracious hospitality that many thought had died.

History, relaxation, fishing and boating, and gracious dining are all a part of the Northern Neck, but they do not tell the whole story. There is something more to the area, something that makes visitors want to come back again and again. It is the charm of everyday country life and the lure of town market days and bustling country fairs. It is local crafts and music. It is seafood fresh from the boat and crisp garden produce fresh from the fields. It is the people who smile and say hello, and who want to help make the most of each visitor's stay.

PRACTICAL INFORMATION
FOR VIRGINIA'S NORTHERN NECK

Note: The area code for the Northern Neck is 804.

THINGS TO SEE AND DO

HOW TO GET THERE. Northern Neck is made up of four rural counties: Lancaster, Richmond, Northumberland, and Westmoreland. The area can be reached via US 360, northeast from Richmond, or US 17, north from Newport News or south from Fredericksburg. Rte. 3 crosses the Rappahannock River from Middlesex County into Lancaster near the Bay, then threads its way northwest up the middle of the Neck.

WHERE TO STAY

HOTELS AND MOTELS. Virginia's Northern Neck, lying south of the Potomac River, is "country"—quiet towns, quiet farmlands, quiet river and Bay-front coves. Like neighboring Maryland counties on the north bank of the river, the Neck's small towns and villages boast only few really notable accommodations. However, Williamsburg and Norfolk are but a few hours drive to the south, via US 17, and Richmond is even closer to the southwest (US 360).

The Tides Inn. *Deluxe.* Located a quarter of a mile south of Irvington on VA 200, King Carter Dr.; 438–5000 or (800) 446–9981. 113 rooms in an inn that belies our opening statement. Golf lodge. Private beach, paddleboats, sailboats, canoes, and yacht cruises. Private patios and balconies. The inn is situated on 25 landscaped acres on a hill and is surrounded on 3 sides by water. Bar and a notable New Orleans restaurant, Cap'n B's, which has a plantation ambience. AE, MC, V for both inn and restaurant.

The Tides Lodge. *Deluxe.* VA 200, just south of Irvington; 438–6000 or (800) 446–5660. 60 rooms, with golf course, tennis, yacht cruises, and heated pool. Luxury in a rural setting. AE, MC, V.

Windmill Point Marine Resort. *Expensive.* Located 9½ miles southeast of Irvington (Rte. 695); 435–1166. 66 rooms with private patios and balconies, marina with slips, and golf privileges. Bar and pool. AE, MC, V.

The Inn at Montross. *Moderate.* Courthouse Square, Montross; 493–9097. Six rooms in a charming old Colonial inn. Continental breakfast included. Fine dining. AE, CB, DC, MC, V.

Whispering Pines. *Moderate.* Located in Whitestone, 2 miles east of Irvington on Rte. 200; 435–1101. 29 rooms with golf privileges and picnic tables on wooded grounds. Restaurant near. AE, MC, V.

PLACES TO EAT

RESTAURANTS. Although our selection of restaurants in the Northern Neck area is not extensive, we are open to suggestions. Seafood, especially crab, is stressed here—and who could ask for anything more? Prices in general reflect the area's rural atmosphere; this is back-country Bay-side, not Norfolk or Richmond or Virginia Beach.

Northern Neck Seafood. *Inexpensive.* Located on Rte. 1, Red Hill, Warsaw; 333–3225. Open all year, this carry-out (only) offers steamed crabs, softshelled crabs, or—in fact—crabs just about any way you want them. Eight in the morning till 8 at night. Shell's credit card only.

Pearson's Seafood. *Inexpensive.* 610 Colonial Ave., Colonial Beach; 224–7511. Live, steamed, and softshelled crabs. Open April to November. Carry-out only. Open to 6 P.M. No credit cards.

THINGS TO SEE AND DO

TOURING INFORMATION. For advance Northern Neck touring information, write or call Colonial Beach Chamber of Commerce, 2 Boundary St., Colonial Beach 22443, (804) 224–7531, or Northern Neck Travel Council, Drawer H, Callao 22345.

Lancaster County

Lancaster County, which was formed in 1651, is a blend of salt-water vitality with venerable Colonial history. Site of numerous outstanding marinas, quiet coves and anchorages, and beautiful scenery along the Rappahannock and Chesapeake shores, Lancaster County is "Chesapeake Bay Living" at its best.

Lancaster Courthouse. The county seat since 1742, the town of Lancaster offers a trip into the past of early Tidewater Virginia. Around Court House Green are the original clerk's office (1797), jail (1819), and courthouse (1860). **Mary Ball Washington Museum and Library** and Lancaster House (1798) are located on Court House Green. Mary Ball, George Washington's mother, was a native of Lancaster County.

Windmill Point. Located on the southeastern tip of Northern Neck, Windmill Point offers a spectacular view of the Rappahannock, where the river joins the Bay. Nearby between White Stone and Kilmarnock is Christ Church, which has been described as "the most perfect example of Colonial church architecture now remaining in Virginia." It was completed in 1732 as a gift from Robert "King" Carter of nearby Corotoman. The **Merry Point Ferry,** one of the few remaining river ferries in Virginia, offers a delightful free crossing of scenic Corotoman River.

Northumberland County

Northumberland is known as the "Mother County" of the Northern Neck because several Virginia counties were carved from its original land. First settled in 1635 and officially formed in 1648, the county is bordered by the wide Potomac and sparkling Chesapeake Bay, blending recreational opportunities with the quiet, historic atmosphere for which the Neck is famous.

Reedville. Located near the northern tip of the Neck, Reedville is one of the busiest fishing Bay ports in Virginia. The village provides a living image of the past with its magnificent Victorian mansions and seafaring atmosphere. Accessible by regularly scheduled boat cruises from Reedville, Smith and Tangier Islands are quaint and historic. Their residents depend upon the Chesapeake completely for their livelihood. Phone 333–4656 for information.

Chesapeake Bay and the Potomac provide excellent fishing and crabbing as well as 438 miles of shoreline (including inland waterways). Public boat ramps are available throughout the county. Other attractions include charter fishing, marinas, and campgrounds. The fresh seafood available at local oyster and crab houses enhances any visit.

Sunnybank Ferry. The Ferry at Sunnybank offers free crossing for vehicles over the beautiful Little Wicomico River, and *Heathville,* Northumberland's picturesque county seat, provides historic attractions including the **County Courthouse, Ball Memorial Library and Museum,** and **St. Stephens Church.**

Richmond County

Richmond County was formed in 1692 and named for the reigning favorite at the Court of William and Mary. The county stretches along the beautiful and unspoiled Rappahannock River. *Warsaw,* the county seat since 1730, was originally called Richmond County Courthouse. The village was renamed in 1831 in sympathy with the Polish struggle for liberty. Warsaw is the site of the **Courthouse** and **Clerk's Office,** built in 1816. The town is a commercial center, with a variety of shops and is the home of the North Campus of **Rappahannock Community College.**

North Farnham Church. Built in the form of a Latin cross, North Farnham Church is a beautiful example of Colonial architecture. Naylors, located beside an attractive Rappahannock River beach, was the seat of Richmond County's government from 1692 to 1730. The Rappahannock River offers beaches, crabbing, fishing, and water sports, plus lovely, peaceful countryside stretching back from the river's edge.

Oak Grove. Ingleside Plantation Vineyards and Winery, VA 638; 224–8687. Historic attractions and daily winery tours. Free.

Warsaw. Rappahannock River Cruises—Rappahannock to Ingleside Winery and Wheatland. Call 333–4656 for schedules.

Westmoreland County

Westmoreland County, named for a British shire, was founded in 1652 by the Colonial government in Jamestown. The birthplace or home of more statesmen of national stature than any other county in the country, Westmoreland produced such leaders as George Washington, James Monroe, and Robert E. Lee.

The Historic Courthouse Area in Montross features the old courthouse (circa 1707), standing on the site of the original courthouse (circa 1667), and the *Westmoreland Museum.* **Colonial Beach** on the Potomac has been a popular river resort for more than a century. The town sponsors the **Potomac River Festival** and an outdoor art festival.

Stratford Hall. Perhaps the most majestic of the Colonial plantations in Virginia, Stratford Hall was the ancestral home of the Lee family, and the birthplace of two signers of the Declaration of Independence and Robert E. Lee. Built in the 1720s, the restored mansion is furnished with exquisite period pieces. The 1,600-acre plantation includes gardens, stable, a working gristmill, and cliffs overlooking the Potomac. Open daily except Christmas. Phone 493–8038.

Washington's Birthplace National Monument. Located in Wakefield, this is the site of our first President's birth. Wakefield provides a wealth of insight into life on an 18th-century plantation. Of special interest are the Visitor's Center, a memorial house of 18th-century design, a Colonial working farm, and the family burial plot. Daily 9–5. Adults $1, senior citizens and children free. House tours. Phone 224–1732.

Westmoreland State Park. The park, also on the Potomac, offers cabins, camping, picnic areas, hiking, a public boat ramp, and swimming at the beach or in a new Olympic-size swimming pool.

This visit to Virginia's Northern neck completes this guidebook's clockwise tour around Chesapeake Bay, for just to the north, across the Potomac, are Maryland's Calvert, Charles, and St. Mary's Counties, back where we began.

INDEX

Index

Fodor's Travel Guides

U.S. Guides

Alaska
Arizona
Atlantic City & the
   New Jersey Shore
Boston
California
Cape Cod
Carolinas & the
   Georgia Coast
The Chesapeake Region
Chicago
Colorado
Disney World & the
   Orlando Area

Florida
Hawaii
Las Vegas
Los Angeles, Orange
   County, Palm Springs
Maui
Miami,
   Fort Lauderdale,
   Palm Beach
Michigan, Wisconsin,
   Minnesota
New England
New Mexico
New Orleans

New Orleans (Pocket
   Guide)
New York City
New York City (Pocket
   Guide)
New York State
Pacific North Coast
Philadelphia
The Rockies
San Diego
San Francisco
San Francisco (Pocket
   Guide)
The South

Texas
USA
Virgin Islands
Virginia
Waikiki
Washington, DC

Foreign Guides

Acapulco
Amsterdam
Australia, New Zealand,
   The South Pacific
Austria
Bahamas
Bahamas (Pocket
   Guide)
Baja & the Pacific
   Coast Resorts
Barbados
Beijing, Guangzhou &
   Shanghai
Belgium &
   Luxembourg
Bermuda
Brazil
Britain (Great Travel
   Values)
Budget Europe
Canada
Canada (Great Travel
   Values)
Canada's Atlantic
   Provinces
Cancun, Cozumel,
   Yucatan Peninsula

Caribbean
Caribbean (Great
   Travel Values)
Central America
Eastern Europe
Egypt
Europe
Europe's Great
   Cities
France
France (Great Travel
   Values)
Germany
Germany (Great Travel
   Values)
Great Britain
Greece
The Himalayan
   Countries
Holland
Hong Kong
Hungary
India,
   including Nepal
Ireland
Israel
Italy

Italy (Great Travel
   Values)
Jamaica
Japan
Japan (Great Travel
   Values)
Kenya, Tanzania,
   the Seychelles
Korea
Lisbon
Loire Valley
London
London (Great
   Travel Values)
London (Pocket Guide)
Madrid & Barcelona
Mexico
Mexico City
Montreal &
   Quebec City
Munich
New Zealand
North Africa
Paris
Paris (Pocket Guide)
People's Republic of
   China

Portugal
Rio de Janeiro
The Riviera (Fun on)
Rome
Saint Martin &
   Sint Maarten
Scandinavia
Scandinavian Cities
Scotland
Singapore
South America
South Pacific
Southeast Asia
Soviet Union
Spain
Spain (Great Travel
   Values)
Sweden
Switzerland
Sydney
Tokyo
Toronto
Turkey
Vienna
Yugoslavia

Special-Interest Guides

Health & Fitness
   Vacations
Royalty Watching

Selected Hotels of
   Europe

Selected Resorts and
   Hotels of the U.S.
Shopping in Europe

Skiing in North America
Sunday in New York